Underwater Forensic Investigation

Underwater Forensic Investigation

RONALD BECKER, J.D.
Chaminade University of Honolulu

Upper Saddle River, New Jersey 07458

Library of Congress Cataloging-in-Publication Data

Becker, Ronald F.
 Underwater forensic investigation / Ronald Becker.—1st ed.
    p. cm.
 Includes index.
 ISBN 0-13-114828-1
 1. Underwater crime investigation. 2. Crime scene searches. 3. Police divers.
4. Evidence, Criminal. I. Title.
 HV8080.D54B44 2006
 363.25'62—dc22

2005022505

Executive Editor: Frank Mortimer, Jr.
Assistant Editor: Mayda Bosco
Editorial Assistant: Kelly Krug
Production Liasion: Brian Hyland
Managing Editor: Mary Carnis
Director of Production and Manufacturing: Bruce Johnson
Manufacturing Buyer: Cathleen Petersen
Production Coordination: *TechBooks/GTS*
Senior Design Coordinator: Miguel Ortiz
Cover Design: Amy Rosen
Cover Art: Henry Ray Abrams/Stringer/Reuters/CORBIS

This book was set in Times by *TechBooks/GTS*. It was printed and bound by RR Donnelley
Harrisonburg. The cover was printed by Phoenix BookTech.

Pearson Education Ltd.
Pearson Education Singapore Pte. Ltd.
Pearson Education Canada, Ltd.
Pearson Education—Japan

Pearson Education Australia Pty. Limited
Pearson Education North Asia Ltd.
Pearson Educación de Mexico, S. A. de C.V.
Pearson Education Malaysia Pte. Ltd.

10 9 8 7 6 5 4 3 2 1
ISBN 0-13-114828-1

Dedication

The author would like to dedicate this text to the following:

To my son Gavin Dixon Becker (born Oct. 8 1994),
Bob Teather, and those public safety divers who have given their
lives so that we can learn.

Brief Contents

Contents

Foreword

Law enforcement personnel will most certainly benefit from this needed book. The science of water-related investigations is in its infancy and needs accurate and useful sources of education.

Consider the following. A hunter finds the body of a young man in the woods. Law enforcement personnel arrive to secure and process the scene. Standard practice dictates that the scene and body are carefully examined and documented with sketches and photographic media. Potential evidence is collected and the body is bagged prior to removal from the scene.

Now visualize a scene where a fisherman discovers a body lying in twelve feet of water. Standard practice dictates that a fire, law enforcement, or civilian dive team is called to recover the body. The postural position and exact location of the body are most likely not documented. The body is lifted off the bottom without being examined or bagged, and the scene is not processed. Sadly, this scenario is more common than not.

Professor Ron Becker is absolutely correct that water-related incidents are typically not treated with the same professionalism as are most land-based situations. He demonstrates an astute understanding of the importance of educating law enforcement personnel and dive teams about the need to treat water-related scenes properly, and he provides valuable lessons on how to do so.

Professor Becker brings a welcome breath of academic objectivity and thorough research to a dive industry that is still too largely grounded in anecdotes and untested beliefs. In addition, his background as an attorney provides all levels of law enforcement with valuable insights on how to conduct an underwater investigation that will stand up in court, and he teaches readers how to prepare for court experiences.

The information provided in this book is equally valuable for dive team members and detectives. Personnel in both jobs need to better understand their own and each other's roles in open water scenes. The chapters on vehicle- and boat-related incidents are particularly useful and should be studied and incorporated into the investigation procedures of any department that could respond to such incidents.

The issue of on-scene documentation is crucial. Our experience in this field over the last thirty years working with dive teams around the world has shown us that only a tiny percentage of dive teams know how and what to document. Would a crime scene technician measure distances on a land-based scene by tying knots at approximately every ten feet on a rope? Of course not. Sadly, many dive teams still conduct low-visibility searches with such knotted tether lines, or worse, with no tether lines at all. Hopefully they will seek out training with much safer and more accurate procedures after reading this book. Additionally, investigators will be able to better understand their local dive team's effectiveness and capabilities, thereby increasing the chances of a successful investigative outcome.

It is not enough to just secure a tow hook to a vehicle and bring it up. This book makes it clear that investigators should ask dive teams to provide them with information about the vehicle before its condition, position, and location are changed during its transport to shore. Until the publication of this book, there was no good, readily available source of information on what data to collect from submerged vehicles, airplanes, and boats. It is not effective for a police diver to say in court, "The defendant is lying; the gun was not under the bridge where he stated he threw it off." Dive teams need to have a proven, documentable decision-making process to convince a judge and jury that the gun was not there, rather than saying that "the divers missed it."

The incorporation of the procedures presented in this book will make a true difference in the final outcome of water-related incidents. More water-related incidents will be investigated in the first place, and those investigations will be handled with a greater degree of professionalism, objectivity, thoroughness, and accuracy. All of us at Lifeguard Systems are very pleased to see the publication of this worthy text.

Andrea Zaferes and Walt "Butch" Hendrick

Preface

All of us who watch the Discovery Channel on television know Earth is the water planet. The United States has water boundaries on three sides and inland waterways too numerous to measure. More and more human activity is taking place on America's waterways as we become fully franchised citizens of Planet Ocean. As our water-borne activities increase, so do the problems associated with enforcing laws on the nation's most popular playgrounds.

Legislatures have passed laws governing citizens' conduct on our diverse waterways, and police have met the challenge of enforcing those laws. When crime is committed in, on, or around open water, the police have no trouble employing traditional investigative techniques designed to assist in the apprehension of offenders.

Everything taught in investigators' schools and police academies pertaining to crime scene management and processing is seen as inapplicable when dealing with evidence retrieved from under water. In many instances fire departments have responsibility for underwater recovery operations.

Since 1963, a small group of dedicated archaeologists, with a love for the sea and scuba diving, has given birth to, nourished, and raised underwater investigation to a science. By utilizing the same types of concepts and techniques as field archaeologists, these individuals have been able to retrieve the remains of ancient ships and their cargoes. Because of painstaking application of patience, scientific method, measurement, photography, sketches, and recovery, marine archaeologists have been able to reconstruct vessels and their cargoes from retrieved bits and pieces. They have devised a technology all their own. They have devised a language all their own. The have devised tools and equipment all their own and have discovered a past that the sea has been extremely reluctant to give up.

The work of the marine archaeologists is very similar to that of the police investigator. A trained police investigator can readily see that many of the concerns and objectives of the marine archaeologist are analogous to the concerns and objectives of the police investigator, the only difference being that of the medium in which each operates.

One of the purposes of this text is to bring together marine archaeology, forensic investigation, criminal procedural law, and underwater search and recovery. Much evidence is lost, unrecognized, destroyed, contaminated, or rendered inadmissible at the time of trial because of improper handling during the underwater recovery process. Underwater crime scenes should be graphically located both geographically and temporally, just as dry land crime scenes are. Chains of custody and demonstrative evidence should be utilized in the presentation of evidence resulting from underwater investigations just as they are in any other investigation.

As the number of people using recreational waterways increases, so does the number of accidents, drownings, and violent crimes, including homicides, that occur in such settings. This increase, coupled with the influx of criminals seeking a watery repository for weapons and other evidence of wrongdoing, has caused law enforcement agencies to become more involved in underwater recovery operations.

Historically, fire departments provided personnel trained in search-and-rescue diving to the police when incidents occurred that required the retrieval of evidence submerged in water. For many years, law enforcement agencies believed that divers required no other special skills to provide this service. Agencies viewed the handling and processing of underwater evidence as nothing more than a salvage operation. Over time, however, law enforcement agencies have begun to raise questions about the wisdom of this belief. What information do they lose in the salvage process? What could investigators infer from measurements, sketches, and photographs, if not at the time of discovery, perhaps later? What parts of the story remain untold because of a failure to properly handle and package evidence, thereby preventing forensic examination? What value is salvaged material if it cannot be entered into evidence because of a failure to connect it with the defendant? These questions demonstrate that all of the resources of the investigator, criminalists, and crime laboratory could be rendered useless if evidence remains undiscovered, ignored, or contaminated. An integrated approach to the study of underwater recovery operations would include an appreciation for the full spectrum of activities found in dry-land crime scene processing as they relate to the underwater crime scene. It is to that end that this text is written.

In the management of underwater recovery operations it should be remembered that there is nothing in the water worth the life of a diver. Two maxims should guide our endeavors: First, do no harm—which applies to those of us who dive as well as to everyone else; and second, everybody goes home. The work we do is dangerous, and the only thing that keeps us from becoming a statistic is our collective and individual judgment. My nine-year-old son is on a quest to look and act as "cool" as his little buddies. I constantly have to remind him that "cool" isn't how you look, talk, or dress; cool is being able to think when other people around you can't. I learned that at thirty-five feet in black water.

Reviewers for *Underwater Forensic Invesigation*

Dr. J. D. Jamieson
Southwest Texas State University

Dr. Tomas C. Mijares
Southwest Texas State University

Chapter 1

Introduction

NEW WORDS AND CONCEPTS

salvaging

enriched air nitrox

fsw

University of California at San Diego

Chaminade University of Honolulu

black water diving

hand searches

Southwest Texas State University

public safety diver

recovery myths

background contamination

barrel blowback

search integrity

LEARNING OBJECTIVES

- Understand the evolution of public safety diving
- Explain the common myths associated with underwater investigations

MAN AND THE SEA

More than 70 percent of Earth's surface is covered with water. Since earliest time humans have been drawn to Earth's waters for trade, transportation, recreation, and food. Greeks were free diving in the Mediterranean as early as 4500 B.C. Accounts of Herodotus, the Greek historian, describe the efforts of free divers in **salvaging** sunken treasure (Diolé 1954). Entry into the underwater realm was undoubtedly linked with the transit of goods by vessel. Ocean trade and war gave rise to the need for salvage activities. Free diving was limited in depth and duration. It was inevitable that efforts would be made to use machines to allow divers to increase both depth and duration (efforts that have yet to cease). Aristotle wrote in 330 B.C. of divers using a diving bell made of leather and later of pitch-bound wood (Diolé 1954).

Today divers using compressed air can safely dive unfettered to depths in excess of 100 feet. With the quest for deeper and/or longer still fresh in our collective memories, recreational divers are flocking to dive shops for advanced instruction in using mixed gases, primarily **enriched air nitrox** (EAN). Increasing the percentage of oxygen in a compressed air tank from the normal 21 percent oxygen (79 percent nitrogen) to as much as 40 percent oxygen (60 percent nitrogen) reduces the amount of nitrogen being absorbed by the body at depths below thirty-three feet, allowing longer dives with a reduced fear of decompression sickness (nitrogen coming out of solution, or "the bends"). Breathing enriched oxygen not to exceed a depth of 100 **fsw** (feet of seawater) has proven to be safe, presuming the diver using the mixture has had the appropriate accompanying training.

In the past thirty years, technology and education have moved diving from the purview of the strong and courageous and placed it in the world of recreation and sport.

In the world of science, underwater archaeology is in its infancy. The popularizing of wartime diving by the media gave rise to a national curiosity about navy "frogmen" and to the 1960s television program *Sea Hunt*, starring Lloyd Bridges as Mike Nelson, ex-navy frogman. Interest increased with the Jacques Cousteau television specials and the James Bond film *Thunderball*, starring Sean Connery. People were no longer content watching others dive. Sport diving was born, and its popularity has continued to grow.

Many archaeologists were interested in employing scuba equipment and scuba diving in the unearthing and recovery of submerged archaeological artifacts. These pioneers were convinced they could employ acceptable scientific archaeological field principles underwater. Many archaeologists were of the opinion that marine archaeology would never meet the rigors of the science of archaeology. Critics viewed early underwater archaeological activity as a salvaging or looting of artifacts. They were convinced that those involved in these operations were opportunists and treasure hunters who were not properly handling, processing, or preserving the artifacts that they were recovering or would recover (Taylor 1969). There was a concern that no information was being gathered in situ.

It is the field archeologist's belief that it is his responsibility to record the location of each artifact or piece of artifact because, as in a criminal investigation, what may have little relevance or significance now may prove invaluable later. It took time and attention to detail, but a slowly evolving science emerged from the watery depths applying the same techniques that field archaeologists applied. The underwater archaeologist is, in every sense of the term, an underwater investigator.

These individuals now have the keys to unlock the richest museum in the world. Using excavation techniques similar to those used in land excavations, these emerging scientists have been able to recover artifacts from sunken cities and reconstruct much of those cities' history and culture. They have been able to excavate entire vessels, and from their cargoes deduce place of origin, trade routes, and personal information about crew and passengers.

It was not until 1974 that academe was ready to embrace scuba diving as an appendage of archaeological field work. In that year the **University of California, San Diego** became the first to offer an undergraduate degree in underwater archaeology. It is the purpose of this text to employ marine archaeological techniques in police underwater operations whenever possible and whenever such application will preserve submerged evidence.

The world of underwater forensic investigation is as new today as was marine archaeology in 1974. Many of the obstacles that marine archaeologists had to contend with then are revisited today by underwater investigators. As you will discover in succeeding chapters, fire departments have historically provided recovery divers for police purposes. In some instances that precedent has been impossible to dislodge. Police administrations confronted with the proposition that fire departments may not be adequately prepared for handling evidence have chosen to ignore the evolution of underwater investigation. That ignorance is often based on budget considerations. Building, properly equipping, and training an underwater recovery team is expensive and labor intensive. Why absorb the costs associated with creating a new specialty when the fire department is ready, willing, and able to continue providing the same service, free of charge, to the police agency? The answer is the reason this book exists: so that homicides and other crimes do not go undetected or uninvestigated. A more insidious reason exists within some agencies. By recognizing underwater forensic investigation, agencies would be forced to acknowledge that they have not been as diligent in investigating criminal activity in the past as perhaps they should have been. Ignorance in this instance is a way to avoid community umbrage.

In June 2003 **Chaminade University of Honolulu** was the first four-year university to offer as part of their criminal justice curriculum a course in underwater forensic investigation. What the University of California did with marine archaeology in 1974, Chaminade University has chosen to do with underwater forensic investigation.

LAW ENFORCEMENT AND UNDERWATER EVIDENCE

People flock to recreational waterways in vast numbers. As the number of people using recreational waterways increases, so does the number of accidents, drownings, violent crimes, and homicides. Criminals often seek a watery repository for weapons and other evidence of wrongdoing. It has become an integral part of the police function to provide resources that can be deployed to retrieve this evidence. Historically, fire departments have provided theses services to the police since they already had firefighters who were trained in search-and-rescue diving. It was believed that no special skills other than diving were required to provide these services. The handling and processing of underwater evidence was a salvage operation.

The first accounts of a dedicated (specific as to function) police underwater recovery team appeared in Miami-Dade County, Florida. The Miami-Dade County Underwater Recovery Unit began in 1960 and has had the responsibility for 28 cities, 400 miles of inland canals, more than 400 rock quarries, and 75 miles of bay front (Robinson 1969).

As we view existing dedicated dive recovery operations, it is apparent that they have evolved and been criticized much the same as were early underwater archaeologists. Police recovery of underwater evidence could also be criticized for an absence of scientific rigor, focusing on salvage rather than recovery and reconstruction.

What information is lost in the salvage process? What might be inferred from measurement, sketches, and photographs, if not at the time of discovery, then perhaps later? What parts of the story remain untold because of a failure to connect the evidence with the defendant? If a piece of evidence were located on land, no competent investigator would pick it up, hold it over his head, and say, "I've found it." Contrary to popular belief, forensic evidence is not necessarily lost when it has been immersed in water.

Many nondivers and most police administrators believe that the police diver's job is fun, much like the film footage seen on television during Discovery Channel underwater specials and in the movies (usually filmed in the Caribbean). Film footage is shot in water with visibility (viz) in excess of 100 feet. The divers blithely soar through the water, enthralled with the sea's abundance and diversity. The world of the underwater forensic investigator is much different from that depicted on television and in the movies, unless that depiction takes place in a quarry, cesspool, or sewage treatment settlement pond or on the bottom of some river, lake, or stagnant pond or under the crashing surf in between the crevices of ocean rock and sand. Most underwater investigation is conducted in water with visibility of less than three feet. That three feet of visibility is often turned into zero visibility when the sediment from the bottom stirred up by the diver is added to the ambient sediment that was responsible for the originally reduced the visibility. This is not a place for the claustrophobic. Recovery diving is done on the bottom. There is no soaring; most recovery divers lie on the bottom tethered to a tended line reaching back to shore. Additional weight is often added (a dangerous practice) to allow the diver sufficient purchase on the bottom to be able to pull against the tended line. It is this line tension that determines the quality (integrity) of the search.

When water is so limited in its visibility that divers cannot read the numbers on their depth and air pressure gauges, it is said to be **black water diving.** Black water diving does not depend on the sense of sight. In many instances a reliance on sight when visibility is limited is detrimental, if not fatal. In an environment with very little gravity and without sight, how does one determine "up"? Without sight, how does a diver determine her depth? Without sight, how does a diver tell in which cardinal direction he is traveling? Without sight, how does a diver tell how much air is left in the tank? Without sight, how does a diver tell how long she has been submerged? The diver who can rely upon his sight need address none of these questions. Depth gauges, air gauges, compasses, watches, and computers are the tools divers have historically relied upon to provide input about their support systems and environment. The black water diver depends on his teammates to convey the necessary information to him. The dry land investigator can be a lone wolf or work with a single partner. The underwater investigator is part of an investigative work group that must coordinate its efforts not only for success, but also for the survival of the investigator. More equipment is being developed as you read this to address the specific needs for the technical diving often required of underwater investigators. But much of the technique used has been a process of trial and error, injury and death.

Touch is the sense upon which the low-visibility underwater investigator must depend, although most teams use underwater metal detectors or search methods that can reduce reliance on **hand searches.** The hand search is the foundation upon which all underwater searches are based. Most body recoveries are hand searches. With all other senses rendered dysfunctional, the focus of sensory input is upon the hands. All data upon which the diver is normally dependent must reach him through his tactile senses. In underwater recovery operations, that data is often relayed by team members through tactilely sensed communications (line tugs). It is imperative that each team member trust explicitly those who comprise the underwater investigative team. The confidence that underwater recovery team divers have in each other is based literally on blind faith.

In February of 1994, **Southwest Texas State University** purchased what had been Aquarena Springs theme park. The area that had been used for an underwater theater was left intact and unused. Various faculty at the university began to consider possible uses for the park and the theater.

The criminal justice department at Southwest Texas State University embarked upon its sojourn into the world of **public safety diver** training in July of 1994, with the birth of the Underwater Institute. The author created and is the director of the institute. In creating a public safety dive training institute, it was necessary to determine the state of public safety diving in Texas. It was noted that diver recovery operations were actually salvage operations conducted with little regard for investigatory protocol or the possibility of the existence of forensic evidence. As the training curriculum for the Underwater Institute began to take shape, it became apparent that there were some misconceptions involved in the processing of submerged evidence. It was to these misconceptions that the Underwater Institute began to devote its attention. Over time a series of misconceptions became obvious and began to lay the foundation for the course of instruction and the direction that the Underwater Institute was to take. Those misconceptions regarding recovery were identified as **recovery myths** because of their pervasive nature.

The concept of the underwater recovery of evidence as nothing more than a salvage operation represented a major myth that surrounded the police underwater recovery operation. While some law enforcement agencies have relegated this myth to the past, many still maintain that view. By doing so, these agencies also cling to other myths or misconceptions about the underwater recovery of evidence. These include the ultimate objective and composition of the dive recovery team, the forensic value of submerged evidence, the assumptions concerning accidents, and the ability to locate submerged items geographically. Most criminal investigation textbooks describe the objective of criminal investigation as the "search for truth" or the "reconstruction of the past." Both are laudable perspectives but of little help in recognizing the interrelationship of police, forensic, and legal contributions. Presuming that in the search for truth, while reconstructing the past, it is determined that a crime has been committed and that a person committed it, we might wish to begin viewing the task of the criminal investigator as one of gathering evidence that can be used at the time of trial. In this context, then, it becomes important to realize that a conviction cannot be obtained if:

a. evidence is illegally obtained

b. evidence is destroyed

c. evidence is contaminated

d. chain of custody is breached

In this context we can see that what criminal investigators do is directly related to trial outcomes.

MYTH 1: The dive recovery team's ultimate objective is to recover a submerged item. If agencies continue to view this process as a salvage operation, then they will conclude that the ultimate objective of dive teams is to find and recover the item sought and return it safely. Both represent admirable objectives but remain short-sighted and a product of traditional law enforcement policy, practice, and perspective. However, convicting criminals of the unlawful acts they commit (simplistic, but fundamental to scientific processing of an underwater crime scene) represents the true objective of a dive recovery team.

MYTH 2: The dive team is made up of a primary diver, safety diver, line tender, on-scene commander, and others involved solely in the recovery process. Embracing the former myth gives rise to this one. However, when agencies recognize that winning convictions constitutes the primary objective of dive recovery teams, they realize that first responders, investigators, crime laboratory personnel, and prosecutors are dive recovery team players as well. Although generally seen as an unimportant element, first responding officers set the tenor of underwater investigations, just as they do in land-based operations. These officers have the responsibility of ensuring crime scene integrity and witness identification, segregation, and initial interviews; barring access by all unauthorized personnel, including the media, medical personnel, and curious bystanders; and recognizing the potential location of all forensic evidence, including routes of entry and exit, and protecting these sites. Because these officers play a pivotal role in underwater investigations, agencies should train them in the fundamentals of processing an underwater crime scene, including exactly what they must protect, and provide them with descriptions of other team members' roles. Often investigators, crime laboratory personnel, and prosecutors also lack an understanding of the scientific approach to processing an underwater crime scene. For example, if only divers realize that submerged evidence has as much forensic value as evidence found on land, then investigators may fail to understand the crucial steps that divers must take to preserve the items recovered and the need to collect water and samples of the bottom and surrounding areas as a control for laboratory analysis. Applying the concept of **background contamination** to underwater evidence collection demonstrates how bottom samples can allow laboratory personnel to exclude the background as the source from which any trace evidence might have originated.

MYTH 3: All submerged evidence is bereft of forensic value. Often water serves as a preservative for forensic evidence that becomes lost only as a result of the recovery method employed, that is, salvaging. For example, in the true account of a modern murder mystery, a serologist determined that a blood specimen that was submerged for three years in salt water was human blood (Bugliosi 1992, 279). Also, investigators found fiber evidence on the body of a murder victim even though the perpetrator had disposed of the body in a river (Deadman 1984). Therefore, while most submerged evidence possesses potential forensic value, all too often investigators unknowingly overlook, contaminate, or destroy this evidence during the recovery process.

MYTH 4: All submerged firearms are bereft of forensic value. Firearms constitute the most neglected evidentiary item recovered from water. A variety of places that may retain forensic material exist on a firearm. For example, fingerprints often remain on protected surfaces, especially on lubricated areas, such as the magazine of a semi-automatic pistol or the shell casing of the rounds in the magazine. Also, if the perpetrator carried the weapon in a pocket, under an automobile seat, or in a glove compartment, the firearm could retain a variety of fibers on its sharp edges, especially on sights and magazine levers. Finally, weapons used in contact wounds may have **barrel blowback** (e.g., blood, tissue, bone, hair, or fabric) stored in the barrel of the firearm (Spitz 1993, 319). When deposited in water, a weapon primarily fills through the barrel. The water serves as a block for any material deposited inside the barrel. The material resides there until a pressure differential (e.g., raising it to the surface) releases the water in the barrel. Unfortunately, such critical evidence frequently is lost due to traditional recovery methods, expedience, and ignorance. If divers hold recovered firearms by the barrel and raise them over their heads as they surface, they drain the contents of the weapons and lose potentially crucial evidence. To avoid this, divers should package weapons in water, while in the water, and obtain a bottom sample to ensure that any fibers or other material found on the weapon are not the product of immersion.

MYTH 5: Submerged vehicles are simply stolen. To resolve this myth, investigators should consider two questions. Are all stolen vehicles immediately reported as stolen? Are all crime vehicles immediately reported as having been used in a crime? Most investigators realize that they should consider all stolen submerged vehicles as crime vehicles (i.e., stolen for use in the commission of another crime) until proven otherwise. In doing so, they can understand that the conventional recovery method (towing by the axle) seriously alters, contaminates, or destroys any evidence. What should they do instead? Before instituting the recovery of a submerged vehicle, investigators should catalog any information that may later become important but that the recovery method may alter or destroy. Divers can conduct this cataloging process by compiling a "swim around" checklist. Divers can complete this checklist even in the worst water conditions through touch alone or other means, such as recording the vehicle identification number and license number by using a water bath (i.e., a clear plastic bag filled with water). By pressing the water-filled bag between the license plate and their masks, divers get a clear medium through which they can see the information; a camera can take a picture using the same process. The swim around allows divers to record the location of any occupants of the vehicle; the condition of the windshield, windows, headlights, and taillights; and the contents of the glove compartment. It also helps divers determine if the keys were in the ignition and if the accelerator was blocked. This information can prove essential during the subsequent investigation of the incident.

MYTH 6: All drownings are presumed accidents. Experienced homicide investigators generally presume that all unattended deaths are murders until proven otherwise, except when they occur in the water. Many investigators have participated in the recovery of a presumed accidental drowning victim only to have some serious subsequent misgivings as to the mechanism of death. Therefore, investigators should employ the same investigatory protocol afforded deaths on land to deaths on or in the water. By correctly processing the bodies of drowning victims, investigators can obtain a variety of forensic evidence. For example, divers should place bodies in body bags to avoid losing transient evidence, such as hair or fibers, and to ensure that any injuries that occur during the recovery process are not mistaken for wounds inflicted before death. Bagging bodies in the water reveals damage to the body bags that corresponds to injuries to the bodies that may occur during the recovery process. Bagging bodies in the water also keeps the clothing intact. For example, shoes can contain dirt, gravel, or other debris from a prior crime scene, which may prove valuable to investigators and laboratory personnel. Because shoes become lost easily, divers should bag feet, with the shoes intact, to prevent loss and possible contamination during the recovery operation or subsequent transportation of the body to the medical examiner's office.

MYTH 7: All air disasters are presumed accidents. This myth coexists with another one: Air crash disasters happen somewhere else. Since September 11, 2001, this particular myth has taken on poignancy heretofore absent in America's collective consciousness. Aircraft crashes can and do occur in every part of the world. Moreover, because most of the world is covered in water, many aircraft crashes occur in the water. Also, for every large commercial airliner that crashes into water (or on land), several hundred airplanes, with a seating capacity of less than ten, crash into oceans, lakes, and rivers (Teather 1994, 117). With this in mind, jurisdictions with any type of body of water within its boundaries can recognize that they may have to conduct an underwater recovery of an aircraft. If they assume that such incidents always are accidents, they may overlook, contaminate, or destroy critical evidence that may indicate that the crash resulted from criminal intervention. Investigators also must understand the purpose of the recovery operation in aircraft crashes. To identify passengers and to determine what caused the crash constitute the two primary purposes. However, investigators must remember that when an aircraft crashes, even in water, it generally becomes a mass of twisted, convoluted, and shredded metal, and the occupants usually have sustained massive, often disfiguring, fatal injuries (Teather 1994, 117). Conducting underwater recoveries of such incidents requires the establishment of contingency plans before an aircraft disaster occurs. In addition, divers involved in the underwater recovery of aircraft and the victims involved in such disasters must have the necessary training and equipment to effectively carry out the operation.

MYTH 8: It is not necessary or possible to locate submerged items geographically. This myth has evolved because most underwater recovery operations occur in conditions of limited visibility. However, divers can find a 2,000-year-old submerged vessel; sketch the area where they found it; recover, label, and measure all of the pieces in relation to each other; reconstruct the vessel on land; and tell by the placement of the cargo in the hold what ports the vessel visited and in what order it visited them (Becker 2000). The techniques exist if the need does. Situations where dive recovery teams need to employ such techniques could include an accident reconstruction where one vehicle came to rest in the water. The position of the vehicle would reveal the direction of travel as well as the approximate speed on impact. In a weapon recovery, the position of the weapon in the water may determine its relevance. If divers discover a weapon 500 yards from where a witness places the individual disposing of the weapon, some serious questions could arise about the case. Investigators must understand the importance of properly marking and recording the location of the recovery site. Failure to do so may result in the

- loss of the site, in the event that more than one dive is necessary, and considerable expense of time and effort in relocating the site and the evidence at the site.
- inability to orient parts of a dismantled motor vehicle, vessel, airplane, or dismembered body.
- evidence subsequently being rendered inadmissible at the time of trial (Becker 1995).

MYTH 9: The only successful recovery operation is one that discovers the evidentiary item sought. This is a relatively recent myth added as the result of the author's experience in serving as a consultant for the Honolulu Police Department during a recovery operation for a pipe that had been used in a homicide. The possibility of trace evidence remaining on the pipe was slim but possible (especially on ragged or threaded ends). The media was present in force. The number of homicides in Hawaii is small, and an underwater search for a murder weapon is a major media event. Based on the information provided by the suspect, a search area was selected and a search pattern employed and executed. The pipe was not found. Everyone left disappointed. That disappointment led to the inclusion of this myth. In reality, a successful underwater search occurs in one of two ways:

1. The item sought is found.
2. There is sufficient confidence in the team, their equipment, and **search integrity** that it can be unequivocally stated that the item sought is not there.

The second point allows the focus of the search to confidently shift to a new location.

MYTH 10: All underwater operations begin at the water's edge. In considering how crime scenes are generally treated, it should be apparent that whatever is in the water did not materialize there. It had to get there in some fashion. Just as in any dry-land investigation, there are points of access, exit, and staging that must be considered as part of the crime scene. Whoever put the item in the water got there somehow. That somehow is part of the crime scene. This became most apparent in a recovery operation for a firearm wherein the author was asked to consult. The dive team brought a tarp, laid it on the ground, and staged their dive equipment upon it. After the discovery of the pistol, the dive gear was packed, the tarp removed, and five expended shell casings found underneath. Although it was apparent that they were from the recovered pistol, they had been trod upon to the point that their forensic usefulness was compromised.

For decades, many law enforcement agencies have viewed underwater recovery operations as nothing more than retrieving submerged items. In the past few years, however, the increasing number of such cases has caused some agencies to take a closer look at this idea. They have encountered several myths or misconceptions that have demonstrated the need for on-scene investigators to understand the complexities associated with the underwater recovery process and to no longer view it as a salvage operation. Dispelling these myths has led agencies to appreciate the forensic value of submerged evidence, the importance of establishing contingency plans for aircraft crashes, and the effectiveness of highly skilled underwater recovery dive teams in solving crimes. Law enforcement agencies must encourage their officers to see the benefits of exploring new methods of investigating underwater crime scenes and not rely solely on past policies and procedures.

REVIEW QUESTIONS

1. Describe the difficulties that marine archaeology encountered on its way to becoming a legitimate academic inquiry.
2. Describe the parallels in the quest for academic legitimacy between marine archaeology and underwater investigation.
3. Who is on the underwater investigation team?
4. What is the objective of an underwater recovery operation?
5. What should the presumption be in unattended drownings?
6. What should the presumption be in in-water airliner crashes?
7. What mediates against treating a submerged vehicle as simply a stolen one?
8. Where might a firearm retain forensic evidence?
9. What are the possible consequences of not geographically locating a recovered item?
10. What is barrel blowback?

REFERENCES

BECKER, R. F. 1995. *Processing the underwater crime scene.* Springfield, IL: Charles C. Thomas.

——. 2000. *Criminal investigation.* Gaithersburg, MD: Aspen.

BUGLIOSI, V. 1992. *And the sea will tell.* New York: Ivy Books.

DEADMAN, H. A. 1984. Fiber evidence and the Wayne Williams trial. *FBI Law Enforcement Bulletin,* May.

DIOLÉ, P. H. 1954. *4,000 years under the sea.* New York: John Jay Press.

MARX, R. F. 1990. *The underwater dig.* Houston: Gulf Publishing.

ROBINSON, P. 1969. County frogmen always ready for anything. *The Christian Science Monitor,* March 17.

SPITZ, W. U. 1993. *Medicolegal investigation of death.* 3rd ed. Springfield, IL: Charles C. Thomas.

TAYLOR, J. P. 1969. *Marine archaeology.* London: Tavistock.

TEATHER, R. G. 1994. *Encyclopedia of underwater investigations.* Flagstaff: Best Publishing.

Chapter 2

A Brief History of Diving

NEW WORDS AND CONCEPTS

breath-hold	open circuit
diving bells	closed circuit
diving dress	Jacques-Yves Cousteau
Augustus Siebe	Émile Gagnan
John and Charles Deane	Aqua-Lung
caisson disease	public safety divers
bends	Robert Boyle
decompression sickness	John Dalton
Paul Bert	William Henry
nitrogen narcosis	Jacques Charles

LEARNING OBJECTIVES

- Discuss the history of diving
- Appreciate some of the major contributors to the evolution of diving
- Explain basic diving "laws"

If we include **breath-hold** diving in our historical treatment, we discover that men and women have been infatuated with the sea throughout recorded history. Indirect evidence from recovered ancient archaeological artifacts depicts divers harvesting shells and sponges and performing what appear to be military operations.

As stated in Chapter One of this text, early sojourns into the underwater world were most likely precipitated by the hunt for food, the recovery of artifacts, or the repair and salvage of vessels. The view that was available to early breath-hold divers was limited. Each dive was dependent upon the ability of the breath-hold diver to maximize one lungful of air. Even those involved in early breath-hold diving for recreation shared the vision of unlimited access to their watery world, and so began the quest for machines that would extend the human capacity to explore under water.

It is not hard to imagine early efforts revolving around the use of long, hollow reeds; they are often used in the movies by heroes who successfully elude their pursuers. Although some exploration was expected, it would be discovered in short order that the narrow reed did not admit sufficient air for lengthy use and that the buildup of carbon dioxide would prevent prolonged use. Even snorkels today must be forcefully cleared periodically to expel accumulated carbon dioxide that settles to the bottom of the snorkel tube.

The first successful experiments with prolonged human submersion were done with primitive **diving bells.** Pictures depict such devices as early as the sixteenth century in England and France.

The diving bell is bell-shaped, with the bottom open to the sea. The first diving bells were large, strong tubs weighted to sink in a vertical position, thereby trapping enough air to permit a diver to breathe for several hours. The trapping of air in these early devices follows the same principle as when an empty tumbler is immersed mouth first in a sink full of water. Observation will reveal that the glass has remained empty of water and is filled with breathable air.

FIGURE 2-1 Halley's Diving Bell
(*Source:* U.S. Navy 1993)

Early diving bells were suspended by a cable from the surface and had limited independent underwater maneuverability. The diver could remain in the bell hovering above the area of interest, or he could breath-hold and leave the bell for short excursions. In 1690 the English astronomer Edmund Halley developed a diving bell in which the atmosphere was replenished inside the bell by lowering weighted barrels of air down from the surface. In a demonstration of his system, Halley and four companions were able to descend into the Thames to a depth of 60 fsw and remain there for an hour and a half (U.S. Navy 2003).

The advent of bell diving was succeeded and moved along by the nineteenth-century development of a hand-operated pump capable of delivering air under pressure. Diving bells no longer needed to be replenished with air in barrels lowered from the surface.

DIVING DRESS

The need for salvage diving in England developed before the Industrial Revolution of the mid-eighteenth century. Diving bells allowed shallow-water salvage operations. Although there was interest in underwater treasure, most salvage operations were concerned with the more mundane task of recovering valuable scrap. Today we recover ancient ship cannons from their watery repository as part of our archaeological quest for understanding of earlier times and peoples. Englishmen were interested in cannons because they were made of brass and had intrinsic value because of the metal used in the manufacturing process. With civilian and military wrecks abounding in and around the English isles, there was a strong interest in developing a diving suit (**diving dress**) that would permit greater maneuverability than the diving bell and would increase the efficiency of salvage operations.

The first practical diving dress was developed by **Augustus Siebe.** Two salvage operators, **John and Charles Deane,** in 1823 patented a basic smoke apparatus that would allow firefighters to enter smoked-filled buildings. By 1828 the Deanes had converted their firefighter suit into Deane's Patent Diving Dress, consisting of a heavy suit, a helmet with viewing ports, and hose connections for delivering surface-supplied air. The helmet was not fastened to the suit, but rested on the

diver's shoulders, held in place by its own weight and by straps to a waist belt. The exhausted air passed out from under the edge of the helmet. The open bottom posed no problem as long as the diver remained upright. However, should the diver fall, the helmet would quickly fill with water. Augustus Siebe modified the Deane Diving Dress by sealing the helmet to the suit at the collar and adding an exhaust valve to expel the used air. This device is the pattern upon which the U.S. Navy standard diving dress, the MK V, was based. The MK V was not replaced until the 1980s with the adoption of the MK 12 surface-supplied diving system (U.S. Navy 1993).

By 1840 several types of diving dress were being used in actual diving operations. At that time, a unit of the British Royal Engineers was removing the remains of the sunken warship HMS *Royal George.* The ship was blocking a major anchorage just outside Portsmouth, England. Colonel William Pasley, the officer in charge, decided that his operation was an ideal opportunity to test and evaluate various types of diving dress. Because of the possibility of flooding of the Deane helmet, Pasley recommended that the Siebe dress be adopted for future operations. When Pasley's project was completed, it was noted that "of the seasoned divers, not a man escaped the repeated attacks of rheumatism and cold." The divers had

FIGURE 2-2   Siebe's Enclosed Diving Dress (*Source:* U.S. Navy 1993)

been working seven hours a day at depths in excess of 60 fsw. Pasley and his men did not realize the implications of the observation. What appeared to be rheumatism was instead a symptom of a more serious physiological problem (U.S. Navy 2003).

Caisson Disease

While a practical diving dress was being perfected, inventors were working to improve the diving bell, increasing its size and adding high-capacity air pumps that could deliver enough pressure to keep water entirely out of the bell's interior. The improved pumps soon led to the construction of chambers large enough to permit several men to work on the bottom. This was particularly advantageous for projects such as excavating bridge footings or constructing tunnel sections where long periods of work were required. These dry chambers were known as *caissons*, a French word meaning "big boxes." Caissons were designed to provide ready access from the surface. By using an air lock, the pressure inside could be maintained while men or materials could be passed in and out. The caisson was a major step in engineering technology, and its use grew quickly (U.S. Navy 2003).

With the increasing use of caissons, a new and unexplained malady began to affect the caisson workers. Upon returning to the surface at the end of a shift, the divers frequently would be struck by dizzy spells, breathing difficulties, or sharp pains in the joints or abdomen. Caisson workers noted that they felt better working on the job. As caisson work extended to larger projects and to greater operating pressures, the physiological problems increased in number and severity. Fatalities occurred with alarming frequency. The malady was called, logically enough, **caisson disease.** However, workers on the Brooklyn Bridge project in New York gave the sickness a more descriptive name that has remained—the **bends (decompression sickness).** Today the bends is the best-known danger of diving. Although men had been diving for thousands of years, few had spent much time working under great atmospheric pressure until the time of the caisson. Individuals such as Pasley, who had experienced some aspects of the disease, were simply not prepared to look for anything more involved than indigestion, rheumatism, or arthritis.

The Cause of Caisson Disease

The actual cause of caisson disease was first clinically described in 1878 by French physiologist **Paul Bert.** In studying the effect of pressure on human physiology, Bert determined that breathing air under pressure forced quantities of nitrogen into solution in the blood and tissues of the body. As long as the pressure remained, the gas was held in solution. When the pressure was quickly released, as it was when a worker left the caisson, the nitrogen returned to a gaseous state too rapidly to pass out of the body in a natural manner. Gas bubbles formed throughout the body, causing the wide range of symptoms associated with the disease. Paralysis or death could occur if the flow of blood to a vital organ was blocked by the bubbles (U.S. Navy 2003). For a more complete understanding, see the discussion of the laws of Boyle, Charles, Dalton, and Henry on pp. 19–22.

Preventing Decompression Sickness

Paul Bert recommended that caisson workers gradually decompress and divers return to the surface slowly. His studies led to an immediate improvement for the caisson workers when they discovered their pain could be relieved by returning to the pressure of the caisson as soon as the symptoms appeared. Within a few years, specially designed decompression chambers were being placed at job sites to provide a more controlled situation for handling the bends. The pressure in the chambers could be increased or decreased as needed for an individual worker.

Nitrogen Narcosis

Divers soon were moving into deeper water, and another unexplained malady began to appear. The diver would appear intoxicated, sometimes feeling euphoric and frequently losing judgment. In the 1930s this "rapture of the deep" was linked to nitrogen in the air breathed under higher pressures. Known as **nitrogen narcosis,** this condition occurred because nitrogen has anesthetic properties that become progressively more severe with increasing air pressure. To avoid the problem, special breathing mixtures such as helium-oxygen were developed for deep diving.

Self-Contained Underwater Breathing Apparatus

The diving equipment developed by Charles and John Deane, Augustus Siebe, and other inventors gave humans the ability to remain and work under water for extended periods, but movement was greatly limited by the requirement for surface-supplied air. Inventors searched for methods to increase the diver's movement without increasing the hazards. The best solution was to provide the diver with a portable, self-contained air supply. For many years the self-contained underwater breathing apparatus (scuba) was only a theoretical possibility. Early attempts to supply self-contained compressed air to divers were not successful due to the limitations of air pumps and containers to compress and store air at sufficiently high pressure. Scuba development took place gradually. However, we are concerned primarily with two types of diving:

1. Diving with compressed air supplied from the surface. The diver is separated from the supply of fresh air, which is kept on the surface. Air reaches the diver through a long umbilical, which in its simplest form ends in a regulator and mouthpiece carried by the diver. In more sophisticated systems, the umbilical leads into a dive suit or some larger enclosed space containing the diver. Devices in this category include caissons (huge spaces supplied with compressed air, employed mainly for bridge and tunnel work), underwater habitats used for saturation diving, diving bells, and rigid-helmet diving suits. In underwater recovery operations, divers often wear helmets that accommodate scuba tanks or have ports for hoses supplying air from the surface. In all these devices, the diver breathes air at the same pressure as the surrounding water pressure, and so is at risk for decompression problems. Mixtures of hydrogen-oxygen, helium-oxygen, or helium-nitrogen-oxygen are used to dive deeper than would be possible diving with compressed air alone.

2. Diving with compressed air or other gas mixtures that are carried by the diver (scuba diving). There are two principal types of scuba: open and closed circuit. An **open circuit** vents all expired air into the water and is the method used in recreational diving. **Closed-circuit** systems, in which exhaled air is rebreathed after carbon dioxide is absorbed and oxygen added, were widely used before open circuit became available, particularly by military divers who wished to avoid showing any air bubbles. As with divers using surface-supplied compressed air, scuba divers are at risk for decompression problems if they ascend without proper decompression. Helium-oxygen and other mixtures can be used to go deeper than is possible with compressed air.

It is to the open-circuit system that underwater recovery operations have turned. In the open-circuit apparatus, air is inhaled from a supply cylinder, and the exhaust is vented directly to the surrounding water. The first and most important component of an open-circuit system was a demand regulator. Designed early in 1866 and patented by Benoît Rouquayrol, the regulator adjusted the flow of air from the tank to meet the diver's breathing and pressure requirements. However, because cylinders strong enough to contain air at high pressure could not be built at the time, Rouquayrol adapted his regulator to surface-supplied diving equipment. In 1933 Commander LePrieur, a French naval officer, constructed an open-circuit breathing apparatus using a tank of compressed air. LePrieur did not include a demand regulator in his design, and the diver spent most of his time manually opening and closing the valve on the tank in an effort to control his air supply. Without a demand regulator, this system had limited practical application (U.S. Navy 2003).

During World War II two Frenchmen achieved a significant breakthrough in open-circuit scuba design. Working in German-occupied France, **Jacques-Yves Cousteau** and **Émile Gagnan** combined an improved demand regulator with high-pressure air tanks to create the first truly efficient and safe open-circuit underwater breathing apparatus. The device was called an **Aqua-Lung.** Recreational dive equipment manufacturer U.S. Divers still bears the Aqua-Lung trademark on many of its products. Cousteau used his gear successfully to 180 fsw without significant difficulty, and with the end of the war, the Aqua-Lung quickly became a commercial success.

The underwater freedom brought about by the development of scuba equipment led to a rapid growth of interest in diving. Sport diving has grown astronomically, and in its wake underwater recovery operations have rapidly followed. The original underwater recovery teams were made up of sport divers volunteering their time. Many fire departments began to provide recovery service for police agencies. It was the logical progression, since fire departments had taken on the responsibility for water rescues. They had boats, wet suits, ropes, fins, and face masks already, and with the addition of regulators, they had dive recovery teams. Since it was the common assumption at the time that submerged evidence had no forensic value, there was no reason for police to either expend the money for equipment and training or allocate manpower to a function that was already being provided by the fire department. It was not until 1983 that the conventional wisdom was challenged in a book by Robert Teather (Royal Canadian Mounted Police) entitled *Underwater Investigation.*

The following year brought the second salvo in the war against salvage operations with the publication of *Processing the Underwater Crime Scene* by the author.

UNDERWATER INVESTIGATION

Slowly police agencies around the country began to recognize that underwater recovery operations were an integral part of police investigation. That perspective was formalized in instruction provided by Dive Rescue International, Southwest Texas State University, the Criminal Justice Department's Underwater Institute, and Lifeguard Systems. Other training entities around the country began to emphasize the fact that submerged evidence was part of a secondary crime scene. Organizations began to sprout up all over the country offering training in underwater police recovery operations. The people involved in police underwater operations began to call themselves **public safety divers,** considering the public safety service provided by the teams. Many fire departments continued to process underwater crime scenes, but they did so after attending the necessary training to do it within an investigatory framework. Many of the fire departments got out of the evidence recovery business, recognizing it as a police function and feeling uncomfortable in a pseudo–law enforcement role. They often spoke of police not fighting fires and firefighters not investigating crimes.

The public safety dive team proved to be an excellent investment in most instances. The media exposure associated with dive recovery operations was always positive even though the service dealt with homicides and other crimes. Police agencies have begun to recognize the good public relations benefits from their recovery operations. Police agencies have also begun to recognize water as an integral part of many secondary crime scenes and have accepted the depths of the operations as "commuting time" to the scene. It would be nice to report that all agencies that have responsibility for recreational waterways and potential water repositories for bodies and other evidence have gotten on board the public safety dive team bandwagon. Unfortunately that is not the case. Many locations with vast oceanic borders still use fire departments to recover bodies and other evidence. They are entrenched in the belief that submerged evidence has no forensic value and continue to enjoy the budgetary relief of not having to fund a police dive team. In time those agencies will recognize the value of processing underwater crime scenes and will prefer the added expenditure to the constant nagging thought that someone has committed a crime for which they might have been caught if all investigatory avenues had been pursued.

Public safety diving is the rubric used today to describe the amalgam of entities that provide law enforcement with underwater dive team capabilities. In essence, firefighters and volunteer teams are doing the job that is integrally a police function. As good a job as is being done by the public diving sector, it is hoped that one day in the not-too-distant future all police agencies recognizing the forensic value of submerged evidence will expend the time, manpower, and resources necessary to bring underwater investigation into the realm of criminal investigation and law enforcement. Those agencies that do not have the resources to field an underwater investigation team will be able to enter into interagency agreements with those neighboring agencies or state agencies that do have proper police underwater recovery resources, just as many rural communities enter into agreements with larger jurisdictions for special team assistance in hostage negotiation and special response (SWAT) needs. Those same types of agreements can spread underwater investigation teams to cover those areas lacking the manpower or resources.

AN EXPLANATION OF PRESSURE AND THE LAWS OF BOYLE, CHARLES, DALTON, AND HENRY

All matter, including air, has weight. Anything exposed to air is under pressure—the weight of the atmosphere above it. This weight of air is known as atmospheric pressure. Air pressure is commonly measured in scuba diving as pounds per square inch, or psi.

At sea level the pressure exerted by the atmosphere is approximately 14.7 psi. The surrounding pressure, on land or under water, is referred to as the ambient pressure. If the surrounding pressure is from the weight of air, it is atmospheric pressure. If the surrounding pressure is from the weight of water, it is hydrostatic pressure. One atmosphere (atm) is the air pressure at sea level and equals 14.7 psi. Two atm is twice the sea level pressure. Two atm = 29.4 psi, a pressure reached at 33 fsw. At 33 feet under water, a diver is under *two* atmospheres of pressure: one atmosphere from the air above sea level and a second atmosphere from the 33 feet of water.

Air is a mixture of gases, mainly oxygen (21 percent) and nitrogen (78 percent). The other 1 percent of air is made up of several other gases such as carbon dioxide (CO_2), argon, krypton, and neon. In any mixture of gases, the individual gases don't chemically combine with each other. The gases maintain their individual identity and percentages regardless of the pressure to which the mixture is subjected. This fact takes on importance as water pressure increases with increasing depth because, although the percentages are unchanged, the total pressure exerted by each gas component increases proportionally. The increases in component gas pressures account for some of the problems inherent in compressed-air diving: nitrogen narcosis, decompression sickness, and oxygen toxicity (Martin 1997).

Air under water obeys the same laws as air in the atmosphere. In underwater operations the four most important gas laws are those of the Englishmen **Robert Boyle** (1627–1691), **John Dalton** (1766–1844), and **William Henry** (1774–1790), and the Frenchman **Jacques Charles** (1746–1823).

Boyle's law:

At constant temperature, the volume of a gas varies *inversely* with the pressure, while the density of a gas varies *directly* with pressure.

Mathematically,

$$PV = K$$

If temperature is kept constant as air pressure increases, the volume of a gas decreases, and vice versa.

P and *V* are the pressure and volume, respectively, and *K* is a constant. Change *P*, and *V* will change in the opposite direction, so their product is maintained at a constant value. Suppose you have a container open on one end that is inverted over water; as the container is lowered into the water, the trapped air will be compressed by the water pressure. Assume the container holds one liter of air at sea level pressure (one atmosphere). $PV = 1$ liter $\times$ 1 atm $= 1$. Increase the air pressure to 2 atmospheres, and Boyle's law predicts the volume of air in the container will be 1/2 liter. Note that Boyle's law also relates to gas *density*. Increase the pressure of a fixed volume of gas, and the density increases. Of the four laws we will study, Boyle's is the most important for underwater operations.

Charles's law:

At a constant volume, the pressure of gas varies directly with absolute temperature.

Mathematically,

$$\frac{P_1}{P_2} = \frac{T_1}{T_2}$$

Given a constant volume of gas, the higher the temperature, the higher the gas pressure, and vice versa.

P_1 and P_2 are the beginning and final pressures, and T_1 and T_2 are the beginning and final temperatures. The law is useful to keep in mind when filling air tanks when there is a large difference between air and water temperatures. Charles's law predicts that a steel scuba tank holding 80 cu. ft. of air at a pressure of 3,000 psi, filled when the air temperature was 90°F and taken into water that is 75°F, will have an in-water tank pressure lower than 3,000 psi.

Dalton's law:

The total pressure exerted by a mixture of gases is equal to the sum of the pressures that would be exerted by each of the gases if it alone were present and occupied the total volume.

Mathematically,

$$P_{TOTAL} = P_1 + P_2 \cdots + P_{OTHER}$$

The pressure of any gas mixture is equal to the sum of pressures exerted by the individual gases. In air those individual gases would be oxygen, nitrogen, and the minor gases.

P_{TOTAL} is the total pressure of a gas mixture, and P_1 and P_2 are the *partial* pressures of component gases (oxygen and nitrogen). The term P_{OTHER} is used to signify partial pressures of all other gases in the mixture.

Partial pressure is the pressure exerted by an individual gas, whether that gas is part of a mixture (such as air) or dissolved in a liquid (such as blood) or in any body tissue. Partial pressure of a gas (P_G) is determined by the fraction of the gas in the mixture (F_G) times the total pressure of all the gases:

$$P_G = F_G \times \text{total gas pressure (excluding water vapor)}$$

In air at sea level, the partial pressures of oxygen and nitrogen are:

$$PO_2: \quad .21 \times 1 \text{ atm} = .21 \text{ atm}$$
$$PN_2: \quad .79 \times 1 \text{ atm} = .79 \text{ atm}$$

Henry's law:

> **The amount of any gas that will dissolve in a liquid at a given temperature is a function of the partial pressure of the gas in contact with the liquid and the solubility coefficient of the gas in that particular liquid.**
>
> Mathematically,
>
> $$\frac{VG}{VL} = aP_g$$

As the pressure of any gas increases, more of that gas will dissolve into any solution with which it is in free contact.

VG is the volume of a particular gas; VL is the volume of a particular liquid; a is the solubility coefficient for the gas in that liquid; and P_g is the pressure of the gas in contact with the liquid.

Taken together, Henry's and Dalton's laws predict two very important consequences:

1. When ambient pressure is lowered (as at altitude), the partial pressure of oxygen and nitrogen in the body must fall, and there will be fewer molecules of each gas dissolved in the blood and tissues.

This first consequence is the physiologic basis for latent hypoxia (shallow-water blackout). The most common form of shallow-water blackout is associated with breath-hold free diving. In an effort to increase the amount of time a breath-hold diver can spend submerged, many hyperventilate prior to entry into the water. Hyperventilation is the practice of excessive breathing with an increase in the rate of respiration or an increase in the depth of respiration, or both. This will not store extra oxygen. The magical benefit of hyperventilation is what it does to carbon dioxide levels in the blood. Rapid or deep breathing reduces carbon dioxide levels rapidly. It is high levels of carbon dioxide, not low levels of oxygen, that stimulate the need to breathe.

The trained breath-hold diver has blown off massive amounts of carbon dioxide with hyperventilation, thus outsmarting the brain's breathing center. Normally metabolizing body tissues, producing carbon dioxide at a regular rate, do not replace enough carbon dioxide to stimulate this breathing center until the body is seriously short of oxygen.

Hyperventilation causes some central nervous system changes as well. Practiced to excess, it causes decreased cerebral blood flow, dizziness, and muscle cramping in the arms and legs. But moderate degrees of hyperventilation can cause a state of euphoria and well-being. This can lead to overconfidence and the dramatic consequence of a body performing too long without a breath: blackout.

Pressure changes in the free diver's descent-ascent cycle conspire to rob him of oxygen as he nears the surface by the mechanism of partial pressures. Gas levels, namely oxygen and carbon dioxide, are continuously balancing themselves in the body. Gases balance between the lungs and body tissues. The body draws oxygen from the lungs, as it requires. The oxygen concentration in the lungs of a descending diver increases because of the increasing water pressure. As the brain and tissues use oxygen, more oxygen is available from the lungs while the free diver is still descending. This all works well as long as there is oxygen in the lungs and the diver remains at his descended level. The problem is in ascent. The reexpanding lungs of the ascending diver increase in volume as the water pressure decreases, and this results in a rapid decrease of oxygen in the lungs to critical levels. The balance that forced oxygen into the body is now reversed. It is most pronounced in the last 10 to 15 feet below the surface, where the greatest relative lung expansion occurs. This is where unconsciousness may happen. The blackout may be instantaneous and without warning. It is the result of a critically low level of oxygen, which in effect switches off the brain.

2. When ambient pressure is raised (as when diving), the partial pressure of oxygen and nitrogen in the body must rise, and there will be more molecules of each gas dissolved in the blood and tissues. This second consequence is the physiologic basis for three important problems associated with compressed air diving: decompression sickness, nitrogen narcosis, and oxygen toxicity (Martin 1997).

IMPORTANT DATES IN THE HISTORY OF SCUBA DIVING

1667—Robert Boyle observed a gas bubble in the eye of a viper that had been compressed and then decompressed. This was the first recorded observation of decompression sickness, or the bends.

1823—Charles Anthony Deane patented a "smoke helmet" for firefighters. This helmet was used for diving, too. The helmet was fitted over the head and was held on with weights. Air was supplied from the surface.

1828—Charles Deane and his brother, John, marketed the helmet with a "diving suit." The suit was not attached to the helmet, but was secured with straps.

1837—Augustus Siebe sealed the Deane brothers' diving helmet to a watertight, air-containing rubber suit.

1839—Siebe's diving suit was used during the salvage of the British warship HMS *Royal George*. The improved suit was adopted as the standard diving dress by the Royal Engineers.

1865—Benoît Rouquayrol and Auguste Denayrouse patented an apparatus for underwater breathing. It consisted of a horizontal steel tank of compressed air on a diver's back, connected to a valve attached to a mouthpiece. The tank was surface-supplied with air.

1878—Paul Bert published *La Pression Barométrique*, a book-length work containing his physiologic studies of pressure changes.

1908—John Scott Haldane, Arthur E. Boycott, and Guybon C. Damant published "The Prevention of Compressed-Air Illness," a paper on decompression sickness.

1912—The U.S. Navy tested the dive tables published by Haldane, Boycott, and Damant.

1930s—Guy Gilpatric pioneered the use of rubber goggles with glass lenses for skin diving.

1933—Louis de Corlieu patents swim fins.

1933—Yves LePrieur modified the Rouquayrol-Denayrouse invention by combining a demand valve with a high-pressure air tank to give the diver complete freedom from hoses and lines.

1942–43—Jacques-Yves Cousteau and Émile Gagnan redesigned a regulator that would automatically provide compressed air to a diver on intake of breath. They named the device Aqua-Lung.

1946—Cousteau's Aqua-Lung was marketed commercially in France (Great Britain in 1950, Canada in 1951, and USA in 1952).

1957—The first segment of *Sea Hunt* aired on television, starring Lloyd Bridges as Mike Hunt, underwater adventurer.

1959—The YMCA began the first nationally organized course for scuba certification.

1960—NAUI (National Association of Underwater Instructors) was formed.

1966—PADI (Professional Association of Diving Instructors) was formed.

1970s—Important advances relating to scuba safety that began in the 1960s became widely implemented in the 1970s, such as certification cards to indicate a minimum level of training, change from J-valve reserve systems to nonreserve K valves, and adoption of the BC and single-hose regulators as essential pieces of diving equipment.

1980—Divers Alert Network was founded at Duke University as a nonprofit organization to promote safe diving.

1983—The Orca Edge, the first commercially available dive computer, was introduced.

1990s—An estimated 500,000 new scuba divers are certified yearly in the United States, new scuba magazines appear, and scuba travel is big business. There is an increase in diving by nonprofessionals who use advanced technology, including mixed gases, full face masks, underwater voice communication, propulsion systems, and so on (Martin 1997).

REVIEW QUESTIONS

1. What is breath-hold diving? How does it differ from scuba diving?
2. What is shallow-water blackout?
3. What is open-circuit scuba?
4. What is closed-circuit scuba?
5. Who is Augustus Siebe, and what was his contribution to the diving world?
6. What is the bends?
7. Who are Jacques-Yves Cousteau and Émile Gagnan, and what was their contribution to scuba diving?
8. What is nitrogen narcosis?
9. How can nitrogen narcosis be avoided?
10. How can decompression sickness be avoided?
11. What does atm stand for?
12. What is ambient pressure?
13. What is the ambient pressure in psi at sea level?
14. What is the water pressure at 33 fsw in atm and psi?
15. Explain Boyle's, Charles's, Dalton's, and Henry's laws as they apply to scuba diving.

REFERENCES

MARTIN, L. 1997. *Scuba diving explained.* Flagstaff: Best.
U.S. NAVY. 1993. *U.S. Navy diving manual.* Flagstaff: Best.
U.S. NAVY. 2003. *U.S. Navy diving manual.* Flagstaff: Best.

Chapter 3

The Underwater Investigator

NEW WORDS AND CONCEPTS

underwater investigation dive team

bottom time

standard operation and procedures manual

job-related

contaminated water

decontamination

team leader

tenders

personal flotation device

swimming skills

diving skills

National Fire Protection Association

primary diver

safety diver

incident commander

security zones

nighttime dive operations

dive team coordinator

incident safety officer

tool pusher

team structure

90 percent diver

coordinating board

intelligence officer

photographer

lift specialists

archivist

training coordinator

LEARNING OBJECTIVES

- Discuss dive team dynamics
- Explain the structure of public safety dive teams
- Explain the roles of each member of a public safety dive team

An **underwater investigation dive team** is a dynamic creature that must be nourished and cultivated. Nothing about diving or dive operations remains the same. An integral part of a dive operation is the bringing together of persons best suited for the task. Historically, anybody who wanted to be on the dive team could be. Over time, as promotion and status began to be accorded dive team members, others began to vie to fill vacancies on the team, and much of the recruitment was based on politics and personal relationships. Suitability today cannot be based on gender, rank, seniority, or personal relationships. If something or someone becomes an obstacle to the overall productivity of the team and its function, there must be a built-in mechanism to replace that component, wherever it may be. No person or component is more important than the team or the organization from which the team emerges.

As was mentioned in the introduction, we often think of the underwater investigative team as made up of members directly involved in recovery operations. That is a conventional perspective and is accurate as far as it goes. If we stop there, we allow ourselves to compartmentalize the underwater investigation function, which results in isolation and miscommunication. We will discuss the membership of the underwater investigation team, but it is important to remember that all investigations including underwater investigations are just a cog in a much larger machine. For our purposes, that machine is made up of everyone who is instrumental in getting the evidence recovered from its underwater location into a courtroom, before a jury, where it is hoped it can serve as the foundation upon which a conviction is made.

The dive team and the underwater investigators on that team cannot operate in a vacuum. It serves little purpose to train underwater investigators if other members of the criminal justice family do not appreciate what it is underwater investigators do or can do. Since the objective of all investigations is to obtain a conviction, it becomes apparent that underwater investigators are part of a larger team, a team made up of those who will assist in preparing, testing, and preserving evidence recovered by underwater investigators. The original challenge in underwater recovery work was to teach dive teams a scientific protocol to apply to recovery operations and the evidence obtained as a result of those operations. The world of the underwater investigator began with reinventing the role of public safety diving based on solid forensic perspectives. The public safety diving industry has done a good job in educating those who are interested in being educated. Most dive teams have underwater investigators who understand the steps involved in processing an underwater crime scene. The weak link in the chain has been the lack of success in bringing other members of the criminal justice team to the table. Administrators, dry-land investigators, forensics personnel, and prosecutors have not been as available as have dive teams around the country to learn about a new perspective in underwater recovery operations. The work of underwater investigators will not reach its maximum potential until the other members of the criminal justice team become as knowledgeable as those processing underwater crime scenes (Becker 1995).

THE TEAM

Dive calls are often the most difficult to staff. Callouts may find the number of responding personnel limited and on occasion lacking. Most police agencies have volunteer teams (within the agency) made up of officers from various sections or divisions on different shifts and at different locations. It is difficult for dive team members to drop what they are doing to respond to an operational callout. Those who do arrive may be too few in number and limited in the roles they can fill. Many teams have land-based personnel who are not divers. The scene commander cannot command from underwater. Although many agencies require all their dive team personnel to be cross-trained, most still use nondiving staff for land-based functions. It becomes apparent that among the variety of skills dive team members must have, one of the most valuable is reliability. On every underwater investigation dive team, there are those who carry more than their fair share and who log the greatest amount of **bottom time.** Some spend the time to get bragging rights; some do it out of necessity. Reliability includes availability for callouts and for training and exercises. It is one of those personal characteristics that is difficult to evaluate prior to an individual's joining the team. Another difficult attribute to evaluate is that of being a team player; not everyone "plays well with others." Some people may be great at the individual role they are assigned or are performing, but if they cannot work as an integral part of a team, someone is at risk. All things considered, it is better to have an average diver who is a team player than an above-average diver who is not. Teamwork cannot be overemphasized in the kind of work involved in underwater operations. Injury and death await the unprepared, poorly equipped, or poorly trained, and those teams that do not work as a team are doomed to failure. Specific requirements for participation on an underwater investigation team vary from agency to agency in that there are no national, regional, state, or local standards that can be employed. A set of desirable requirements are discussed later in this chapter.

When we think of teamwork, we generally think of the working dynamics of a particular dive team. In large operations, teams from different agencies will gather to provide the necessary manpower for large-scale underwater recoveries. The recovery of shuttle debris would be such an occasion, as would the crash of a passenger aircraft into a lake or offshore body of water (see Chapter Eight dealing with "mass disaster"). Interagency teamwork is the key to successful large-scale operations. Interagency agreements should be considered before a recovery requires interagency cooperation. These agreements anticipate the need for cooperation among communities and their public service agencies. In the case of mass disasters, it is too late to wait until the disaster occurs to gather all that is necessary to properly handle such an event. It is contingency planning that allows communities to evaluate what resources that community has and does not have. Contingency planning provides the community with a "needs list." What it lacks must be either bought or borrowed. The purpose of interagency agreements is to make that borrowing easier and more effective.

Prerequisites

What makes an underwater investigation dive team diver? A good place to start is with recreational certification. There must be some minimum entry-level requirements, and most teams write their own **standard operation and procedures (SOP) manual** (perhaps a better term is standard operation guideline [SOG]) that describes what these entry-level requirements are. At this juncture it would be good to proffer a caveat regarding job requirements and SOPs. All requirements for a position within a police agency must be **job-related.** If there are requirements that are not job-related, they could be challenged if they discriminate based on gender, age, or race. All prerequisites for entering the dive team must be job-tested. Whether SOPs or SOGs, they should contain all the information regarding the prerequisites for entry to the dive team, training, equipment, and operational procedures and forms. We will discuss SOPs more fully later. Suffice it to say that from a legal perspective, if it is not contained in the SOPs, it does not exist. If it is contained in the SOPs, it is the standard against which all team activities will be measured. Teams want members who are mentally and physically fit, and to that end may promulgate examinations both physical and mental to assist in making those determinations.

All applicants for positions on the underwater investigation team (dive recovery team) must pass a physical. Those team members who will be land-based support personnel must have yearly physical examinations and have those results provided to the person within the agency with responsibility for the continued existence of the team. Some agencies have an administrator who handles the personnel issues dealing with membership on the team. That person's title may be dive team director, commander, supervisor, etc. For the purposes of this discussion, we will refer to this person as the dive team administrator. It makes little difference what the name is as long as there is someone providing budget, personnel, and equipment oversight. This person is generally not a part of the operational team, does not respond to callouts, and does not get wet. All team members who will be diving must have annual dive physicals by a dive medicine physician. Additionally, team members should undergo a dive physical after any dive-related injury, major injury, illness, or medical procedure. Those records must also be provided to the team administrator.

DAN (Diver's Alert Network) offers divers the latest in medical perspectives regarding diving. Their Web site is full of information for the new and seasoned public safety diver. They provide dive insurance and the location of various hospitals with hyperbaric (dive) physicians and chambers.

Contaminated Water

Contaminated water is a major concern for divers. There are things in the water that we cannot see that can hurt us. A partial list would include:

- Bacteria
  - Salmonella—an infection characterized by fever, headache, constipation, abdominal pain, and a rash

- *V. Cholerae*—an infection involving the small bowel characterized by watery diarrhea, vomiting, muscular cramps, and dehydration
- *E. Coli*—causes urinary tract infections, necrotic lesions, and diarrhea
- Aeromonas—often involves the lungs and is characterized by upper respiratory congestion
- Pseudomonas—often involves the ear, eye, or sinuses and is characterized by purulent drainage
- Pfesteria—a microbe that kills fish and that has transcended the species boundary and may cause lesions in humans
- Viruses
  - Hepatitis A and B—both create flulike symptoms, nausea, vomiting, and fever. After three days, dark urine and jaundice occur. Symptoms subside, but jaundice worsens. May cause tender and enlarged liver. All dive team members should receive inoculations against hepatitis A and B.
- Parasites
  - Giardia—may cause intermittent nausea, flatulence, abdominal cramps, and diarrhea
  - Amebiasis—a protozoal infection characterized by diarrhea or dysentery (Beers and Berkow 2004)

When called out to a dive, a team should have some way of determining the contamination level of the water. Is it tangentially contaminated but not harmful for human submersion? Is it highly contaminated, and do we know the nature of those contaminants? Over time we discover that criminals have favorite water repositories for their weapons and associated contraband. They pick places that secret their deposits and may intentionally pick a place that is contaminated to avoid possible discovery. In a Texas case of homicide by an off-duty police officer, the weapon used (a kitchen knife) was thrown into a sewage settlement tank. Although the tank was contaminated and disgusting, that recovery was performed using the right equipment, personnel, and **decontamination** protocol. The common depositories have characteristics that make them attractive to criminals. Those very characteristics are what make these places the most undesirable for underwater investigators to navigate. Time and again investigators are called to the same or approximately the same locations to provide recovery services. It should be a fairly straightforward proposition to note the obvious contaminants, their sources, and their intensity. It may require the help of health department personnel to provide on-site testing to determine the nature and extent of contamination, but that time is well spent. It is important to remember that there is nothing in the water so important as to risk the life or health of another human. There is always a cost-benefit analysis under way that should include the level of contamination in the area to be searched and the concomitant training and equipment available to search it safely. In a nutshell, it is the **team leader's** responsibility to see that as much information as possible is gathered regarding the various areas in which the team operates. It is that person's responsibility to match the divers to the conditions and the conditions to the equipment available. An equipment inventory will quickly begin to determine the scope of a team's area of operations. If wet suits and regulators make up the equipment inventory, dives should be made in only the cleanest of water.

All surface water in the United States is contaminated. The amount of that contamination varies, but no surface water is fit for human consumption without some type of prior preparation. If surface water is unfit to drink, it should be axiomatic to say that the same water poses a potential danger when given access to a person's system through the nose or mouth by a dislodged or replaced face mask or regulator.

It is difficult if not impossible to dive in traditional scuba diving equipment without swallowing or allowing entry of water through the ears. In that vein, it is prudent for all team members, both land-based and, especially, waterborne, to have hepatitis and tetanus vaccinations. If all surface water is unfit for human consumption, consider its fitness as an underwater investigator crawls along the bottom of highly contaminated waterways or through highly contaminated bottom sediment. Upon decontamination, everyone involved in the decontamination process is susceptible to contagion. It is this simple proposition that prompts most teams to invest in dry suits, hoods, and full-face masks or helmets.

The question we should be asking ourselves is: Do we need to be diving in this situation, and if so, how can we protect ourselves from biologicals? This is an important consideration wherever we operate. It is important to remember that "clean water" often is not clean. If diving in water we know to be "safe" in wet suits with partial face masks and regulators, we should wash down the dive gear at the dive site with an antibacterial soap and mild chlorine solution followed by a clean water rinse.

Eardrops should be a standard part of every underwater investigator's dive locker. A good antibacterial eardrop can be made from 16 oz. of acetic acid with a Domeboro tablet added.

When diving waters we know to be contaminated, all underwater operators should dive dry with a positive-pressure, full-face mask or helmet. Some dry suits are more suitable to certain kinds of contamination than others. It is necessary to determine the nature and potency of any contaminants in determining whether or not the dry suit available will withstand exposure to the contaminants. It is important to remember that all land-based support personnel who are handling divers, dive equipment, and search lines are equally susceptible to contamination and should be outfitted accordingly. They should also be part of the decontamination protocol. Divers exiting contaminated waters should be sprayed with clean, fresh water as they exit. An area should be set aside as a decontamination area, and all decontamination personnel should be clothed in hazmat suits prior to the beginning of decontamination. The freshwater wash down (including the bottom of the feet) should be followed by an antibacterial soaping. The soap should be sprayed clean before the dry suit is removed. The diver should also be washed down once the dry suit has been removed. Any undergarments worn under the dry suit should be isolated and washed with antibacterial soap along with any clothing worn by the dive **tenders** or other support personnel who may have gotten wet. All divers

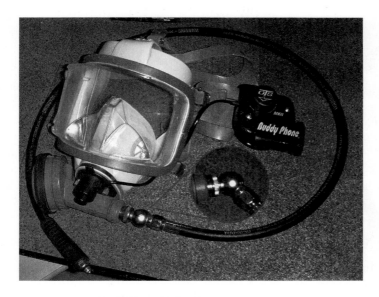

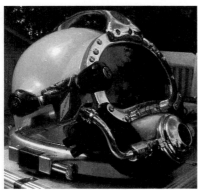

FIGURE 3-1 AGA full-face mask, Kirby Morgan superlight, and dry suit.
(*Source:* R. F. Becker)

FIGURE 3-2   Wet suit, exposure suit, regulator, and face mask.
(*Source:* SMART Divers)

should use eardrops immediately after completion of their personal wash down. The removed dive gear must be subjected to a more thorough washing after the decontamination process has been completed. It is impossible to give all dive equipment the decontamination attention it requires at the dive site. Further cleaning should be thorough and specific. In the highly contaminated waters of the Florida Everglades, the search operation for ValuJet flight 592 had searchers in the water wearing appropriate hazmat apparel but also wearing their own hats and caps. The decontamination process included the destruction of the hazmat apparel, but searchers who had been wading around in highly contaminated water took their hats or caps home with them. It is important to remember that anything exposed to contaminated water is contaminated.

Some points worth reiterating:

- "Clean water" may not be.
- All surface water is contaminated.
- If you wouldn't drink it, you shouldn't be getting it in your ears, nose, lungs, or mouth.
- Develop dive site libraries that contain contamination levels.
- Use full-face masks and dry suits whenever possible.
- Decontaminate the whole team, not just the divers.
- All personal clothing, if exposed, must be decontaminated or destroyed.
- Don't dive in waters you are not trained or equipped to dive in.

FIGURE 3-3 Stratford, Texas, recovery operation, decontamination in progress.
(*Source:* L. Dixon)

Swimming Skills

The world of the underwater investigator revolves around water. There are no safe water locations. Each watercourse has its own characteristic risks, but the most common is the water itself. Every member of the dive team must be a competent swimmer. Every member of the team on site who is not "dressed out" to dive must wear a **personal flotation device** (PFD) regardless of water depth, ambient temperature, or **swimming skills.** There is a direct correlation between the outside temperature and the complaints about having to wear a PFD. Part of every team's SOPs must be a written requirement for all on-site personnel not dressed out to wear a PFD. It is the only way the agency and the team can insulate themselves from allegations of negligence should support personnel drown. It's really very simple: no PFD, no access.

Most elite police teams have physical standards that are required for membership and continued qualification as a member. Dive teams historically have had no such physical requirements because it was felt that working underwater was not strenuous and did not require physical fitness. In a study conducted by the author to determine the effects of nitrox (enhanced oxygen diving) on divers, we discovered among other results that all divers using compressed air or nitrox had elevated blood pressure and pulse rates. The greatest elevations were among those divers who exceeded height-to-weight ratios (overweight). Keeping those results in mind, it becomes apparent that underwater operations are more physically demanding and stressful than we heretofore believed (Jamieson, Becker, and Dixon 1999). In addition to yearly physicals, it is a good idea to record blood pressure and pulse rates for each diver prior to that diver entering the water. Blood pressure and pulse rates should be recorded and kept in a file for each diver. Maladies that are obvious and that should preempt membership on dive teams for operational personnel would include:

- Hypertension (blood pressure seems to increase with increased depth)
- Fear of heights
- Fear of confined spaces
- Heart condition
- Middle ear problems
- Respiratory disorders
- Diabetes
- Pregnancy
- Specific physical disabilities

It would be prudent to assess and monitor physical conditioning through the assessment of swimming skills. In this way the physical requirements are shown to be work-related. Some teams have running, lifting, push-up, pull-up, and sit-up requirements. Although an excellent way to condition and stay in condition, these are not necessarily job-related and may be challenged as discriminatory and designed to bar specific groups from entry to the team. Physical testing that is job-related can withstand such allegations. Whatever skill set is assessed, that assessment must be continued throughout an individual's tenure on the team to validate the job-related nature of the skills being tested. If the entry-level skills are not retested once the applicant has made the team, those skill tests may be considered suspect and may be challenged as discriminatory.

Many teams require swimming skills testing as an entry requirement for the underwater recovery team. Often an agency will cross-train team members and have no nondiving personnel. In other instances support staff do not dive and are not divers. In order to have entry-level requirements that are job-related, it is necessary to have two sets of swimming skills testing: one for diving personnel and the other for nondiving personnel.

Here is an example of a swim skills test that may be offered:

1. Breathe comfortably with regulater in place. This may be the single most important exercise that teams can regularly practice.
2. Perform an ascent from thirty feet of water without the use of scuba equipment other than face mask and fins.
3. Perform an ascent from twenty feet of water without the use of scuba equipment other than a face mask and fins while carrying a five-pound weight.
4. Perform an ocean entry into surf with scuba equipment.*
5. Perform an ocean exit with surf using scuba equipment.*

*Only if ocean entries and exits are part of the dive operations for the team.

6. Be able to don scuba equipment while underwater.
7. Be able to remove scuba equipment while underwater.
8. Be able to access a backup air supply while submerged.
9. Be able to use another diver's backup air supply while submerged.
10. Assist an unconscious diver to the surface.
11. Tow an unconscious diver 100 feet.
12. Tow an unconscious diver 100 yards fully dressed out absent weight belt.
13. Lift twenty-five-pound weight belt waist high with each hand, and walk fifty feet.
14. Rappel down a twenty-foot embankment fully dressed out.
15. Retrieve a rappelled, fully dressed-out diver from a twenty-foot embankment.

It should be noted that all the activities in the preceding dive team skills test are directly related to the job. This list could be a good starting place for a dive team that wishes to develop a set of team entry guidelines. Those teams that have skills tests that require distance swimming and water treading durations will have difficulty withstanding attacks alleging discrimination. The skills suggested above are a starting point for a team to:

- Determine membership
- Assess skills
- Devise a gender-free skills set
- Implement in-service training and periodic skills assessment
- Establish a basic training protocol

During the tests divers must be monitored, and after each test their vital signs should be recorded. Physical responses to the tests may reveal unknown or unrecognized medical or psychological issues. Those issues should be recorded and made part of each applicant's permanent dive team record.

For land-based support personnel who are not divers, it would be necessary to create a separate set of swimming skills testing that is job-related. Considering that they may fall into the water, some swimming acumen would be required. What follows is a job-related list of skills that could be employed to determine applicant suitability:

- Pull a fully dressed-out, 200-pound diver 100 feet through the water to the surface.
- Drag a 200-pound diver twenty feet on land.
- Swim 100 yards fully clothed and wearing a personal flotation device.

- Float upright or on the back for fifteen minutes while fully clothed and wearing a PFD.
- Lift a twenty-five-pound weight belt waist high with each hand, and walk fifty feet.

Diving Skills

Many teams recruit members from among their nondiving colleagues. These teams believe that recreationally trained divers are not only unfit for dive recovery operations, but may even be a liability to the team. They prefer to get men and women who are clean slates, thereby precluding any bad habits a recreational diver may have developed. It is dangerous to presume that a recreational diver has any type of standardized training. Although recreational certifying agencies attempt to standardize training, there is a gap between policy and application. All too often at shops throughout the country, the primary concern is to certify new divers and sell them the most fashionable diving ensembles. If you pay the fee for training, you get certified. That practice became most obvious at the Underwater Institute at Southwest Texas State University. Divers came from all over the country with a variety of certifications that the staff at the Underwater Institute relied upon. That reliance was to their detriment. Many certified divers lacked basic **diving skills,** from clearing a face mask to recovering a dropped regulator. The solution was to precede every Underwater Institute training session with a pool checkout of basic scuba skills. It was very revealing. The single most common oversight, and perhaps the most dangerous, was emergency ascents. Few knew how to do it; some had tried it once; a few had practiced it after their original exposure.

Part of the dilemma is that recreational divers have nothing with which to compare their training. They did what they were requested to do and received a basic scuba diving certification card. Nowhere on the card does it stress the limits of the certification. Divers with recreational certification enter caves, examine underwater tunnels, attempt submerged automobile recoveries, etc. They believe that their certification has prepared them to do anything underwater. It is these bad habits that agencies attempt to avoid by recruiting nondivers.

Some states adhere to the **National Fire Protection Association** (NFPA) standards for rescue divers. It should be borne in mind that this text leaves the subject of rescue to those more expert in that field. It is the author's belief that fire departments should handle rescues, and police agencies underwater recovery of evidentiary items. But for the purpose of providing a framework within which we can consider levels of training, those training standards are included here. The NFPA provides three levels of competency for rescue divers that can be applied to recovery teams:

1. Awareness competency
   a. Assess the site and determine the platform for the operation (boat, shore, dock, etc.)
   b. Assess the site as to obstacles and hazards
   c. Determine the nature of the operation

      d. Contact backup (support) agencies

      e. Secure the scene

         i. Identify witnesses

         ii. Prevent unauthorized entry

         iii. Delineate the scene with police tape

      f. Determine entry and exit routes

      g. Assess contamination levels

2. Operational competency

      a. Stage equipment

         i. Check equipment

      b. Rig equipment

      c. Reassess obstacles and hazards

      d. Reassess contamination levels

      e. Select a command site

      f. Determine the need for the dive

         i. Cost-benefit analysis

      g. Assist in dressing divers

      h. Assist in deploying divers

      i. Provide dive tender support

         i. Direct the dive

         ii. Monitor communications (or line pulls)

         iii. Maintain search integrity

      j. Don PFDs

      k. Prepare **primary diver,** backup diver, and **safety diver**

      l. Assess the quality of search for each sweep

      m. Monitor the diver in the water

      n. Assist in diver recovery and gear removal

      o. Flush all gear in clean water

      p. Provide decontamination assistance where needed

      q. Stow gear

3. Technical competency

      a. Assess the obstacles and hazards

      b. Assess the quality of the diver platform

      c. Determine whether or not this is a good day to dive

         i. Only divers decide if it's a good day for that diver

      d. Discuss contamination levels

         i. Determine the type of equipment to be used.

            1. Hazmat or conventional scuba gear

      e. Check gear

      f. Dress

      g. Discuss search pattern and objective

         i. Line signals

         ii. Contingency plan

    h. Tether to the search line
    i. Deploy
    j. Maintain search integrity
    k. Upon relief, report
        i. Obstacles
        ii. Hazards
        iii. Bottom structure
    l. Complete all necessary paperwork
    m. Record vital statistics

INCIDENT COMMAND STRUCTURE

Determining who's in command at a dive site is generally a relatively simple proposition. There really is no command center other than where the team leader, who usually is working as the **incident commander,** is. There are no collateral agencies involved, and the team handles the operation the same way it's handled similar operations in the past. It does not get complicated until other agencies are factored into the equation. Those complications can become almost insurmountable in mass disasters where contingency plans and interagency agreements are not in place. Periodic conflict can arise between agencies if more than one is dispatched to an operation. The most common conflict is a long-running dispute between rescue-oriented fire departments and recovery-oriented police agencies. This conflict goes back in history and arose as a result of fire departments providing dive services for rescue operations and recovery services for police underwater recoveries. It made sense to have fire departments doing the diving, since they had rescue responsibility to begin with. They had the boats, equipment, and divers. It was not until recently that their domain over public safety diving has been challenged. In various venues around the country, police agencies were becoming aware that submerged evidence might retain forensic information. It became readily apparent to everyone except fire departments that police recovery operations were a secondary crime scene and firefighters had no business in them. That news was not welcomed by fire departments around the country. It came to a head in Seattle, Washington, where police and firefighters came to blows over who had the right to provide dive services to the community. To exacerbate the situation, both the police and fire departments were unionized and it devolved into issues of overtime, promotion, and job security—everything the debate needed to turn it into an inferno.

It is hoped that by the time you read this, the debate over recovery versus rescue will be resolved. It may appear to be a straightforward dichotomy: Fire departments rescue and police process underwater crime scenes. If only it were that easy. If police arrive before the fire department, have they some legally recognized responsibility to attempt a water rescue. If they do not, can they be held legally liable? If, in the midst of a water rescue by the police, the fire department arrives and the police withdraw, resulting in the drowning of the victim, can both agencies be sued? If, during a police dive recovery operation, a police diver is at risk, must police wait for the fire department to arrive to effect a rescue? What appears to be a simple issue on the surface is much more complicated. It would be good if common sense would prevail, but collateral issues have arisen, clouding the real issues and fueling the fire.

If the issue of who has command responsibility can be resolved amicably among various agencies (fire department, police, emergency medical services, STAR Flight rescue, etc.) at a critical incident, the operation will run smoothly. The Texas Department of Public Safety has some fairly straightforward written guidelines. Their dive team will not deploy subordinate to any other organization. The team will not deploy on rescues other than those that occur during a recovery operation involving recovery personnel. It is common knowledge among agencies throughout the state what the working orders of the TDPS are, and there is little dispute when they arrive on a scene. That working arrangement may evolve over time, especially with an agency that has statewide jurisdiction. It is a better policy to resolve these types of disputes prior to encountering them. The tool for that is the interagency agreement, wherein the parties express their respective authority and responsibilities. It seems a simple process to define a rescue as any recovery operation that takes place within an hour or two (to be determined by the agency based on water temperatures) of the person's last sighting. If it is a rescue, it should be a fire department function. After the predetermined time has passed, it should become a recovery operation and be turned over to the police. The scene changes character from a rescue site to a prospective primary or secondary crime scene, which is and should be police territory.

Incident Commander

In an incident that involves more than one responding agency, site command will have to be initiated. As mentioned above, that can be a complex proposition. Once it is determined who has support responsibility and who has operational responsibility, a command post can be established. In crime scene recovery operations, this may be a reflection of police administrative hierarchy. Generally the incident commander in these types of incidents is not a diver and has command interaction only with the team. It is the incident commander's responsibility to coordinate activities as needed among the various agencies participating in a large-scale recovery operation. If a large perimeter needs to be established, it is the incident commander who has supervisory authority over the patrol personnel who are assisting in establishing the boundaries of the scene and who are responsible for maintaining the security of the scene. Patrol staff have to provide exits and entryways for personnel who are authorized to have access to the scene. The incident commander authorizes access. The patrol force has to establish an exterior staging area that is within the perimeter but does not interfere with parking and staging of support personnel and equipment.

It is generally to the patrol force that the responsibility falls to establish and secure the search scene perimeter. In dive operations there should be three secure zones. These zones allow access control and assist in the staging of operational and support personnel.

- *Zone one:* Most agencies believe this zone begins at the water's edge. That perspective is a mistake and can result in the destruction of or the failure to discover relevant information or evidence. As in all crime scenes, the actors had to arrive and depart the scene. Often the point of arrival or departure can be determined and may contain evidence relevant to the investigation. The underwater investigative team must address the issues of arrival and departure. If the area in question is highly trafficked, it may have been necessary for the actor to have waited prior to depositing the item of interest in the water. Often a casual search of the area will reveal evidentiary items that are not directly associated with the item sought but may nonetheless prove important. If a perpetrator sat on a bench adjacent to the area in which the item is believed to repose, there may be food remnants (wrappers, pull tabs, cans, etc.), cigarettes, footprints, or tire marks. Every crime scene is examined for points of entry, departure, and anticipation; underwater crime scenes should be treated no differently. Once zone one has been thoroughly searched, dive personnel can begin the in-water recovery operation. This zone is reserved for dive team personnel only. The media and administrative personnel should not enter this area but will attempt to. Patrol personnel cannot be expected to deny administrative officers access, although they should. Because it appears that all the real activity is taking place underwater, various unauthorized individuals will attempt to engage team members in conversation. To the untrained eye, it does not appear that much is going on. The fact that the diver's survival is based on support personal and their ability to pay attention is lost on the untrained individual. The only way for the team to maintain focus, with the tender, safety diver, and scene commander watching the progress of the diver, is to have no external distractions. It is therefore vital that they be protected from those who are not part of the dive operation.

    The media will often press forward based on their First Amendment credentials. It is important to note that the First Amendment freedom of the press clause refers to a press free from government censorship and grants them no greater right to access a crime scene than any other citizen would have.

    Zone one serves as the area that belongs to the dive team. The team will usually set up a canopy or tent to serve not only as a command center, but also as a place to get out of the sun or cold with food and drink available. Spare tanks, compressors, and equipment vans are often backed into the area for ease of access. Although it would be best to leave all these things out of zone one, it will not happen. Teams will stage equipment, gear, and trucks as close as possible to the area of operations to reduce the distance they have to carry things. If the area has been adequately searched, it probably does little harm to stage their gear inside that zone. Many teams have had gear "walk off" when left unattended in vehicles or at a distance from the operation. The one thing that does belong inside zone one is the decontamination equipment that is going to be used. The decontamination process begins while divers are still in the water and progresses to a decon station as close as possible to the water's edge.

    Many teams have no patrol cadre to assist in establishing security areas. In this case, instead of three zones they will have one larger zone encompassing the area of operation and a bit beyond. They will not be able to look to patrol staff to provide security but will be required to provide it themselves. In the best of all possible worlds, there are three zones and a patrol force to man them.

Zones of security again shrink when operations are in open water and conducted from a platform (boat or barge). Again, security is left to the dive team. The scene perimeter should be marked with buoys and dive flags with a team member stationed in a small, fast, motorized craft such as a rubber inflatable raft (RIB) that can redirect any surface traffic.

It should also be readily apparent that zone one moves as the search operation moves. It is just as likely as not that the item sought will not be found in the first place searched. Adjacent areas will have to be searched, and the zones of security may have to move with the search.

- Zone one summary
  - Three **security zones** when possible
    - Necessary in mass disaster recovery operations
  - Patrol force provides security
  - Access is monitored
  - Incident commander provides overall security
  - Zone one should not be penetrated by anyone other than operational personnel
  - Zone one does not start at the water's edge
  - Zone one can begin at the water's edge once the area adjacent to the water's edge has been cleared (searched)
  - Zone one is movable
  - Zone one should be designated by police tape
  - Media should be managed and not allowed direct access to zone one

- *Zone two:* Ideally, zone two would be the area within which all equipment and personnel not directly involved in the search activity would be located. This second zone is designed to assure a sense of security for support personnel and their equipment, a place for them to park and to prepare whatever contingency plans may be part of their responsibility without interfering with the dive operation or team member focus. This zone is for all collaterally authorized personnel. In large operations it is to this area that the command center would be relegated. Medical support personnel can record vital signs pre- and post-dive at this location.
  - Zone two summary
    - For authorized support personnel and command staff only
    - Access is monitored
    - Support equipment and vehicles are staged here
    - Pre-dive briefings conducted here
    - Pre-dive medical assessment done here
    - Post-dive briefings conducted here
    - Post-dive medical assessment done here
    - R&R (rest and rehabilitation) area (tent, canopy, food, and drink) located here

- *Zone three:* There must be an area for family and friends of the victim in a body recovery to gather. They need to be close, but not as close as they may wish. Along with next of kin, this area would house media representatives. A managed media pool is a resource. An unmanaged media pool can be a nightmare (Becker 1995).

It is the incident commander's responsibility to notify all supervisory personnel from the various operational components of the chain of command and the location of the command center and to establish communication elements necessary to coordinate overall command and control. Often the incident commander has responsibility for coordinating the activities of the following:

- Patrol officers
  - Scene entry
  - Scene security
  - Equipment and vehicle staging
- Fire Department
  - Emergency service
  - Decontamination
  - Recovery assistance
- Ambulance service
  - Rehabilitation services for divers
  - Emergency medical assistance
  - Transportation to recompression chamber
- Vessel accrual and deployment
- Investigator deployment
- Underwater investigators
- Dive team
- Dive planning
  - Briefing
  - Deployment
  - Recovery
  - Processing
  - Debriefing
- Personnel assignment
  - Responsibility
  - Chain of command
- Documentation
  - Witness statements
  - Dive team assessment
  - Dive plan
  - Operational plan
- Conduct a constant and recurring risk assessment
- Determine needed resources
  - Allocate necessary resources
- Manage the media
  - Public information officer
  - Media packages (prepared statements)
- Stand down

In most dive situations, there is no formal command and control structure other than the team leader serving as the scene commander.

Often the work of recovery operations is measured in time. Since time is a constraint that operates on all police functions, it is not surprising that it should appear as an element in underwater investigations. Once the need for rescue has passed, whatever is in the water is not going anywhere. The risk involved in underwater investigations does not need the added pressures of artificially imposed deadlines or time-based expectations.

The first concern regarding time is the practical consideration of what happens as we approach the hour when team personnel go off duty. Do we conduct night operations? Do we hurry to wrap it up before quitting time? Do we pretend that we have satisfactorily completed a search to accommodate departure? All of these considerations are unnecessary if we take time out of the equation. For underwater investigations it is the author's belief that the additional risks associated with **nighttime dive operations** are unwarranted and unacceptable. There is nothing in the water that will not be there tomorrow or the next day. Time is an additional pressure that is not a welcome or necessary part of underwater investigations, especially if time constraints and pressures compromise diver safety (Becker 1994).

In the past we have protected the nonrecovery world from the realities of in-water air crashes. Deployment in these cases begins in a rush to recover survivors. When a plane crash-lands, there may be survivors, but when an aircraft uncontrollably crashes into the water, there are no survivors and generally no intact bodies. The American public has been protected from that reality until recently. Following the TWA flight 800 crash off Long Island in 1998, for the first time it was reported what was involved in the recovery operation. More will be discussed about this flight in Chapter Eight. Suffice it to say that all the pressure that is brought to bear on an underwater investigation to rescue survivors has been unnecessary in the past and should be absent in the future.

An additional time pressure brought to the aircraft recovery scene is the need for closure for next of kin. As important as this concept may be, it is subordinate to the criminal investigation. We don't hasten to complete dry-land searches and investigations in the name of closure. Why should underwater investigations have to contend with this pressure? In the past, aircraft crashes have been treated as accidents and no one was overly concerned with an investigative protocol for the recovery operation. It is hoped that with this text and the abandonment of the accidental crash myth, we will be allowed to get on with the business of investigation without the artificial time constraints imposed by the public and media-conscious politicians who have no business directing an investigation of any description (Becker 1995).

Dive Team Coordinator

In large-scale operations where more than one team responds, it is necessary to have someone who is responsible for coordinating the activities of the various teams so that they are not working at cross purposes. In the TWA flight 800 operation, the U.S. Navy provided the organization, equipment, structure, and coordination. The

numerous teams assisting the Navy divers all worked under a naval officer responsible for coordinating the dive operation. Once again we can refer to that endeavor
as a model for large-scale operations. In addition to the naval officer who served as
the **dive team coordinator,** the number of divers and teams was such that naval chief
petty officers served as assistant coordinators. Lines of communication were open
and employed to good effect. Much police work is paramilitary in its organization.
That becomes most advantageous in large-scale operations where military models of
planning, command, and coordination can provide a framework for police underwater operations. The team coordinator should keep a record in both picture and word
of the operation, the area searched, and the items recovered. That information should
be made part of the incident documentation and included in a profile of the operation. That profile will include all documentation pertaining to the following:

- Each team
  - Diver names
    - Tender names
    - Performance levels
  - Vital signs
  - Air consumption
  - Bottom time
  - Surface intervals
  - Abilities
    - Inabilities
  - Risk-benefit analysis
  - Equipment available
  - Equipment used
- Standard operating procedures
- A graphic reproduction of the team's search and recovery efforts (Hendrick, Zaferes, and Nelson 2000)

Public Information Officer (PIO)

Every team and every incident needs to have someone designated as a media repre-
sentative for the dissemination and management of the media. It is essential that teams
and operations have cordial working relationships with the media and their representatives. The public relations benefits that can be bestowed on a cooperative team or
operation are immeasurable and do not happen accidentally. The worst thing that can
come out of an operation team member's mouth is "No comment." It is a suggestion
of lack of cooperation and respect. It should not be surprising when a similar inference is made in media reports about the operation and its participants. Conversely,
media representatives who are treated with courtesy and respect respond in kind. The
appropriate response from a participant in any underwater recovery operation is: "We
have been trained to direct all media inquiries to our public information officer." It
may also be helpful to identify that person or to suggest, if true, that a PIO press

release is planned. In the world of underwater investigations that involve just one team, the PIO, incident commander, scene commander, and team leader are all the same person.

Incident Safety Officer

This may be the most important role played by the personnel responsible for command of the operation. It is this officer who has the overall responsibility for assuring that every aspect of the operation is completed safely—not just the activities taking place in and around the water, but also within the entire incident structure. It is a large responsibility that one person may not be able to accomplish. In the event that the operation is so large as to tax the efforts of a single individual, it may be necessary to have assistant safety officers who report back to and are subordinate to the **incident safety officer.** To the safety officer falls the responsibility for:

- Constant vigilance
- Continued risk-benefit analysis
- Equipment compatibility with the operational requirements
- Personnel compatibility with the operational requirements
- Training compatibility with the operational requirements
- Hazmat assessment
- Providing input to the incident commander
- Participating in incident planning
- Reviewing the plan
- Participating in incident briefing
- Preparing and initiating the hazmat decontamination plan
- Having sufficient hazmat decontamination equipment and personnel available
- Having appropriate medical personnel, equipment, and transportation available
- Requiring that all personnel adjacent to or on the water have PFDs
- Investigating and documenting accidents
- Reserving the prerogative to remove a diver, a team, or any other personnel who constitute a danger
- Terminating the operation if safety considerations so warrant
- Documenting safety considerations during the operation
- Participating in the operation's debriefing

Tool Pusher

This position can be referred to by many names, but the best analogy for the function of this position comes from the oil fields of Texas, Oklahoma, and the Gulf of

Mexico. There are a variety of supervisory personnel on an oil rig. The bigger the rig, the greater that variety, but the **tool pusher** is responsible for getting men and equipment together at the right place and the right time with the right stuff. So too is there an officer at a dive site who has the same equipment and manpower responsibility. In all operations it is best if manpower and equipment are located at a particular place and deployment of both is based upon need and propriety. It is this officer's responsibility to know who the operators are, what equipment they have, and whether or not those operators and that equipment are sufficient for the task.

In large operations, each component is made up of men and women who have brought with them their own chain of command and operational protocols. It is necessary for these individual components to subordinate themselves to the command structure in place and to communicate their readiness to that command structure. Once that communication has taken place, the teams may be disbanded and individuals assigned to already-existing operational entities. The teams may be deployed intact subject to the supervision of the incident commander. However the teams are employed, it is the responsibility of every participating agency to contact the command center, learn the command structure, and become an integral part of it.

After each incident, there is an inclination to disband and depart as rapidly as possible. With diverse agencies operating together for the duration of the operation, many of the agencies will see their participation as ended once the order to stand down from the operation is given. There is a wealth of information available to the participants in the operation. That information does not reside in any one person, agency, unit, or team. Each of the participants in a large-scale operation has a part to be placed into the informational puzzle. It is not until all the pieces of the informational puzzle have been placed that the opportunity to learn can occur. An integral part of the operation includes the planning, briefing, and deployment stages. The final part of the operation deals with "what we learned from this operation," and it's called a debriefing. Debriefing is valuable upon completion of any underwater recovery operation, regardless of size, but it is of most value in large operations because of the diversity of responsibilities, perspectives, and opportunities. "It's not over until the paperwork has been completed" is true, but not complete. For dive operations, it's not over until the debriefing has been completed. It is at this time that we get the chance to compare our operational manuals to operational functions. It is at this time that we see if our plans and preparation were the right plans and the right preparation. We discover our limitations, and we discover our equipment's limitations. We find out if we and those working with us were prepared as well as we believed we were. It is a time for reflection and introspection.

TEAM STRUCTURE

The basic **team structure** of a dive recovery team includes, minimally, the following:

- Scene commander
- Dive line tender

- Primary diver
- Backup diver (**90 percent diver)**
- Safety diver

This is the minimum number of team members necessary to begin an underwater recovery operation. What follows will describe a number of other team roles that are important and may be performed by team members filling other roles. Some are desirable but not absolutely necessary (Hendrick, Zaferes, and Nelson 2000).

Dive Team Coordinating Board

Although not a part of the operational end of the dive recovery team, a dive team **coordinating board** is the political action group for the team. The coordinating board should include in its membership a doctor, lawyer, deputy chief or the equivalent, and senior dive team officer or dive team leader. This organization handles the daily and long-range administrative needs of the department dive recovery team, which may include:

- Spokespeople for agency administrators
- Politicians
- Media and external funding agencies
- Policymakers
- Budget oversight
- Equipment selection and updating
- Discipline
- Team selection, recruitment, and termination
- Record-keeping entity for dive recovery operations
- Creating, updating, and maintaining a standard operations policy and procedures manual
- Training
- Insurance

Team Members

The role of team members should be explicitly understood. Recovery team members may exchange roles or perform more than one, but each role should be specifically described in the SOP, and areas of responsibility clearly defined. For each team function there should be a job description and a list of prerequisite skills necessary to perform that function. Not all members will be interested in all the jobs on a dive team. Some team members will be interested in all the jobs on a dive team. All team members will be interested in some of the jobs on a dive team. As the team develops confidence, experience, and credibility, it will also garner some publicity within and outside the agency. Administrators will come to value the role the team plays for the department and the community. A well-trained and well-used dive team gathers in its wake excellent publicity. Good public relations are a long-sought-after and seldom-found objective for most agencies. It will become apparent to all concerned that the dive team is a highly visible and positive reflection of all that is best in law enforcement. Over time the team will take on a glamorous hue with the public and police who are nondivers. There will be a lot of ribbing and joking, but it will be good-natured, with a hint of envy. As the team grows, so will its reputation (good or bad). If that growth is positive, the people associated with the team will improve their reputations and standing in the law enforcement community. Promotions will come more quickly to members of the team, and in short order a berth on the team will be a highly sought-after and contested matter. It is at this juncture that a dive team's own success becomes its demise, or at least the cause of difficulties. As positions on the team become available and coveted, the standards used to determine who gets the job will come under strict scrutiny. We are no longer talking about a group of folks involved in a somewhat novel and crazy activity; it becomes a stepping-stone for career enhancement, bringing into play egos and money—a volatile combination at best. The best way to deal with this inevitability is to plan for it. The key to successfully countering charges that the entry requirements for membership to a dive team are discriminatory is to assure at the outset that all skills tests are job-related and periodically retested. Remember that *saying* that a team's requirements are or are not something is an exercise in legal futility; under the law, if it's not written down, it doesn't exist. Furthermore, if it's important enough to write down, it should be contained in the SOP. One of the problems with an SOP is that it starts to be ignored. It ceases to be updated and operational changes are not reflected in the manual. When that happens, the team is one step closer to being found liable for discrimination. You cannot update the requirements for entry to the team unless those requirements are reflected in the SOP, including subsequent additions and deletions.

Team Leader

It is the team leader's responsibility to organize and supervise the operation. It is his or her responsibility to coordinate activities between the team and other teams or agencies with which the team may be operating. It is imperative that the team leader be available to make decisions pertaining to the operation at any given time. Those decisions cannot be appreciated or made while in the water. The position of team leader does not include diving. If the team leader is placed into the diving rotation, he or she must abrogate the role of team leader until he or she is ready to resume command of the team and remain topside.

The team leader is responsible for all aspects of the operation, but the most vital responsibility lies in the team leader's responsibility to conduct a risk-benefit analysis based on the requirements of a dive operation, the training and experience of the team, and the equipment available (and which the team is trained to use). The risk-benefit analysis is an ongoing responsibility, beginning at the time of the first dispatch and continuing until the last diver is out of the water. In the usual under-water investigation the team leader is responsible for the following:

1. Risk analysis
2. Callout (contacting team members)
3. Pre-dive briefing
4. Role assignment
5. Deployment
6. Establishing crime scene parameters
7. Determining the search method(s) to be employed
8. Operational oversight
9. Post-dive briefing

If a problem arises in the water that threatens divers (and it will), there must be someone available who knows the respective strengths and weaknesses of all the team's members. There must be someone who is capable of bringing to bear all necessary logistics and manpower.

The morale and discipline of the team are a reflection of the team leader's philosophy. By setting and enforcing hiring, qualification, and training standards promulgated by the coordinating board, the leader enhances or denigrates the status of the team proportionally. The safety of the team in the water may depend upon the equipment the team leader selects and how that equipment is maintained and updated. Courtroom success will be dependent to a large degree on the documentation and records kept by the team leader, which should include:

- Training files
- Medical records
- Offense reports
- Incident reports
- Complaints
- Records of disciplinary actions
- Commendations
- Dive logs and debriefings
- Decompression records and dive narratives
- Recovery documentation
- Evidence logs
- Photographic records
- Operational records
- Location documentation

The dive team leader's responsibility begins long before the team is dispatched to a dive site. It is the leader's responsibility to select team members for the operation in question and gather all equipment and logistical support the operation may warrant. He or she is responsible for the team briefing wherein entry sites, obstacles, contamination issues, dive equipment, communication gear, and evidence processing requirements are discussed. The team leader is responsible for the pre-dive briefing wherein water depths, temperatures, currents, and tides are discussed, along with methods of entry and exit and the type of search pattern to be employed. Anticipated dive depths are considered along with a prospective dive profile. Any prior operational documents for the area in question are gathered and examined prior to the deployment of team personnel. It is the team leader's responsibility to determine, based on intelligence provided and gathered, the focal point of the search, the perimeter of the search, and the pattern that will best facilitate completing a search of the predetermined area. The leader assures that all relevant information about the dive, geography, personnel, bottom structure, objectives, and outcome is recorded. It falls to the team leader to assign roles and determine who is going in the water and who is tending. The dive team leader debriefs each diver immediately after his or her bottom time has been reached and determines the nature of the bottom and the environment in which the search is taking place. Upon completion of the operation, the team leader conducts an operational debriefing and includes all relevant information about the diver, personnel, and site and assures that all the appropriate information finds its way into team data files (Becker 1995).

Tenders

The dive tenders are the eyes and ears of the underwater investigator. Although underwater voice communication systems are available, often the price is more than the dive team budget will allow. The underwater recovery process began with divers being tethered to a tended line. This is still the most common method employed.

Communication between the line tender and the diver takes place through a process of predetermined line tugs. Change of direction, ascent, entanglement, etc., are all communicated by line pulls, the most common method of communication during police dive recovery operations. During operations of limited or no visibility (which comprise the bulk of police dive operations) the underwater investigator is dependent on line pulls to guide and communicate. Those teams that rely on communication systems have to fall back on line pulls when communication systems go awry.

Once the item has been located, the preferred protocol is to tell the tender either with line tugs or, if underwater voice communication is available, verbally. Line tug protocols vary among teams, but one successful set of signals would be:

Tender tugs

One pull   Are you OK?
Two pulls   Stop, turn, and go the other direction

Three pulls	Come up
Four pulls	Stop and stay down

Diver tugs

One pull	I'm OK
Two pulls	I need slack
Three pulls	I found target
Four pulls	I need help

Four pulls from the diver are repeated until help arrives.

> In dealing with divers of any stripe, it is important to keep it simple whenever possible. Teams throughout the southwestern United States use the above-described line pull signals very effectively. As progress would dictate, the needs of recovery divers nationally have led to additions to line pull signals. Many of the northern teams have adopted Team Lifeguard Systems' line pull signals. They are more complicated but do provide greater control.

Team LGS Line Pulls

Tender to Diver

One pull	Stop/face and tighten line/Are you OK?
3 pulls	Go right (diver's)
4 pulls	Go left (diver's)
2 + 2 pulls	Search immediate area
3 + 3 pulls	Stand by to leave bottom
4 + 4 pulls	Come up

Diver to Tender

1 pull	Diver is OK
2 pulls	Tender to make a notation
2 + 2 + 2 pulls	Tangled but OK; alert backup diver
3 + 3 + 3 pulls	OK, but need help from backup diver
4 + 4 + 4 pulls	Need help immediately

Additionally, it is the tender who assists in the staging of all operational equipment and who is responsible for dressing each diver. The donning of dive gear is cumbersome, especially when dealing with dry suits, weight harnesses, and tanks. It is the tender who does the lifting and exertion, reserving the strength and composure of the diver for the operation.

Divers

Three divers work together in providing support and confidence for each other. The primary diver has the operational oar. It is upon this diver that the integrity of the search being conducted is based. The quality of a search depends on the search pattern selected and the methodology employed. It is axiomatic to say that a successful search is one that:

- Discovers what is being sought
- Is conducted in such a fashion that search integrity is maintained and confidence in the pattern selected and employed is so high as to be able to conclude unequivocally that the item sought is not within the searched area.

It is to the primary diver that the success or failure of the mission is attributed. This diver must be so situated in the water that he is able to crawl across the bottom and keep line tension. It is the tension that determines the quality of the search.

The backup (90 percent) diver is the next person in the rotation to take the place of the primary diver. Most operations limit each diver's underwater time to twenty minutes. Having sufficient divers to continue a rotation until the item sought is found is the responsibility of the team leader. The backup diver is 90 percent prepared to enter the water. In addition to being the next diver in the search rotation, this diver serves as safety diver should the main safety diver be deployed (Hendrick, Zaferes, and Nelson 2000).

The safety diver's sole responsibility is to be 100 percent suited and prepared to enter the water. This diver is often deployed in the water to remain cool because body temperature increases the temperature inside the diver's wet or dry suit. It is this diver's responsibility to track the course of the search and make suppositions as to what the searching diver is encountering. Should there be a need for assistance, this diver can be deployed immediately. Once the safety diver is deployed, the 90 percent diver finishes dressing and becomes the default safety diver.

Intelligence Officer

Each team should have a person designated as the team **intelligence officer.** Often this role is served by the team leader. No matter who provides this service to the team, it is fundamental to the safety and success of the operation. It is the intelligence officer who liaises with the dry-land investigators and gathers what information they may have that will assist in the formation of the operational plan. Criminal investigators interview witnesses and generally convey that information to the dive team intelligence officer. Any information derived from interviews with witnesses should not be relied upon. Dry-land investigators may not know the kinds of questions and the kinds of information that the dive team needs to build an operational plan. In many instances they will interview a witness at a place of convenience for themselves or the witness, not knowing that the information possessed by the witness cannot be adequately evaluated unless it is gathered at the location of the event. Distances are unreliable. Locating a last-seen point of a drowning or the approximate location of a gun thrown into the water can best be done by directing a surface swimmer, using hand signals, to the location that best represents what was seen. That cannot be in the comfort of an automobile, living room, or investigator's office; it must be done on location and conducted by people who know what it is that is most helpful to an underwater investigation. All information gathered by the intelligence office should become a part of the permanent record associated with the underwater investigation (Becker 1995).

Photographer

Many people not associated with limited-visibility diving presume that the world of the underwater investigator does not lend itself to photography. Nothing could be further from the truth. Even if visibility does not allow pictures to be taken underwater, there is a vast array of above-water subject matter available. Some of the things that can be filmed by the **photographer** are the:

- Probable entry route
- Probable exit route
- Area adjacent to the water
- Team personnel present
- Equipment and the way the equipment was worn
- Search pattern selected
- Staging of equipment
  - If there arises a question as to the type of equipment used or available
- Staging of personnel
  - If there arises a question as to safety or 90 percent diver availability

In many instances there is more visibility than would seem apparent. A camera lens needs less light to capture an image than does our eye. It may also be possible to use a plastic bag of clear water pressed against an object to provide the necessary clarity to take a picture.

Lift Specialist

All team members should be specialists in the location, measurement, identification, tagging, handling, and processing of underwater evidence. Subsequent chapters will describe the types of forensic evidence that are not destroyed by water and the prospective sites of such evidence. In addition to the forensic characteristics of the evidence that may be recovered, there must be some consideration of how the item discovered is to get to the surface. There is a saying that if you're underwater working strong, you're working dumb. That axiom carries with it the knowledge that anything in the water can be made to float (there may be a point of diminishing returns, but for underwater investigations that is not a consideration). Making things float is a skill that can only be acquired with training and experience. At least one member of the dive team should be trained and certified to rig and lift items off the bottom. The heaviest things that need to be raised to the surface would include:

- Automobiles
- Small aircraft
- Large aircraft pieces
- Safes
- Bodies

Most other things are small enough that they can be hand carried to the surface. Those things that cannot be safely and easily carried to the surface must nonetheless arrive there in order to be useful as evidence. There are various techniques available, but the most appropriate technique is to use lift bags or pontoons to get what is underwater to the surface. Using lift bags is a technical proposition and can include certain inherent risks that must be considered. Anything in the water of interest to investigators can be lifted to the surface. The rigging of air bags and their deployment must be done only by those with the specialized skill that can only come from training and experience. These individuals are **lift specialists.** In most departments, all underwater investigators are trained in the use of lift bags, and since the whole team is familiar with their employment, it is not seen as a specialty. However, it is, and it is one that should not be attempted without proper training and supervision.

Equipment Specialist

In the best of all worlds, underwater investigation dive teams would have a dive locker that would store and issue all dive equipment necessary for a particular underwater operation. Most teams do not have the luxury of budgets that would allow for departmental equipment, so the team members end up using their own equipment. From the best to the most common equipment, a team fields as great a diversity of equipment as it does of personnel. The idea of uniformity of equipment operates in every other sphere of police endeavors. Police within a particular agency will generally carry the same firearms. That sameness allows interchangeability of ammunition, firearms, and parts. No operation is canceled for lack of functional equipment. When equipment is interchangeable, there are always replacement parts available to avoid the cancellation of an operation. SWAT teams carry the interchangeability to its finest point. Unfortunately, interchangeability has not made its way to the underwater investigation team. If the team is issued standard equipment, it is necessary to maintain, issue, and account for that equipment. It is the equipment specialist who routinely checks all equipment and every six months performs required maintenance on it. Periodic maintenance checks are documented for each piece of diving equipment used by all dive team members. Any equipment issued by the department is kept under lock and key, for use in police operations only. All equipment is checked prior to issue and again upon return. Divers are discouraged from using personal equipment. It is understood by all team members that any equipment used on a dive other than departmental equipment is not authorized, and any such use would absolve the department of liability for injury or death resulting from such use. Teams are moving to standardized equipment, but, alas, it is a slow and expensive process. It is in equipping and training a team that an agency should address the issue of whether or not a dive team is needed. It is better not to have a team than it is to undertrain and underequip them (*City of Canton, Ohio v. Harris* 1988). There is no legal liability associated with the former, but there is with the latter (Becker 1995).

Archivist

Any on-site measurements, sketches, records, or reports should be kept by someone other than the person providing the information. Few police officers enjoy paperwork; however, concise records allow for more efficient report writing and testimony. It is of little value to be an excellent investigator if reports are embarrassingly illegible and in-court testimony is ponderous, convoluted, and not consistent with the documentation. No matter who is responsible for the documentation for the team, that documentation is the history of the efforts of the team to reach a level of professionalism upon which the agency and community can rely. It should be remembered that no matter how hard we try to convince someone of our competence, our behavior speaks the loudest. All documentation should be a reflection of our behavior and a reflection of what we as a team are and aspire to be. It is important to select someone for the position of **archivist** who shares that perspective.

Medical Officer

The well-being of each team member is the concern of the entire team, not only in altruistic terms, but also in terms that are integral to the survival of the whole team. Every team member is responsible for his or her own safety as well as the safety of the other team members. That same perspective is shared in terms of medical concerns. Often fatigue, shock, stress, and anxiety are not as readily apparent to the sufferer as they are to those around him or her. Each team should supplement this vigilance and concern with a member who has the responsibility for the medical well-being of the team during operations and during training. This person must have specialized training and may be an emergency medical technician. This person is responsible for maintaining medical records for the team members, assuring they are up-to-date with their dive physicals, and recording vital signs for each diver before and after each dive. It is this officer's responsibility to monitor divers for dehydration and hypothermia. All medical perspectives and treatment must be documented and kept as a part of each team member's permanent file.

Training Coordinator

One member of the team should be identified as having training responsibilities. That does not necessarily mean that the **training coordinator** is expected to conduct all training. This team member is responsible for organizing all activities, consistent with in-service and initial training requirements as set forth in the standard operation and procedures manual. An integral part of training is document maintenance. Accurate records should be maintained detailing dates, times, and content of all training provided. In addition to training activities, conducting annual or semiannual qualification exercises is the responsibility of the training coordinator. It would prove helpful if this team member not only had a scuba instructor's rating but also was certified as a public safety diver instructor. If possible, additional training and/or certification in underwater air bag rigging and lifting would be very useful.

Today there is some type of public safety dive team training going on someplace at some time. It should not be difficult to find various training programs in the area in which the team operates. The difficulty is twofold:

1. Finding the funding to attend
2. Ascertaining the quality of the instruction available

Just as there are many recreational certification programs that may or may not be relied upon, there is a growing number of PSD training programs that deserve some investigation prior to enrolling. With no national standards, the only way this plethora of program offerings can be evaluated is by word of mouth. The costs can be so high that it is foolish not to do the homework necessary to find out what the quality of any given group or organization may be. The only quality control presently available is community censure. If a training program or group is substandard, the people working in the industry hear about it and pass the word around. It is good to remember that the only thing we have of real value in this business is our reputation. It is the stock in which we trade amongst our peers and in the courtroom.

In the beginning, anyone with basic recreational dive certification was considered for participation on public safety recovery dive teams. Over time it became apparent that recreational diving and recreational training had little to do with the responsibilities of the public safety diver. Formalized training began at various venues around the country. Dive Rescue International began providing public safety diver instruction. Lifeguard Systems also provided training. Southwest Texas State University started a training program at its Underwater Institute. Slowly, training programs began to develop around the country to address the unique characteristics of public safety diving. An integral part of that advancement was the recognition that what public safety divers did was evidence recovery, and the next evolution in training included forensic considerations in the processing of underwater crime scenes. Southwest Texas State University was one of the first universities in the country to offer training in underwater investigation. It was at a small university in Honolulu, Hawaii, that the first underwater investigation course was included in a criminal justice curriculum. In the summer of 2003, Chaminade University of Honolulu offered CJ 480—Underwater Forensic Investigation—for college credit.

REVIEW QUESTIONS

1. What is public safety diving?
2. Who does public safety diving?
3. If an underwater recovery operation involves the recovery of evidence, who should recover it? Why?
4. What is the purpose of a standard operation and procedures manual for an underwater investigation dive team?
5. What role does the coordinator play in underwater operations? Who should be the coordinator?
6. Discuss the following statement as it applies to SOPs: "If it's not written down, it doesn't exist."
7. Discuss the following statement as it applies to underwater investigations: "If you're working strong, you're working dumb."
8. Is it possible to perform recovery operations in contaminated water? If yes, how?
9. Describe a decontamination protocol.
10. List the types of swimming skills you would require for an underwater investigation dive team.
11. List the types of diving skills you would require for an underwater investigation dive team.
12. Describe the method of command and control that can be employed in a large-scale underwater investigation operation.
13. Discuss the role of the dive tender.
14. Discuss the respective roles of the primary diver, safety diver, and 90 percent diver.
15. What is the job of the safety officer?
16. What is the job of the team leader?
17. What is the job of the intelligence officer?
18. What are the jobs of the medical officer and team archivist?
19. What is the job of the team equipment specialist?
20. What are the jobs of the team lift specialist and training coordinator?

REFERENCES

BECKER, R. F. 1995. *Processing the underwater crime scene*. Springfield, IL: Charles C. Thomas.

JAMIESON, J. D., R. F. BECKER, and L. C. DIXON. 1999. Public safety diving and nitrox (unpublished report).

HENDRICK, W., A. ZAFERES, and C. NELSON. 2000. *Public safety diving*. Saddle Brook, NJ: PennWell.

BEERS, M. H., and R. BERKOW, eds. 2004. *Merck manual of diagnosis and therapy*. Rahway, NJ: Merck.

TABLE OF CASES

City of Canton, Ohio v. Harris et al., 489 U.S. 378 (1988).

Chapter 4

The Law of Search and Seizure

NEW WORDS AND CONCEPTS

due process clause

privileges and immunities clause

equal protection clause

reasonableness

exclusionary rule

derivative evidence

fruit of the poisonous tree

good faith

warrant procedure

warrant affidavit

emergency exception

inadvertent discovery

exigent circumstances

consent search

legitimately on the premises

immediately apparent

open field

curtilage

LEARNING OBJECTIVES

- Discuss the Fourth Amendment as it applies to searches
- Discuss the Fourth Amendment as it applies to seizures
- Discuss the Fourth Amendment as it applies to public safety dive teams

THE U.S. CONSTITUTION AND DUE PROCESS

This chapter will deal with general principles pertaining to searches and arrests. There are some fundamental issues that must be addressed prior to specifically discussing those situations in which search warrants might be required in underwater operations. Through an understanding of some of these general principles, applications for underwater investigations will become more apparent.

The U.S. Constitution is a blueprint for the building of a democratic government. It outlines the structure of our government and the powers granted to the three branches. It was an oversight of the original drafters of the Constitution that they did not include guarantees of individual freedom, especially since the violation of the colonists' inalienable individual rights had laid the foundation for the American Revolution. The founders had to amend the Constitution to include a list of ten guarantees that addressed the original grievances that the English Crown chose to ignore. The first ten amendments of the U.S. Constitution form the groundwork of "due process." Of course, the Bill of Rights was never intended to apply to the states. It was the objective of the drafters of the Constitution to protect the citizens of the colonies from an oppressive central government, a government insensitive to the rights of its citizens, a government that levied abuses upon its citizenry—in short, a government like that of England. It was not until the passage of the Fourteenth Amendment that the United States Supreme Court began in its diverse holdings to interpret the due process guaranteed in this amendment as the same due process guaranteed in the Bill of Rights. Bit by bit, the Bill of Rights was incorporated into the Fourteenth Amendment, until virtually all of it had been made part of this amendment's **due process clause.**

The Fourteenth Amendment contains three separate but equally important clauses:

1. The **privileges and immunities clause**
2. The due process clause
3. The **equal protection clause**

In studying searches and seizures, it is the due process clause we are most concerned with. The Supreme Court has embraced the Fourth, Fifth, and Sixth Amendments as the touchstones that limit the discretion available to police in conducting the searches of people and places and the seizure of people and things.

The Fourth Amendment

The Fourth Amendment provides two guarantees that assure citizens due process when confronted by police seeking to conduct a search or to seize a person or thing. First, it proclaims, "the right of the people to be secure in their persons, houses, papers, and effects, against unreasonable searches and seizures, shall not be violated." The most important part of this procedural safeguard is that all searches and seizures must be reasonable.

The Supreme Court has gone to significant lengths to define what kinds of searches and seizures are reasonable. An understanding of **reasonableness** as promulgated by the court can only be achieved by examining some of the salient cases that provide the definition of reasonableness. Second, the amendment proclaims, "No warrants shall issue, but upon probable cause, supported by oath or affirmation, and

The Fourteenth Amendment to the U.S. Constitution

Section 1 All persons born or naturalized in the United States, and subject to the jurisdiction thereof, are citizens of the United States and of the State wherein they reside. No State shall make or enforce any law, which shall abridge the privileges or immunities of citizens of the United States: nor shall any State deprive any person of life, liberty, or property, without due process of law: nor deny to any person within its jurisdiction the equal protection of the law.

particularly describing the place to be searched and the persons or things to be seized." When we think of seizures, we generally think of things other than persons. The restrictions on police conduct in effecting an arrest are provided for in this part of the Fourth Amendment. Disputes pertaining to this clause generally arise in regard to the probable cause requirement for a warrant to search or arrest. Probable cause to arrest is the minimum information a reasonable person would need to have in order to believe that a crime has been committed or is about to be committed. Probable cause to search is the minimum information a reasonable person would need to have to believe that an item is where it is purported to be. Not only must police have reasonable information that the item in question is contraband, the fruit of a crime, or otherwise illegal to possess, but they must also have reasonable information as to the location of the item.

The Fifth Amendment

Because of the experience of the colonists at the hands of an overbearing government that denied them the right to remain silent and allowed coerced confessions to be used against them in colonial courts presided over by British jurists, the drafters of the Bill of Rights included a provision that specifically forbade the government from requiring that a person incriminate himself or herself. Through later Supreme Court decisions, the self-incrimination clause of the Fifth Amendment took on unprecedented significance in American jurisprudence.

The Sixth Amendment

The Sixth Amendment requires that a person caught up in the criminal justice system be provided legal representation. When dealing with the police, at what point is a citizen entitled to the assistance of counsel? The citizen is entitled to counsel at the point where he or she asks for it. The Supreme Court, however, has determined that this fundamental right may not be known, may be forgotten, or may be frightened away. In a far-reaching decision in *Miranda v. Arizona*, the Court required that a series of warnings be provided whenever a citizen is subjected to an interrogation while in custody of the police. These warnings, in recognition of the landmark nature of the case, are commonly known as Miranda warnings.

It is the United States Supreme Court's holding in *Miranda v. Arizona* that changed the focus of law enforcement from confessions to forensically supported investigations. That same emphasis was instrumental in the rise of underwater investigation. It has become common for offenders to confess to a crime, lead investigators to the watercourse in which they disposed of the weapon, and later recant the confession. At every stage of the investigation, it is a good idea for investigators, including underwater investigators, to:

- Admonish offenders of their right to remain silent
- Acknowledge that anything they say will be held against them in a court of law
- Admonish offenders of their right to the services of an attorney during questioning
- Have offenders acknowledge their understanding of these rights

The Sixth Amendment contributes to the content of those warnings: "In all criminal prosecutions, the accused shall enjoy the right . . . to have the Assistance of Counsel for his defense." Although the amendment speaks specifically of "criminal prosecutions," the Court has presumed that the investigation of a criminal offense begins the prosecutorial process and, thus, brings into play the right to the assistance of counsel.

THE EXCLUSIONARY RULE

History

In 1914 the Supreme Court, in *Weeks v. United States*, decided that evidence obtained (seized) as a result of an illegal search, arrest, or interrogation would not be admissible at the time of trial. This case applied only to the federal government and its law enforcement agencies. Not until 1961 did the states feel the brunt of the holding in the *Weeks* case.

In that year three Cleveland police officers went to the residence of Dolree Mapp, looking for a person who was wanted for a recent bombing. The officers demanded entrance but were refused. After the arrival of other officers, the police broke down the door. Mapp demanded that she be shown the search warrant authorizing the intrusion into and the search of her home. When a paper was held up by one of the officers, Mapp grabbed the paper and placed it in the bodice of her blouse. The police forcibly removed the paper and handcuffed Mapp. A search of the house produced no bomber but did produce some drawings and books that the police believed to be obscene. The materials were admitted into evidence during trial, over Mapp's objection. Dolree Mapp was convicted of possession of obscene materials.

The Supreme Court held that the **exclusionary rule** promulgated in *Weeks* and applicable in federal cases was also applicable in state criminal proceedings. There were three questions that the Court had to address in the *Mapp v. Ohio* case:

1. Was there a warrant?
2. If not, was there an exception to the warrant requirement?
3. If the search was in fact illegal, what remedy should be applied?

In addition to imposing federal constitutional standards on police within the states, the Court, in the *Mapp* decision, indicated that both the Fourth and Fifth Amendments were the genesis of the exclusionary rule, which meant that not only would illegal searches and seizures be governed by the exclusionary rule, but the remedy for illegally obtained confessions would be their exclusion at the time of trial.

The logical extension of the exclusionary rule as a deterrent to police misconduct in conducting searches, seizures, or interrogations is to exclude any evidence discovered as a result of an illegally conducted search, seizure, or interrogation. An illegally obtained confession is excluded, and any evidence discovered as a result of the confession is likewise excluded. Such evidence is referred to as **derivative evidence** and is subject to the exclusionary rule. The rule that evidence can be derivatively tainted is commonly called the **fruit of the poisonous tree** doctrine.

Exceptions

The easiest way to avoid the impact of the exclusionary rule is to obtain a search warrant and execute that warrant reasonably, which means consistent with the authorization contained within the warrant. However, Supreme Court justices are not able to foresee all situations when forming their opinions. As life shows, most rules have exceptions. The exclusionary rule has been further defined by the Court to assist police in determining what conduct is acceptable in conducting searches and seizures. The objective of the exclusionary rule is to deter police misconduct. If important evidence or a lot of evidence is excluded, it may be impossible to obtain a conviction based on the remaining evidence.

Relevant Exceptions

The basic presumption under the law is that, absent a search or arrest warrant, any search or seizure of persons or things is illegal. There are many exceptions to the warrant requirement of the Fourth Amendment, and the conduct of the police is so often based on these exceptions that it begins to appear that having to obtain a warrant is the exception rather than the rule. Underwater investigators may be required to obtain a search warrant to conduct underwater searches on private property.

The "Good Faith" Exception

The most significant exception to the exclusionary rule results from a decision handed down by the Supreme Court in *United States v. Leon* (1984). Police acting on information provided by an informant began a drug investigation. An affidavit for a search warrant was prepared and reviewed by three deputy district attorneys, and in response to the affidavit, a state court judge issued the requested warrant. A search of the premises disclosed large quantities of drugs. The defendant was indicted, but his motion to suppress evidence was granted based on the fact that the affidavit and warrant contained insufficient probable cause. The court dismissed the case against the defendant.

The Fourth Amendment's exclusionary rule allows the use of evidence obtained by officers acting in reasonable reliance on a search warrant issued by a neutral and detached magistrate that is ultimately found to be invalid. Once the officer has complied with the prerequisites for obtaining a warrant, there is little more that the officer can do to comply with the law. Further, there is little deterrence value in penalizing the officer for the magistrate's error. Any evidence seized through a search warrant signed by a neutral and detached magistrate is immune to exclusion. Such evidence must be the product of a search conducted pursuant to a warrant that was issued by a neutral and impartial magistrate, appears valid on its face, and is procured without fraud on the part of the police. It goes without saying that the prudent officer will obtain a search warrant whenever possible. The value of the warrant is not only that it ensures that probable cause in fact exists and that it avoids lengthy pretrial suppression motions, but also that it affords immunity to police pursuant to the **good faith** holding of *United States v. Leon.*

A search warrant represents the authority of the state mediated by an impartial magistrate. It may be easy to find a law and order judge who will give the police anything they want. But remember, if the warrant is patently lacking in probable cause, the officer may still be held liable for criminal trespass and criminal violation of civil rights and may be civilly responsible for the same behavior; the judge has absolute immunity from suit for any action arising out of his or her judicial duties. A good search also benefits the prosecutor, who now can demand that the defendant demonstrate a failure of probable cause before having to prove otherwise. The amount of time and effort required to defend probable cause pursuant to a warrant is less than without a warrant, and evidence obtained pursuant to a warrant is more readily accepted by the court than evidence obtained without the benefit of a warrant. It is far better to find a judge who will require the officer to get the necessary probable cause. This type of judge is an asset and will assist in providing competent assessments of probable cause for good searches and arrests. The **warrant procedure** comprises three individual actions on the part of the police:

1. Drafting an affidavit that on its face establishes, to the satisfaction of a neutral and detached magistrate, sufficient probable cause
2. Serving the warrant
3. Preparing and rendering the search warrant return

Experience and preparation are the keys to preparing an adequate search **warrant affidavit.** It is better to provide too much information than not enough. A competent magistrate will not ask any questions pertaining to probable cause and the information contained in the affidavit. The affidavit must speak for itself. If the content of the affidavit is insufficient to establish probable cause per se, the warrant should not be issued. The language used should be free of jargon and abbreviations, for it will be scrutinized by defense counsel should the matter progress to trial or to a suppression motion. Real skill is required to be able to draft readable, legally sufficient search warrant affidavits. It goes without saying that everything contained in an affidavit should be true or corroborated. Known falsities abrogate the "good faith" defense against defective warrants. The affidavit is a legal road map that tells the magistrate what has been done in obtaining probable cause and what is going to be done with it. Each legally sufficient affidavit includes:

- A statement outlining the facts the officer believes constitute probable cause
- A description of what the probable cause allows to be sought
- Identification of the places the probable cause allows to be searched

Every search warrant must contain certain essentials to meet constitutional and legal muster. All warrants contain the following:

- Authorization by a magistrate in the name of and by the authority of the state
- Authorization to seize specifically described items
- Issuance based on probable cause
- A specific location (to be confused with no other)
- Authorization granted to a specifically named officer
- A return that includes:
  - Date of the search
  - Things seized
  - Name of the serving officer
  - Signature of the serving officer
  - Signature of the issuing magistrate

The return is an itemized inventory of all the property seized by the executing officers. It is prepared in duplicate, and a copy is left with the defendant or, in his or her absence, at the residence. The original is returned to the issuing magistrate no later than twenty-four hours after service of the warrant.

Emergency Searches

There are situations where police or firefighters may find themselves on the premises to provide a service other than to arrest, interrogate, interview, or search. Public safety dive teams may be involved in rescues as well as evidence recovery operations. If a police rescue team were providing assistance to a motorist stranded in high water

---

STATE OF TEXAS
SEARCH WARRANT

THE STATE OF TEXAS
To the Sheriff or any Peace Officer of _____ County, Texas, or any
Peace Officer of the State of Texas
Greetings:
Proof by affidavit being made this day, before me, by _____ (name of
officer), a Peace Officer under the laws of Texas, that there is probable cause to believe
that in the herein described (building, premises or vehicle) is located the following
property, possession of which is a violation of the laws of Texas or constitutes evidence of
a violation of the laws of Texas, and is particularly described as follows:

Controlled substances to include:
     Marijuana and associated paraphernalia
     Cocaine and associated paraphernalia
     Crack cocaine and associated paraphernalia
The described (building, premises, or vehicle) should be searched by reason of the
following grounds:
     Possession of the above-described controlled substances is evidence of violation of
the Texas Penal Code and the Texas Health and Safety Code.

You are therefore commanded at any time, day or night, to make an immediate search of
the residence of *3339 Sisterdale Road, Sisterdale,* Texas, more specifically described as:
A single family dwelling located on the property of Fillmore Duckworth and wife Jocelyn;
attached outbuildings including a farm shop, barn and garage.

Herein fail not, but have you then and there this Warrant within three days,
exclusive of the day of its issuance and exclusive of the day of its execution, with
your return thereon, showing how you have executed the same, filed in this court.

Issued this the _____ day of _____, 2008, at _____ o'clock am/pm

                                                            _____
                                                            Judge's signature

FIGURE 4-1   Search warrant.

and in the process saw items in the vehicle that are illegal to possess, the motorist
could be arrested upon completion of the rescue. If police are brought to the premises to deal with an emergency, any evidence discovered in the course of handling
the emergency would be admissible despite the fact that the police had no probable
cause or warrant to enter the premises. The entry would be reasonable under the
Fourth Amendment and exempt from any warrant or probable cause requirement
(*Mincey v. Arizona* 1978). The discovery would fall within the ambit of the plain-view

doctrine (discussed below), abrogating the need for particularized suspicion, probable cause, or a warrant. The item discovered would have to meet the requirements
set forth below. The **emergency exception** to the warrant requirement only justifies
entry to the premises without probable cause or a warrant. Another exception to the
warrant requirement would be necessary to justify the **inadvertent discovery** of contraband or evidence.

Exigent Circumstances Exception

Similar to the emergency exception, and sometimes considered part of that exception, is the exception for situations in which the police are concerned that a criminal may destroy evidence or abscond from the scene. If the police have probable
cause that a felony has been committed and that the evidence may be destroyed in
the time that it takes to procure a warrant, a warrantless entry may be made. A search
of the premises based on the probable cause justifying the entry is permissible. Any
entry based on **exigent circumstances** will be the subject of rigorous examination
at the suppression hearing. Police will be required to prove the probable cause as
well as the exigency that justified entry without a warrant.

WARRANTLESS SEARCHES BASED ON REASONABLENESS

Consent Searches

The most important tool in a police officer's arsenal against crime is the **consent
search.** A consent search need not be supported by any quantum of cause or any
individual suspicion. The notion of police requesting permission to search is at odds
with the concept many officers have of themselves, according to which they
demand, they do not ask. Getting police out of cars and onto the streets seems to
be a popular step in "communitizing" police services. An officer needs no probable cause to engage a citizen in a conversation, or to request permission to search
a citizen's person, auto, or effects as long as the officer remembers that the citizen
is free to decline to give consent. A citizen's declination should not result in retal-
iation or threat. Consent must be voluntary—free from coercion, psychological or
physical. In *Bumper v. North Carolina* (1968), the United States Supreme Court
determined that consent given based on the false assertion of the police that they
were in possession of a valid search warrant was coerced. The term *consent search*
itself is virtually an oxymoron, in that, since permission was given, the Fourth
Amendment does not apply (as long as consent was voluntary and the scope of the
search was within the given or inferred consent). A proper consent search for Fourth
Amendment purposes is a search in which the Fourth Amendment plays no direct
role. In a sense, a properly conducted "consent search" is not really a search. However, a consent given by one illegally in custody is not really consent, and anything

seized (derivative evidence) as a result of that consent is excluded (*Florida v. Royer* 1983).

Most departments provide consent forms for officers, realizing that written consent is more effective than oral consent at the time of a suppression motion. The question that invariably arises with respect to a consent to search is whether the consent was given voluntarily and knowingly. The voluntary requirement is self-explanatory and predicated upon a coercive free consent. A written consent goes a long way toward proving voluntariness if it also contains an admonition to the citizen that consent must be freely given and not the product of coercion. The knowing requirement is not self-evident, and it, too, is more easily proven if a written consent form provides an additional caveat indicating that consent may be withheld, suspended, withdrawn, or limited in scope or duration (*Florida v. Enio Jimeno* 1991).

The United States Supreme Court, in *Schneckloth v. Bustamonte*, clearly relieved the police of the responsibility of having to provide consent warnings comparable to those required in the *Miranda* decision. But at the same time it indicated that the burden would be on the police and the state to prove that the consent was given knowingly. The Court went on to say that the touchstone of knowing consent was sufficient. In other words, to give consent, a citizen has to be of an age and possess the education, intelligence, cultural familiarity, and language skills to understand that he or she is free to withhold, withdraw, or limit consent without fear of recrimination. The officer obtaining consent therefore has the responsibility of providing testimony that the consent giver had the sophistication necessary to presume that he or she had the right to withhold, withdraw, or limit consent—a heavy burden in light of the situations in which consent is generally sought. The prudent officer will use a consent form with warnings about coercion and the citizen's rights. Absent a consent form, the next best approach is to utter an oral warning outlining the citizen's rights (which must be given in the same fashion in court as on the street). Memory is not a reliable source for ensuring a citizen's rights have not been violated, or his or her will overborne. Departments should provide consent-warning cards for officers similar to those provided for Miranda situations. Although approved by the Court, the worst-case scenario for the officer is to obtain consent without providing some kind of warning. The result will be that the officer will be confronted on the witness stand with the task of explaining the considerations employed in determining the age, intelligence, education, cultural familiarity, and language skills of the person from whom the consent was obtained.

Plain-View Searches

Often evidence will come to the attention of an officer who is on a citizen's premises for a reason other than a search, an arrest, or exigent circumstances. The courts have unanimously recognized that when police are **legitimately on the premises** and recognize contraband or evidence (in plain view), it is unreasonable to think that the same contraband or evidence will be there at the time the police return with a warrant. The Supreme Court laid out the specific requirements for the admissibility of evidence discovered in plain view:

- The officer must be on the premises legitimately.
- The item viewed must have been found inadvertently (access was not gained through subterfuge for the purpose of examining the premises).
- It is **immediately apparent** that the item is evidence, contraband, or otherwise illegal to possess.

The court does not treat a plain-view discovery as a search. Since a search was not anticipated and access to the premises not gained to facilitate entry for the purposes of conducting a search, the Fourth Amendment does not apply. If the item to be seized is immediately recognizable as illegal to possess, no search has been necessary to reveal that to the police, and once again the Fourth Amendment does not apply. If any manipulation of the item in question occurs, however, a search in fact has occurred and must be justified pursuant to the Fourth Amendment or one of its exceptions. The immediately apparent requirement establishes that no search was necessary to discover the items or to identify them as illegal to possess (*Coolidge v. New Hampshire* 1971).

Open-Field Exception

This exception is often confused with the plain-view exception, but when they are examined in light of the Fourth Amendment, it becomes easy to distinguish between the two. The Supreme Court has held that the Fourth Amendment does not protect open fields. The only concern the Court has is in defining an **open field.** The Fourth Amendment protects a citizen's home and by extension the area around the home that is used in the course of daily living, known as its **curtilage.** Any area outside the curtilage of the home is an open field and is unprotected by the Fourth Amendment. Therefore, any examinations of such areas are, in regard to the Fourth Amendment, not searches.

The police need no excuse for treading upon an open field. They need no justification for looking for whatever they choose once in that field. Their conduct is not subject to constitutional scrutiny if it has been determined that the area in question is not a house or its curtilage but rather an open field. There is no "legally on the premises" requirement because there are no premises to be on. If the area of interest to the police is an open field, pond, lake, or river that is fenced and posted to prohibit trespassing, they can enter without further justification. They may have committed a criminal trespass, but they have not rendered their conduct subject to the exclusionary provisions of the Fourth Amendment. Unlike in the case of the plain-view exception, there is no "inadvertent discovery" requirement either. Once the trespass has been completed, the police may search wherever and for whatever they choose without fear of having their evidence suppressed. And once an item is found, it may be handled and examined to determine if it is in fact evidence or contraband without rendering it inadmissible.

In the case of *Oliver v. United States* (1984), the police received a tip that Oliver was growing marijuana on a noncontiguous plot of land. Police located the area in question; determined it was not contiguous to Oliver's home or farm; and, although it was fenced and posted, found a path leading through a locked gate to a field of marijuana surrounded by trees that kept the field from the public view. Oliver was arrested and convicted of manufacturing a controlled substance. The question raised was whether the field searched was protected by the Fourth Amendment. Oliver's position was that the field was not within public view; in fact demonstrated an expectation of privacy by the signs, fencing, and locked entrance; and, therefore, was not an "open field." The Supreme Court determined that since this land was not involved in the activities of daily living, it was not curtilage and, therefore, not protected under the Fourth Amendment. The fact that Oliver had demonstrated an expectation of privacy in the field and that it was not subject to cursory public view was not persuasive to the Court. The justices said that, although the police officers' conduct may have been subject to criminal or civil sanction for trespass, it did not violate the Fourth Amendment, since the area was an open field.

The Court's interpretation of the open-field doctrine suggests that the area in question need not be a field, nor need it be open, to fall within the exception. Fenced yards have been considered open fields when viewed by the police from the air. Because the same view was available to any member of the public, it was also available to the police.

Water-related operations may require a warrant be obtained to facilitate the operation. The Lower Colorado River Authority is a public utility company in central Texas. It has been authorized by statute to establish its own statewide law enforcement agency, and those officers have been called LCRA Rangers until recently, when they underwent a name change to the LCRA Department of Public Safety. Part of their responsibility is the Colorado River, its tributaries, dams, lakes, and associated parks. They have law enforcement responsibility on all the waterways supplied by the Colorado River as it flows through the state. They are a well-trained group of professionals who are also trained in high- and low-altitude rescue, swift-water rescue, and underwater investigation. In addition, they have responsibility for enforcing any and all environmental laws that have an impact on the Colorado River and its tributaries. It is their work in enforcing environmental laws that has required them to obtain search warrants to further their environmental investigations. Portions of the river system may be contaminated by effluent. They must locate the source and effect whatever remedy is available to them to stop the contamination. It is relatively easy to track the contamination by the "tracks" left in the water. Once those tracks have led them to a location, it is necessary for the investigators to swear to an affidavit containing probable cause in support of their application for a search warrant to discover the specific source and nature of the contamination that is occurring. That warrant is necessary if the effluent is tracked back to a particular location that enjoys the protection of the Fourth Amendment. However, if the area is not a home or business, then the "open field" exception may allow them to access the area without fear of a Fourth Amendment violation.

The Texas Department of Public Safety has statewide jurisdiction in the investigation of felonies. The Texas Rangers are more readily identified as a state bureau of investigation. The Rangers came into possession of information that a body might have been disposed of in the septic system of a mobile home. Once the affidavit had been completed and the warrant obtained, an underwater search of this highly contaminated septic system was conducted. The system was approximately twelve feet wide and forty feet long. This was a hazmat dive, and hazmat protocol was employed. The warrant allowed entry upon the premises and the search of the septic system. A body was found, and the case is being prosecuted as of this writing.

A police officer in McAllen, Texas, was suspected of having murdered his wife. Close to where the officer lived was a sewage treatment plant. The Texas Rangers were called in to assist in the investigation. The Rangers called in the Texas Department of Public Safety's dive team. Since this was not a location open to the public, it was necessary to obtain permission from the utility company to have access to the plant's settlement tanks (ponds). Again this was a hazmat operation, and a hazmat protocol was established. The suspected weapon was not found after an exhaustive search of all the settlement tanks.

It must be remembered that underwater investigation is a law enforcement function and as such is amenable to all the constitutional restraints that operate against land-based investigations. In truth, most of the underwater investigations that take place are done in public waterways where access is not restricted, but this is not always the case. It is the responsibility of the team and its members to recognize those situations that require observation of constitutional prerequisites and obtain the appropriate authorization or warrants necessary to execute the operation.

REVIEW QUESTIONS

1. What portion of the Fourth Amendment pertains to arrests?
2. What portion of the Fourth Amendment pertains to searches?
3. In what amendment(s) do we find the equal protection, privileges and immunities, and due process clauses? Of what importance is the due process clause to the rights of citizens of various states?
4. What is the "fruit of the poisonous tree" doctrine?
5. What is the exclusionary rule, and how did it come to be applied to the states?
6. What are the elements of a plain-view exception to the warrant requirement?
7. What exception to the exclusionary rule did *United States v. Leon* establish? How does this exception assist police in avoiding civil liability?
8. What is derivative evidence, and what effect does the exclusionary rule have on it?
9. What is contained in a legally sufficient search warrant affidavit?
10. What is the open-field exception to the warrant requirement, and what role does curtilage play in applying the exception?

KEY UNITED STATES SUPREME COURT CASES

Bumper v. North Carolina, 391 U.S. 543 (1968).
Coolidge v. New Hampshire, 403 U.S. 443 (1971).
Florida v. Enio Jimeno, 499 U.S. 934 (1991).
Florida v. Royer, 460 U.S. 491 (1983).
Mapp v. Ohio, 367 U.S. 643 (1961).
Mincey v. Arizona, 437 U.S. 385 (1978).
Miranda v. Arizona, 384 U.S. 436 (1966).
Oliver v. United States, 466 U.S. 170 (1984).
United States v. Leon, 468 U.S. 897 (1984).
Weeks v. United States, 232 U.S. 383 (1914).

Chapter 5

The Underwater Crime Scene

NEW WORDS AND CONCEPTS

last seen point

contamination

transfer

search briefing

dive report

bottom structure

base line

trilateration

search pattern

line tender

Global Positioning Systems

photographic log

video log

predicate

rectangularization

orienting evidence

photogrammetry

underwater crime scene sketch

First Amendment

LEARNING OBJECTIVES

- Discuss the methods employed in conducting an underwater crime scene search
- Discuss the methods employed in recording an underwater crime scene search

The focus in land investigations is on witnesses. Witnesses are as important to the underwater investigation team as they are to any investigative effort. When dealing with drownings or abandoned evidence, where witnesses are available, the underwater investigator should not rely on dry-land investigators to gather information pertaining to the **last seen point.** The underwater investigator has the responsibility to establish the last seen point independently. A thorough examination of possible witnesses by a member of the underwater investigative team may provide last seen point data overlooked or misinterpreted by the dry-land investigating officers. That information may reduce the time and effort expended in the search of the applicable areas.

In drownings, the victim is often found on the bottom within a radius from the last seen point that is equal to the depth of the water. For example, if the victim was drowned in thirty feet of water, the body may be found on the bottom within a thirty-foot radius from the point on the bottom directly below the last seen point topside. In establishing the last seen point, it is often helpful to place a diver or a boat in the water and allow the witness to direct the diver to the last seen point. All interviews should be conducted at the scene approximating the location of the witness at the time of the sighting.

All information gathered from witnesses or dry-land investigators is geared to assisting in the recovery of physical evidence. Witnesses differ in perspective and may color that information through their own perspectives. Any information provided by dry-land investigators pertaining to the search area should be corroborated if possible. Although the recovery of drowning victims gets the most media exposure, underwater investigators spend most of their time in the water seeking evidence that is usually in the form of a weapon, automobile, stolen property, or abandoned drugs.

As waterway recreation and transportation expand, so will crimes committed on those waterways. Underwater investigators provide a large range of recovery services, including but not limited to:

- Boat arsons
- Boat explosions
- Suicides
- Homicides
- Drownings
- Abandoned contraband
- Abandoned weapons
- Abandoned vehicles
- Vehicle entombment
- Vessel and aircraft crashes
- Contraband attached to keels

The first step in any underwater investigation is to locate the underwater crime scene. It is helpful to think of the recovery of underwater evidence as an extension of the overall investigation. By perceiving the recovery operation as an integral part of the overall investigation, it is but one short step to viewing the underwater operation as the processing of a crime scene. If the offense suspected is such that it would precipitate a crime scene analysis, then the underwater counterpart of that investigation should be conducted as meticulously.

As in any investigation, a search cannot begin until a reasonable search area has been delineated and all information that might reduce the size of the search area has been gathered and considered. Much underwater time and frustration can be avoided by not entering the water too soon.

In most instances of police diving, the life of the victim is not in question. Bad weather and surface conditions should be considered before anyone is ordered into the water. Barring a hurricane, the bottom conditions tomorrow will be virtually the same as today. Postponing the dive until better diving conditions are available should be a constant consideration in the mind of the team leader. There is no evidence so important that it warrants risking the life of a diver.

Underwater investigators are often requested to recover an item of evidence that is partially visible or has already been located. Where the resting place of the item sought can be ascertained from the surface, it is not necessary to initiate search procedures. In those instances where it is incumbent upon underwater investigators to conduct the search, the following general procedures should be employed.

No matter the crime or the location, no two crime scenes are ever the same. The crime scene takes in not only the geography, but also persons and things. It is not sufficient to protect geography if what is contained within that space is not also protected. In addition to the location of the victim or property comprising the corpus of the offense, there are also prospective entryways and exits that must similarly be protected from **contamination.** The geography can be easily secured, as can the things upon it. The most difficult part of a crime scene to preserve is people. It is imperative that people be seen as an integral part of the crime scene and preserved as meticulously as any other evidence.

The skills of the investigator may come into play anywhere; crime has no out of bounds. The crime scene includes all areas over which the participants moved while entering to commit, while committing, and while exiting the crime scene. Generally it is one well-defined area, but it may be several noncontiguous areas. Since most human activity takes place inside, the majority of crimes occur inside. Buildings and vehicles are the primary crime scenes, and the majority of the processing and thought about crime scenes deals with these situations. But as more and more people seek outdoor recreation, the responsibility of the investigator and the scope of the investigation increase.

Reconstructing the scene of the crime is accomplished by recording each piece of evidence in relationship to other permanent nonevidentiary items at the scene. That reconstruction is the same regardless of the location of the crime scene. Indoor or outdoor evidence must be recovered with some record of its relationship to the environment from which it was removed. The inability to demonstrate that relationship at the time of trial may result in that evidence not being admitted.

The protection of the underwater crime scene will reduce crime scene contamination. All crime scenes and all evidence retrieved from a crime scene are already contaminated; the point is not to add to that contamination. Only materials handled in contamination-free laboratories can be said to be truly contamination-free. The trick is to prevent any untoward or unnecessary contamination once the scene and its contents come into the possession of the police. Anyone entering a crime scene leaves something; anyone departing a crime scene takes something with him or her. It is this idea of **transfer** that prompts forensic scientists to search for minute materials that may have been left at the scene of a crime.

Many jurisdictions treat waterways as an anomaly to the investigative process and believe that there is nothing to process in an underwater crime scene. It is through this ignorance that offenders have been acquitted or evidence rendered inadmissible. It does little good to have a properly prepared and trained underwater investigative team if the dry-land investigator in charge sees water recovery operations as a mere retrieval of items from beneath the water. Just as there is an appropriate protocol to be employed in dry-land investigations, there should also be an acceptable protocol for wet investigations. Police often lose sight of the true objective in police investigations. Although it may appear that the discovery of evidence and the arrest of a suspect are the goals of an investigation, those are shortsighted goals. The true objective in all police investigations is conviction of a criminal offender. That objective requires that we stop compartmentalizing law enforcement functions and accept that in underwater investigations that strive for convictions, the team includes:

1. First-responding officers who secure the scene
2. Dry-land investigators who will assemble the evidence into a coherent picture
3. An underwater investigative team that will employ a scientific protocol in the recovery of submerged evidence
4. Laboratory personnel who will provide forensic testing
5. Prosecutors who will pursue a conviction

It is imperative that each member of the investigative team recognize who the other members are, what services they provide, and how they provide them. In that way, team members can work to advance the team's overall objective of obtaining a conviction.

Search Briefing

Once the area of the search has been described, a **search briefing** should be conducted describing the methods to employ and the roles for each participant. Often dive teams are eager to get into the water, and lack of planning results in an initial search that proves fruitless, resulting in a duplication of time and effort.

An integral part of the briefing is documenting the dive. The following information should be obtained and documented for inclusion in the **dive report:**

- Witnesses interviewed: names, addresses, and telephone numbers
- Dive team members
- Date
- Time
- Location
- Persons present
- Purpose of search
- Time arrived
- Time search begun

- Methods of searches conducted
- Weather conditions
- Water conditions: temperature, depth, tide, current
- Bottom conditions
- Equipment availability: vessels, tow trucks, barges
- Time, date, and reason for terminating search

Bottom Structure

Determining **bottom structure** will help in selecting search methods and equipment. Many freshwater sites have silt and mud bottoms. Stirring up sediment can further hamper limited visibility. It is apparent that in searches involving mud and silt bottoms, buoyancy control will be important. Diving depth will have to be maintained above the bottom at a distance that will allow visual examination of the bottom without stirring up mud. When dealing with bottoms of this nature, searches should be conducted in layers, beginning at the farthest reaches of visibility and descending closer to the bottom in stages. Inland lake bottoms may be covered with decayed vegetation on top of mud or silt, additionally hampering a search effort. Often the only sign of evidence may be the depression or disturbance caused by the item as it settled to the bottom. In most instances of limited visibility, a diver will use an underwater metal detector. Using a metal detector correctly is a skill that can be acquired only with long practice. It often seems underwater investigators have too few hands to go around.

Current

Current is important for two reasons. First, it may require that mechanical assistance be provided to the underwater investigator to maintain a position in the current and to prevent being moved by the current. Second, police not familiar with underwater operations may exaggerate the effect of the current when locating the search area. In river searches where fast currents are evident, it may be necessary to affix a line across the river, securely anchored on both sides. Once the line is anchored, another line can be tied into the **base line** perpendicularly to allow a rubber raft to be deployed. Divers can be tended from the raft, and safety divers can be stationed in the raft to facilitate ease of access. Conventional wisdom suggests that in fast currents, items dropped will flow with the current and may move great distances downriver from the entry site. Despite this, it will prove expedient in the long run to begin all searches at the point of entry.

Surf, Waves, and Tide

Turbulent surface activity in shallow water may affect items reposing on the bottom. Again, the effect of surf and waves may not be as great as expected, and search operations should begin at the point of entry. Obviously, tides and crashing surf may move material shoreward or out to sea, but presumptions made as to the degree of movement may be erroneous.

Knowing the tide characteristics of a potential dive site can affect the search in a number of ways that do not directly relate to submerged evidence. When interviewing witnesses about the last seen point, tide must be taken into consideration because it can affect the witnesses' distance perception. If possible, such witnesses should be interviewed at the scene at approximately the same tidal flow as existed at the time of the incident in question. In areas of significant tidal flux, awaiting low tide may allow a search of the area without the necessity of entering the water.

Perimeter Marking

At any crime scene, there are points of access and exit points. Exterior crime scenes are no different. People using lakes and rivers as repositories for bodies, weapons, or contraband have to get to those places and have to leave those places. In many instances a vehicle may have been used and may have left some evidence of its passing. It is fundamental to the establishment of a search perimeter to include points adjacent to the waterway that is to be searched as well as shallow water leading to the area to be searched. In a search conducted at Canyon Lake in Texas for a firearm, divers found shell casings on the bank and in the shallow water adjacent to the area at which witnesses placed the suspect who threw the weapon in the water. The shell casings were of the same caliber as the weapon recovered, and since the shell casings were processed as evidence, the crime laboratory was able to lift a fingerprint from one of them.

The preliminary briefing should be followed by dispatching divers to mark the perimeter of the water area to be searched with buoys and, if necessary, to place a dive flag visible to any vessels that may be using the area. A rectangle is generally used to describe the perimeter, with each corner marked by buoys that are visible not only to team participants, but also to any vessel traffic. These buoys should be large enough so as to be difficult to ignore.

Once the perimeter has been marked, it should be located geographically (by Global Positioning System, compass, tape measure **[trilateration],** or range finder) and sketched or plotted on a site map. If a site map is drawn or available, plastic overlays allow plotting of the search area onto the plat without permanently marking the map itself. If the search area must be expanded, the overlay can be replaced. Each overlay should be kept as a permanent part of the dive record so that testimony regarding the search can be supported by the plastic overlays. Once the search area has been marked, the recovery process can begin.

THE UNDERWATER SEARCH

It is not always necessary to launch a search using large numbers of personnel and expensive equipment. In waters of high visibility, fishermen for centuries have used a simple device to locate underwater schools of fish. This device, a glass-bottom bucket, should be part of every recovery team's equipment. Edmund Scientific of New

Jersey makes an inflatable cone with a glass bottom and a viewfinder top designed specifically for clear-water use. Getting in the water is not always the most effective use of manpower and time.

Boat Searches

Identifying the search area may begin with a slow boat ride over the area while peering through a glass-bottom bucket. Looking through a glass-bottom bucket relegates boat speed to two or three knots. A faster method may be to tow a diver behind the boat using snorkel and fins or a search sled. When towing a diver, it is important to provide him or her towrope of sufficient length to avoid prop wash distortion and motor fumes. If the search is to be a prolonged one, use of a sled will reduce arm fatigue and the necessity for rapid diver replacement. A sled search enables boat operators to follow a surface pattern. It also enables the operator to more easily maintain and control the pattern, resulting in a more efficient use of time and manpower and ensuring a more accurate search. When the diver sees what might be the object of the search, he or she can drop off the rope or drop a small pelican buoy that unreels line as the weighted end drops to the bottom. These buoys are light and can be easily attached to a diver's belt or placed in the pocket of the diver's buoyancy compensator.

If a large area must be searched and visibility permits, two boats can be used to tow divers with a line stretched between the boats. The number of divers who can be towed can be increased, as can the area searched, with each pass. Boat searches must also be conducted based on a repeating pattern that can be plotted by compass and chart. All parts of the search must be geographically located and documented for courtroom use. A number of small buoys will be needed to mark the progress of the sweeps being made by the search boat. These buoys will be dropped at locations intersecting the rectangle that forms the perimeter of the search area. These buoys must be larger then the ones the divers carry for marking evidence. The size of the search area may render smaller buoys nearly invisible. The glass and Styrofoam floats used by fishermen to support their fishing nets work well for marking the route of the search boat. One of these is dropped, with enough line and weight to prevent it from being carried away by waves, at each outermost point of the search before direction is reversed and the search continues. By aligning two of these buoys, the skipper of the search boat should be able to maintain an overlapping search interval within the rectangular search area.

If the search is conducted contiguous to a shoreline, it may be simpler to place markers on the shoreline, allowing the boat to line up on these markers and use its compass to assist in laying down the **search pattern.** If these shore markers are laid with the assistance of a transit or similar device, the boat course can be directed by the transit operator. Once the evidence is discovered, it can be marked with a buoy and immediately triangulated by the transit operator.

In water of limited visibility, magnetometers or towed sonar arrays, if available, may be used to locate large underwater objects. Sidescan sonar covers a larger area than the handheld or installed echo sounders found in many bass fishing boats. A sophisticated system with a competent operator can sweep shallow waters in 500-foot swaths. In deeper water, up to 1,200 feet can be examined in each sweep. The sidescan is not affected by weather or visibility.

Proton magnetometers are affected by focused masses of ferromagnetic metals. The size of the object sought, or, more precisely, the amount of ferromagnetic metals used in the manufacture of the item determines how deeply the magnetometer probe must be towed. The strength of Earth's magnetic field should be fairly constant within the area surveyed; detection of a significant change in that field suggests a concentrated ferrous mass. Again, the size of the iron item sought will determine how close to the bottom the magnetometer probe must be towed. Robert Marx used a proton magnetometer to find the sunken Spanish galleon *Maravilla*. Although she was buried beneath twenty-five feet of sand, he was able to locate her and twenty-four other wrecks, discovering anchors, chains, and a fisherman's tackle box (Marx 1990, 123).

If an item sought is below the surface and not of ferrous material, the magnetometer and towed sonar array are of little use. A specialized sonar echo sounder called a sub-bottom profiler is effective in such searches to a depth of ten feet under the sand. British antiquarians and archaeologists have searched in vain for the infamous *Mary Rose*, sunk in Portsmouth Harbor, England, in 1545. Search efforts had concentrated in a 1,200-square-foot area known to be the sinking site. Attempts to locate her with sonar and magnetometer had failed. A sub-bottom profiler revealed her location beneath ten feet of silt and mud, within that 1,200-foot search area.

Although most police agencies may not have underwater sensing devices, often military or oceanographic organizations are willing to assist in a search operation. When searching for items such as large aircraft or sunken vessels, a compass may reflect the change in Earth's magnetic field resulting from interference from a large metal mass.

Historically, the most common method of boat search was the towed cable search. This technique is only effective in waters with unlittered and geologically undisturbed bottoms. The cable search is applicable in those situations in which large evidentiary items are sought. This method employs two boats towing a heavily weighted cable between them. The length of the cable determines the scope of each pass. The size of the boats and the motors driving them limits the length of the cable that can be towed. It becomes apparent when a large obstruction is snagged. As the boats retrieve the played-out cable, they eventually back over the snagged obstacle. Once the item is directly below, a diver can be dispatched to mark the evidence. Most of the shipwrecks in the Baltic and North Seas have been discovered using this method. The most recent discovery of note was the galliot found in 120 feet of water near the Borsto Islands in the Baltic Sea. The ship, sunk between 1700 and 1710, was found intact and upright. In the cold, impenetrable Baltic waters, divers found, in the main cabin, the skeleton of a man, enameled snuffboxes, pocket watches, and clothing (Falcon-Barker 1964).

Search Patterns

In water of limited visibility or irregular bottom structure, searching may be done in the water by divers using a search pattern. In black water diving, lines must be sunk to which divers can be attached while conducting a search by feel, handheld sonar, or metal detector. Handheld sonar can be used in any of the search patterns described below. A sonar unit emits a beep when it senses an item protruding from the bottom. As the diver descends, the beep becomes louder. It would be helpful if these devices also produced a vibration that increased in intensity as the object being sensed drew closer. Once an item is sensed, that location should be marked with a buoy before the search is interrupted so that if the item sensed is not the object sought, the search can continue at the point where the item was first sensed.

The same approach should be used when the diver is operating a handheld metal detector. Most detectors use dials and audible signals to assist in locating metal. It would prove helpful for these devices also to have a vibratory component to assist in searches involving limited visibility.

Often low-visibility and no-visibility searches are conducted without the assistance of electronic devices. Hand searches usually involve crawling through visually impenetrable mud, wearing gloves, attempting to identify by touch the things the hand grasps or touches. All the senses focus on the hand and fingers, and the sense of touch heightens to the point where a diver wearing gloves can touch a pull tab from a beer or soft drink can and, without picking it up, tell that it is a pull tab. A search must be undertaken with diligence and perseverance. A systematic search method prevents duplication of efforts and facilitates documentation and in-court testimony.

The nature and scope of the search are determined by the offense, existing current, tidal conditions, water depth, visibility, wind direction, and known bottom structure. It is the recovery team leader's responsibility to determine, based on the relevant variables, which search pattern to employ.

Search patterns vary and have different attributes, enabling them to address different search requirements, but all search patterns should have certain basic attributes. The pattern should:

1. Begin at a predetermined point, have predetermined midpoints and changes of direction, and end at a predetermined location or upon discovery of the item sought
2. Include communication from surface personnel to searchers through line signals or voice communication
3. Allow the searcher to deploy buoys to mark points of interest or evidence
4. Be simple
5. Effectively use divers and resources
6. Allow for safe support of the diver or divers

Most searches involve a surface component (**line tender**) and a diver or divers. All divers should be competent in line tending. The diver provides the labor, and the tender provides the direction and support. The tender is the diver's lifeline. The backup tender is responsible for keeping notes of the dive regarding location, direction, duration, and depth. In those instances when a diver is unable to determine air consumption and depth, it falls to the tender to provide that information. Each tender needs a compass (to record search direction and termination points), timepiece (to approximate air consumption and time at depth), flotation device, and notepad.

Random Search

Although not a pattern at all, putting a number of divers at a search site and having them cast about within that area may prove successful in small search areas with maximum visibility. Not generally seen as artful or strategic, it may render a positive result quickly. In clear water with bottoms layered with sediment, it is important not to dive too deep, thereby agitating that sediment and prohibiting a subsequent patterned search if the random search is unsuccessful.

Sweep Search

This is the most commonly employed search method, for searches conducted contiguous to an accessible shoreline, bridge, dock, or pier, or in a river whose current requires a line stretched across the river. The diver swims, tethered to the tender by a 3/8-inch to 7/16-inch polypropylene line, in ever-broadening arcs. The tender line remains taut, and the tender and diver remain in continuous communication through line pull signals. The farthest reaches of the arcs should be determined by the tender using landmarks, placed buoys, or compass bearings. The terminus of the arcs should be recorded in the dive profile (a sketch of the search site and search pattern). When the bottom drops quickly, it may be best to employ a parallel pattern to avoid running the diver into the shore and to reduce the number of times the ear must equalize pressure because of rapid or numerous changes in depth. Underwater obstacles can be addressed in one of three fashions:

1. Raise the line tender.
2. Conduct the search up to the obstacle and begin again on the other side of the obstacle.
3. Pick a pattern that will allow for debris-strewn bottoms.

Parallel Searches

When the area to be searched is relatively free of obstruction and close to the shoreline, this pattern allows lengthy passes along the shoreline, extending outward. Markers should be placed on the shore at the farthest reaches of the pattern. The tender moves back and forth between these two markers paralleling the diver's movement. At the farthest reaches of the pattern, two tugs on the tender line communicates to the diver that it is time to turn back in the opposite direction but at a slightly greater

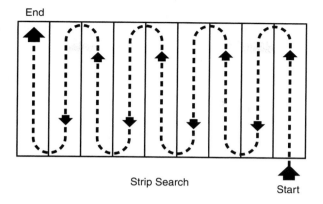

Strip Search

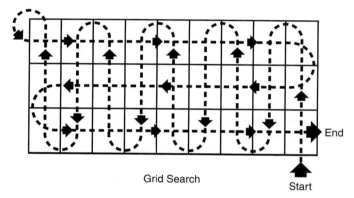

Grid Search

FIGURE 5-1 Search patterns.
(*Source:* R. F. Becker)

distance from the shoreline. The amount of line fed to the diver on each direction change has been predetermined depending upon what is being sought.

Circular Search

This is often a boat-based search. In areas not conducive to search using a land-based line tender, the tender works from a boat. In shallow water, the line tender is at the center of the circle in a boat, feeding line to the diver, who swims in a 360-degree circle, stops, and is fed another one to three feet of line. The line tender directs the search using a landmark, an anchored buoy, or a compass bearing for the stopping point. This same pattern can be employed wherein the diver changes direction after each stop. Changing direction is less disorienting than swimming in concentric circles, does not require the tender to continue turning in circles, and reduces the likelihood of the diver turning in ever-smaller circles should the line get wrapped around a stump or other debris.

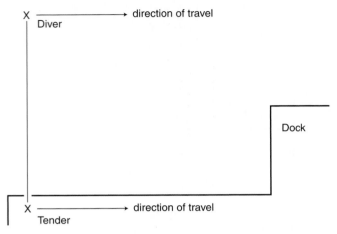

FIGURE 5-2   Parallel search.
(*Source:* R. F. Becker)

In a circle search from a "circle board" resting on the bottom, the line to the diver is either self-fed or fed from a surface line tender. This is a common search method and works best in open water.

Circular searches can be conducted without a boat or circle board, using a submerged diver as the tender and center of the search pattern. Using compass bearings or an orientation line, the anchored diver can direct the search and the needed directional changes.

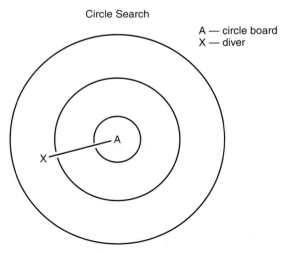

FIGURE 5-3   Circular search.
(*Source:* R. F. Becker)

FIGURE 5-4   Circle board.
(*Source:* R. F. Becker)

Snag Search

The snag search is not a search pattern but a search method. This technique can be used with an arc pattern, parallel pattern, or circular pattern. Just as in boat-towed snag searches, the size of the item sought and the presence of submerged obstructions determine the applicability of this procedure. The value of this technique is that it allows large areas to be searched in a short period of time. The tender allows more line to the diver than he or she would in a hand or vision search.

River Search

River searches can be especially tedious when significant current is present. Depending on the intensity of the current, it may well be that a search is impossible. In currents of manageable proportions, to be determined by the team leader, it may be necessary

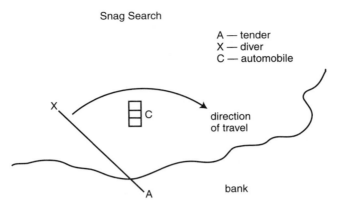

FIGURE 5-5   Snag search.
(*Source:* R. F. Becker)

to provide the river diver line-based assistance. This procedure depends on the availability of land-based anchor points on opposite sides of the river. A line must be extended from one anchor point to the other. The line should be pulled taut, using mechanical devices if necessary (e.g., vehicle, fence stretcher, or winch). A RIB (rubber inflatable boat) with a line tender and safety diver is tethered to the transverse line, allowing movement up and down the river as well as shoreward. Once the primary lines have been set, a secondary line, downstream of the area being worked, needs to be anchored in a similar fashion. The secondary line serves as a safety device and as a method for divers to exit the water by simply letting the river carry them to the secondary line. The secondary line should be angled with the flow of the river instead of perpendicular, allowing easier exit. Swift-water searches are dangerous and should be avoided. If they are unavoidable, maximum safety precautions must be taken and specialized training completed.

Relocating the Search Site

It may be necessary to return to the search site on a day other than the one upon which the search was begun. It may be necessary to continue searching on subsequent days, in which case the accurate plotting of the previous day's search pattern will prevent beginning anew or guessing where the search left off. Once evidence has been found, it may take days to completely process and recover the evidence, in which case it may be necessary to return to the precise location. Floating buoys left unattended may disappear. To ensure a return to the appropriate spot, a dive site profile must be created for each search site. Often divers will attempt to use compass bearings to triangulate their positions. Although this method is subject to significant margins of error, depending on the distance of the objects used for triangulation, in many instances it is all that is available. When using a compass to locate a site, the objects from which bearings are taken should be greater than thirty degrees apart. When plotted on a profile map, these bearings should return the team to the general location.

Profiling

The search area can be recorded as to location and general content by employing a method pioneered by Butch Hendricks (1989, 52) and Lifeguard Systems. They have named the process "profiling," and it is an invaluable tool. It can serve as a sustainable record of any given search, allowing:

- Return to the same location
- Rediscovery of underwater obstacles
- Permanent record of areas searched
- Supportive trial documentation

Using search lines that have been marked at five-foot intervals out to 150 feet gives the profiler the approximate distance to the primary diver from the tender throughout the dive. Compass bearings allow for an approximation of the location of the primary diver from the tender. The scene commander or a profiler can take the bearings and record the measurements. Using predetermined line signals, the diver can request that the profiler record an obstruction. The location of that obstruction is important for a number of reasons:

- Future reference (should another operation occur in that location, bottom structure and obstruction information will be available)
- Should it become necessary to search the site again (for another piece of evidence or because of questions of integrity of the original search), knowing where the obstructions are is a great help for the primary diver
- Identifying the search scene

The profiler locates on the search sketch or profile slate the location of all obstructions communicated by the primary diver. Symbols can be used to represent the types of obstructions, or generic symbols can be used to identify:

- Natural obstructions
- Man-made obstructions and debris

Each obstruction should be given a symbol and a number. The number can be explained as a footnote to the profile as described by the primary diver with communication capabilities or after the dive by the primary diver. All measurements in this method revolve around the position of the tender. That position must be located geographically as well (three land measurements should be sufficient to locate the position to the exclusion of all others [triangulation or trilateration]).

Searches conducted out of the sight of land pose an additional problem. Typical navigational abilities can only approximately locate the position of a vessel at sea. Sailors using sextants to ascertain their position at sea can do so with only a modicum of accuracy. Radio beacons affixed to various permanent and well-known landmarks allow vessels at sea with radio direction finders (RDFs) to triangulate their

scene sketch/profile

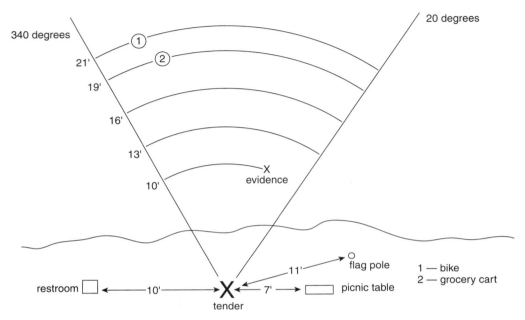

FIGURE 5-6   Scene sketch/profile.
(*Source:* R. F. Becker)

positions with a degree of certainty. **Global Positioning Systems** (GPS) use up to twelve satellites accessible globally to anyone with a handheld GPS device to compute positions to a heretofore unattainable degree of accuracy. The GPS can be used on land or at sea; its only limitation is in its ability to receive signals from one of the satellites to which it is calibrated.

TEMPORAL AND GEOGRAPHICAL LOCATION OF EVIDENCE

After the team has located the evidence, the usual procedure is to retrieve it. It is important to remember that the officer recovering the evidence is responsible for testifying as to the method used in locating, marking, sketching, measuring, photographing, bagging, and tagging the evidence, and maintaining the chain of custody.

All details pertaining to the dive site must be recorded prior to the recovery of any evidence. The boundaries of the recovery site should be marked with buoys, and the entire area plotted on a site chart. This chart must be large enough to contain measurement information about each piece of evidence to be recovered. The methods used to record available information will vary depending on the size of the recovery area, nature of the items to be recovered, available time, weather conditions, water conditions, visibility, bottom conditions, seriousness of the offense, and manpower demands. Failure to properly mark and record the location of the recovery site may result in:

- Losing it, in the event more than one dive is necessary
- Inability to orient parts of a dismembered or dismantled auto, vessel, airplane, or body. In airline crashes, body parts may be strewn over the site (Wagner and Froede 1993, 574). Reconstruction of the bodies may require anthropological assistance. Often the fastest way to associate severed body parts with the torso is by recording the location of the body parts relative to each other or to the seat or seats the parts were closest to. By referring to the seating chart, investigators can readily associate body parts with the passenger who had been occupying the seat nearest where the body parts were found.
- Considerable expense of time and effort in relocating the site and the evidence at the site
- Having the evidence rendered inadmissible at the time of trial

The most effective method of recordation is photography. Where visibility allows, the camera should be the first piece of equipment on the site. All evidence should be photographed, visibility allowing, where it is found. After measurement, sketching, and tagging, the evidence should be photographed again and then bagged.

Photographic Log

A separate **photographic log** should be kept by the photographer. If the underwater investigator takes the pictures, an entry for each photo taken should be placed in the field notes and should include:

- Description of the content of each photo
- Speed of the film
- Shutter speed
- Distance of the camera from the object photographed
- Location and direction from which the photo was taken
- Date, time, and case number or name

Video Log

If the underwater investigator takes the video, then the following information should be recorded in a **video log:**

- Type of recorder
- Type of film
- Type of lens(es)

- Artificial light used
- Evidence recovered and its location
- Geographical and temporal location of evidence

A specific time and place embraces all matter. It is the underwater investigator's job to record sufficient information to adequately place each piece of evidence as to time and place. All measurements should be recorded as well as the identity of the person discovering the evidence. The identification of evidence is accomplished by providing the following information:

- Description
- Location
- Time discovered
- Who discovered it
- Container used
- Method of sealing the container
- Markings used on tags and evidence
- Maintenance log (where it's being kept)

All courtroom testimony will be balanced against the documentation the underwater investigator has manufactured.

Photographing the Underwater Crime Scene

The method whereby the underwater crime scene is first recorded is through photographs and/or video, visibility allowing. The video recorder is becoming a very popular tool in recording the underwater crime scene. Film makes a permanent historical record of how the scene appeared when the film was exposed.

All photographed evidence should be shot in situ before adding anything for size perspective. In order for a still photograph to be admitted into evidence, it is necessary for a witness (underwater investigator) to "prove up" the photograph. Each type of physical evidence that may be brought to trial must first be authenticated as being what it purports to be. Before any evidence can be referred to in front of a jury, the presenting party must first proffer a series of questions, known as a **predicate,** demonstrating to the satisfaction of the court that the item is relevant, unaltered, and identifiable. A predicate for a photograph might be as follows:

Q. Officer, I hand you what has been labeled as the State's Exhibit Number 1. Do you recognize it?
A. Yes, I recognize it.
Q. What is it?
A. A photograph.
Q. Do you recognize the scene portrayed in the photograph?
A. Yes.

> **Q.** Does this photograph fairly and accurately portray the scene in the photograph as you remember it?
>
> **A.** Yes, it does.

The photograph would then be marked as State's Evidence #1 and could be offered to the jury for examination.

Video Recordings

Today's underwater investigator relies on video photography to record the crime scene where visibility allows such a recording. The appropriate predicate combines the audio recording and still photograph predicates.

> **Q.** Was the videotape you have described as State's Exhibit Number 3 prepared on a recording device capable of making an accurate recording?
>
> **A.** Yes.

No technical data need be supplied. However, if the witness is a competent video technician, a brief technical description may ensue. Nevertheless, technical understanding is not required to use video equipment or to establish the predicate for admissibility.

> **Q.** Who was the operator?
>
> **A.** I was [or name of the party who made the video].

It is not necessary for the witness to have actually made the video to be able to prove its authenticity. All that is required is that the testifying officer viewed the scene prior to taping, has viewed the tape, and verifies that the tape is an accurate reflection of the scene.

> **Q.** Have you viewed the tape?
>
> **A.** Yes.
>
> **Q.** Has the videotape been altered in any way?
>
> **A.** No.

Some agencies will add a voice-over to a tape to provide for a better understanding of the video images. Obviously, the voice-over is hearsay and probably inadmissible. If the defense objects to the voice-over, the sound can simply be turned off. It may be necessary to testify that the video has been altered by the addition of a soundtrack, but that the addition has not altered the video images.

> **Q.** When was the tape made?
>
> **A.** [Provide time and date.]
>
> **Q.** Do the pictures of the events contained in the video fairly and accurately reflect the scene as you recall it?
>
> **A.** Yes.

Logging Photos

Underwater crime scene photographs should be taken in a coordinated sequence with that sequence being recorded by photo number and description. Panoramic and general content shots should be taken and logged first, with more specific, detailed, and close-up shots following. The photo log should be a story that flows from the general to the specific. The photo log should contain the following information:

- Identifying information sufficient to describe the photographer, including name, rank, badge number, and agency
- Identifying information pertaining to all equipment and film used. The equipment used may vary from exterior to interior locations, as will film speed and exposure settings. Those variations should be reflected in the photo log. Ambient light conditions and visibility should be described.
- Case number, if one has been assigned, or a geographical location to which the photos can be tied. Date and time of day should also be provided.
- The chronological order in which the photos were taken
- Disposition of the exposed film: whether the film is sent out for processing or is processed in the police lab. If it is processed by the photographer, development and printing information should be provided as an addendum to the photo log.

The log itself is not constructed at the underwater crime scene. All the foregoing information is included in the photographer's field notebook and transferred to a photograph log sheet. Most agencies have preprinted log sheets divided into categories for ease of recording. Often the police get only one opportunity to process an underwater crime scene; subsequent entries may be predicated upon probable cause and warrant acquisition. Everything that needs to be done needs to be done right and completely the first time. There are no guarantees that any single photo or any single roll of film will render usable photographs. Taking multiple shots of all-important aspects of the crime scene may save frustration and embarrassment later. Film is relatively cheap compared to verdicts of acquittal.

Establishing a Reference Point

When discussing measurement methods, it is easiest to use the metric system. Mathematical operations based on ten may prove easier to work with than the changing base of inches and feet. However, when testifying, it may be necessary to convert meters to inches and feet in order for the jury to understand the distances involved. When evidence is recovered from a crime scene in a conventional crime, measurement is generally not a problem. There are fixed landmarks from which measurements can be taken. However, under water there may not be a readily available landmark to which an investigator can anchor measurements. After plotting the recovery area on the site chart, it is generally necessary to establish a point of reference from which measurements can be made.

Crime Scene Measurements

Interior crime scene investigators use one of three basic measurement techniques: **rectangularization,** triangulation, and base line construction. In rectangularization, two right angles are drawn from the item being measured to the nearest permanent object (fixed point).

Rectangularization

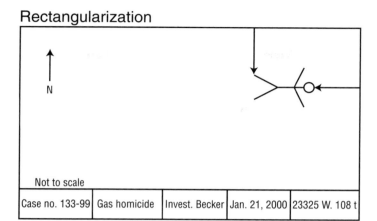

| Case no. 133-99 | Gas homicide | Invest. Becker | Jan. 21, 2000 | 23325 W. 108 t |

FIGURE 5-7 Rectangularization.
(*Source:* R. F. Becker)

When triangulating, as the name suggests, three angles, or a triangle, are measured, with the item of interest at the apex of the triangle and the base angles of the triangles intersecting at permanent objects (fixed points).

When using the base line construction measurement method, it is necessary to establish an arbitrary line (base line) of some measurable distance from two fixed

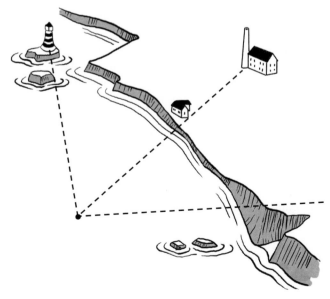

FIGURE 5-8 Triangulation.
(*Source:* R. F. Becker)

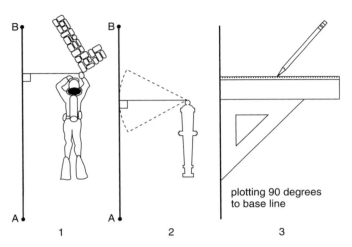

FIGURE 5-9   Base line construction.
(*Source:* R. F. Becker)

points. Measurements can then be made from the base line at right angles to the item of interest.

Both triangulation and base line construction work especially well outdoors, where permanent landmarks are at a distance from the item to be measured. But none of these methods work very well when processing an underwater crime scene, where measurement of the distance from items in the water to permanent objects on land is hampered by limited or zero visibility. Trilateration is a method of measurement in which the underwater investigator need not rely on sight for accuracy. Objects in the water are measured from two known locations on the shore. One end of the measuring tape is on shore at the prelocated position, and the diver moves the other end of the tape to a point on the object being measured. The shore-based end of the tape is then moved from one known position to the other. It is important to note that this measurement will give only the location of the object being measured, not the orientation. To orient the object, two more measurements must be taken from different points on the submerged item.

Orienting Evidence

Measuring evidence in this fashion does not provide orientation information. **Orienting evidence** may be as important as locating it in the first place, particularly for autos, airplanes and their occupants, vessels and their occupants, and debris from fires, explosions, crashes, or collisions. The front, back, and sides of large evidentiary items can be located by gross (large) measurements from what are recognizably the front, back, and sides, with those measurements plotted on the site map. However, when dealing with small items of evidence such as coins or weapons, the size of the item makes it impractical to measure to the front, back, and sides. Obviously, the easiest way to orient an item of evidence is to photograph it, marking north so that the photo can later be oriented with the information plotted on the site map.

TRILATERATION
(orientation)

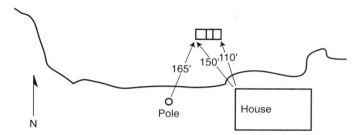

A third measurement is required to
orient (lock in space) the vehicle.

165'   150' 110'

O
Pole   House

FIGURE 5-10   Trilateration; orientation.
(*Source:* R. F. Becker)

Grid Searches

A small grid three meters square made of plastic pipe and subdivided into ten-centimeter squares, with fixed legs six to ten inches long, is invaluable in fixing the position (orientation) of small pieces of evidence such as weapons, ammunition, coins, etc. Having located the item, it is relatively easy to plot its orientation within the grid. First, the

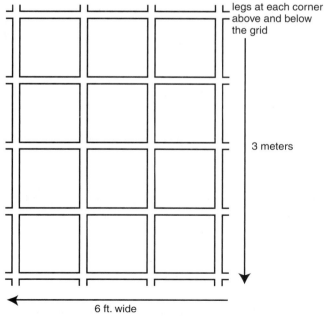

legs at each corner
above and below
the grid

3 meters

6 ft. wide

FIGURE 5-11   Small grid.
(*Source:* R. F. Becker)

FIGURE 5-12   Large grid.
(*Source:* R. F. Becker)

grid must be geographically located and plotted. Once the grid is in place, a photo-graph or tape measurement will allow accurate measurements to the front, back, and sides of the item, thereby orienting the evidence within the grid. The grid can then be plotted on the site map and a separate expanded grid map constructed.

In many instances visibility will not allow the use of underwater measuring devices. It should be noted that measurement of the type described above has been used in waters of minimal visibility. Visibility should not be used as an excuse for not measuring. In those instances where time or visibility is limited, measurement can be done from the shore.

Photogrammetry

Using a photo tower can produce horizontal measurements, but if elevations are important, a photo tower will not provide elevations. Dimitri Rebikoff devised a method whereby a shipwreck can be accurately measured horizontally and vertically via **photogrammetry.** This method does away with the need for hand measurements altogether. A bar is floated above the site at a constant height. A camera designed to take stereo pictures is slid along the bar, and a series of overlapping pictures is taken. The matched photos are measured for differences in parallax with digital measuring devices, thereby locating each item visible in the photograph (Williams 1972, 220).

Not all cases warrant expenditures of time and money, and not all departments have budgets allowing for sophisticated measurement or photographic activities. Time, weather, current, and visibility will undoubtedly play important roles in the recovery process and the method of measurement employed. It should be emphasized that limited visibility, time, or budget is not an excuse for abandoning all attempts at measurement.

The Underwater Crime Scene Sketch

The data upon which the **underwater crime scene sketch** is based is gathered after the scene has been completely processed and photographed but before evidentiary items have been bagged, tagged, and transported. The sketch is a measured drawing showing the location of all important items, landmarks, permanent fixtures, and physical evidence. The underwater investigator usually is responsible for the crime scene sketch, but some agencies have drafting technicians who render the drawing. It should not be surprising in this day of computer software to find that there are a number of programs that assist in this capacity. The future will also provide laptop computer companions for the underwater investigator that will accept a verbal description of the premises and render a drawing to the exact measurements provided. There is surveying equipment presently available that plugs directly into a portable computer, which accepts the measurements directly from the instruments and provides a visual representation of those measurements. However, the majority of crime scene sketches are still drawn by investigators, by hand and not to scale. Everything that is included in the sketch must be geographically located (measurement is one method of geographically locating something). All unnecessary detail should be omitted from the sketch. Only items necessary for locating evidence and establishing scene parameters need be included.

The usefulness of the sketch is based on accurate measurements, not on artistic content. The trial may take place years from the date of the offense. The underwater investigator's on-scene measurements and sketches are not the official crime scene sketch. Measurement notations and initial drawings are done in pencil and later incorporated into a permanent inked or printed sketch. The finished product should contain the following information:

- A scene identifier in the title box of the sketch; that identifier should be either the case number or a recognizable title associated with the offense being investigated
- Also in the title block, the specific location of the underwater crime scene
- The date of the original sketch (rough sketch)

- The name of the underwater investigator and the person drawing the sketch, if other than the investigator
- In the title box, a written statement of the scale to which the drawing is made or of the absence of scale
- A directional rosette, an arrow showing which direction is north. In orienting the drawing on the paper, it is generally presumed in drafting that north is up.

An underwater crime scene sketch is of little value if it cannot be admitted at trial. As with photos and video recordings, there is a particular evidentiary foundation (predicate) that must be established in proving up sketches, maps, or diagrams.

Q.   Did you participate in the preparation of the diagram that you have identified as State's Exhibit Number 2?

A.   Yes.

Q.   Are you personally familiar with the objects and locations contained in the diagram?

A.   Yes.

Q.   Is this a fair and accurate representation of the _____ [search site, recovery site, location of evidence found] as you recall it?

A.   Yes.

Q.   Is this diagram drawn to scale?

A.   No.

Generally, it is easier to testify about a diagram that is not drawn to scale. Defense lawyers may focus on minuscule measurement errors to undermine the credibility of the entire diagram. If all measurements are linked to a permanent landmark that was located on the diagram with the aid of surveying instruments, having a scale drawing may not be a problem. Reasonable approximations are much easier to defend.

Handling Evidence

Physical evidence is usually handled according to a predetermined protocol. That protocol includes recording field information about all evidence discovered. That information may include but is not limited to:

- Identifying evidence by description in field notes and evidence tags
- The location within the underwater crime scene at which the evidence was obtained
- The name of the person who found the evidence
- Time and date of the finding of the evidence
- A description of any characteristics unique to a piece of evidence
- The names of all participants in the search process

The Press

Although a good working relationship with the press is desirable, it is best for recovery team members to leave such relationships to persons designated for that purpose. In dealing with the press, the following may prove helpful:

- Keep the search scene secure and organized, anticipating covert photography.
- All briefings and debriefings of dive team members should be done in private.
- Recovery team members should arrive at the site together rather than straggle in individually, casting about aimlessly.
- Conduct and conversation should reflect the gravity of the situation at all times.
- The release of information pertaining to victims is the province of authorized personnel only.
- All statements to the media should be prepared statements and read to media representatives (copies of such statements should be kept as part of the file).

Considering the sophistication of listening devices and zoom lenses, dive teams should not engage in conduct or conversation that they would not want to hear or see on the evening news.

Representatives of the press have the same impression of underwater recovery operations as do most of the public. They do not see them as a law enforcement function, or the area involved as a crime scene. In their quest for that special picture, interview, or perspective, they may attempt to gain access to a search area.

The most difficult situations to deal with are those involving other agencies and media representatives. Medical examiners, emergency medical personnel, and coroners all have duties to perform and places they would rather be. Bodies cannot be released until investigative analysis has been completed. There will always be someone making a demand for entry who may be upset at being excluded from the scene. It is vital to security that the police and all persons associated with a crime scene in any capacity be aware of and comply with the written policies and procedures that apply to crime scene security. The media often attempts to gain access and information by invoking the **First Amendment** and the people's right to know. Most police officers are only vaguely aware of the First Amendment and have little understanding of the cases that have established the limitations referred to in the First Amendment.

First Amendment

Congress shall make no law respecting an establishment of religion, or prohibiting the free exercise thereof; or abridging the freedom of speech, or of the press; or the right of the people peaceably to assemble, and to petition the Government for redress of grievances. (Source: U.S. Constitution)

Nowhere in the First Amendment to the United States Constitution does it refer to the "people's right to know," nor does it refer to extraordinary rights of the press. It simply refers to the abridging of the press. The First Amendment was created to protect the press and the public from a strong central government that would not allow an uncensored press. Abridgement in this context refers simply to what the press may or may not be allowed to print. Limited access to a crime scene does not abridge the press; they are free to write whatever they wish. In managing the press, it is important to attempt to maintain the highest rapport with all representatives of the media. All statements to the press should be made by the public information officer, and all requests for access or statements should be referred to that office. The media has no greater right to enter a secured area than does any other citizen, nor have they any greater right to information than does any other citizen. Under no circumstances are media representatives to be allowed access to a crime scene. All information provided to the press regarding an investigation should be managed through press pools and public statements.

If proper security zones have been established, media efforts at penetrating the inner zone should prove futile. In many instances, underwater investigators do not establish security zones or even use police tape to delineate the working area. It is good to remember that police presence alone does not assure security if there are no security boundaries. All recovery operations should be within secure areas.

REVIEW QUESTIONS

1. What is meant geographically by the term *crime scene*?
2. Discuss the importance of the first responding officer to the investigative team.
3. What is crime scene contamination, and what role does it play in the processing of a crime scene?
4. What is transfer, and what is its significance to a crime scene?
5. What rights does the press have to view a crime scene?
6. What kind of information should be recorded pertaining to recovered evidence?
7. Where does photography come into play in processing the crime scene? What is photographed, and when is it photographed?
8. What is the appropriate predicate for the admissibility of crime scene photographs?
9. What information is included in a crime scene photo log?
10. What are triangulation, rectangularization, and trilateration?
11. What information should be included on a crime scene sketch?
12. Describe three underwater search techniques.
13. In underwater searches for drowned victims, what is the last seen point, what is its significance, and how is it determined?

REFERENCES

FALCON-BARKER, T. 1964. *Roman galley beneath the sea*. New York: McGraw-Hill.
MARX, R. F. 1990. *The underwater dig*. Houston: Pisces Books.

WAGNER, G. N., and R. C. FROEDE. 1993. Medicolegal investigation of mass disasters. In *Spitz and Fisher's medicolegal investigation of death*, 3rd ed., ed. Werner U. Spitz, 567–584. Springfield, IL: Charles C. Thomas.

WILLIAMS, J. C. C. 1972. Underwater surveying by simple graphic photogrammetry with obliques. *Underwater archaeology: A nascent discipline*. Paris: United Nations.

Additional Readings

BASS, G. B. 1968. *Archaeology under water*. New York: Frederick A. Praeger.

BLACKMAN, D. J. 1973. *Marine archaeology*. London: Martin Robertson.

BRYLSKE, A. 1984. *PADI rescue diver manual*. Santa Ana, CA: PADI.

CLEATOR, P. E. 1973. *Underwater archaeology*. New York: Holt, Rinehart, and Winston.

LONSDALE, M. V. 1989. *SRT diver*. Los Angeles: Lonsdale.

LINTON, J. S. 1986. *The dive rescue specialist training manual*. Fort Collins: Concept Systems, Inc.

WOOD, M. 1985. *Dive control specialist handbook*. Fort Collins: Concept Systems, Inc.

UNESCO publication. 1972. *Underwater archaeology*. Paris: United Nations.

Chapter 6

Medicolegal Aspects of Underwater Death

NEW WORDS AND CONCEPTS

bagged	lazy eyelid
putrefaction	corneal clouding
underwater investigators	postmortem lividity
wear patterns	postmortem interval
bottom structure sample	postmortem immersion
primary identifications	exudate
skeletonized remains	Mary Jo Kopechne
rigor mortis	washerwoman's skin
flotation times	gloving
flotation	background contamination
water soluble	pugilistic position
algor mortis	explosive device
semifetal position	microtaggants

LEARNING OBJECTIVES

- Describe the postmortem changes in a body
- Describe the use of postmortem changes in underwater investigation
- Describe how various medical specialties assist in the underwater investigation

INTRODUCTION

All of us who watch the Discovery Channel on television know Earth is the water planet. The United States has water-shrouded boundaries on three sides and inland waterways too numerous to measure. More and more human activity is taking place on America's waterways, as we become fully franchised citizens of Planet Ocean. As our waterborne activities increase, so do the problems associated with enforcing laws on the nation's most popular playgrounds.

People flock to recreational waterways in vast numbers. As the number of people using recreational waterways increases, so do the numbers of accidents, drownings, violent crimes, and homicides. There are more than 7,500 drownings in the United States each year; it is the fourth leading cause of accidental death in the country. Many of these go uninvestigated on the presumption that a reported drowning is an accident and nothing more. The conventional wisdom is that once something has been submerged, the item no longer has any forensic value.

UNATTENDED WATER DEATHS

In the world of homicide investigators there is an axiom that serves them well: All unattended deaths are presumed homicides until proven otherwise. Sometimes that proof is immediately apparent; sometimes it is not, but the presumption is still the starting point. As unlikely as it seems, that presumption has been relaxed if not ignored in cases of drowning. The common approach to dealing with bodies in the water is that it is presumed accidental until proven otherwise. There is no question that a knowledgeable killer could go a long way in dispatching his victim in the water and reporting it as an "accidental" drowning. If such a homicide were to occur in a rural community, it would go virtually unnoticed, with the local fire department providing recovery services for the police. Most fire departments have little concern for the possibility of a crime and for prospective forensic evidence that might be available on the body. In most instances, any evidence that may have existed prior to the recovery is destroyed, contaminated, or removed in the recovery process.

Body Recovery

In an effort to establish a standardized protocol for the recovery of submerged bodies, accidental or otherwise, all bodies should be **bagged** in the water. There will always be those cases where rigor and **putrefaction** make underwater bagging difficult, but a failure to bag in the water may result in the loss of transient evidence, such as hair or fiber, and the destruction or contamination of trace evidence, such as accelerant residue. Hands should also be bagged in nylon bags with wrist pull ties to preserve any hair, blood, fiber, or tissue under the fingernails; any defense wounds on the hands or broken fingernails; and any fiber or gunpowder that may be retrieved

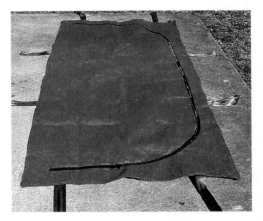

FIGURE 6-1   Picture of body bag.
(*Source:* R. F. Becker)

from the hands and fingers. Hands may also suffer postmortem damage as a result of the recovery operation. If the hands are bagged, the nature of these types of injuries becomes readily apparent. Until the police evidence collection packaging industry becomes aware of the specific need for **underwater investigators,** police dive teams will have to continue to improvise to get the job done correctly. Any efforts to tie plastic bags onto the hands and ankles may result in the bags filling with water, becoming heavy when the body is brought to land, and pulling loose, disarticulating a body part or imparting ligature marks.

Feet and shoes should be bagged in nylon bags to preserve any trace evidence in the shoe soles and to compare internal **wear patterns** of footwear. Footwear is easily dislodged during traditional body recovery operations. Trace evidence lodged in the soles of shoes may also be lost in the recovery process. Glass (auto light lenses or filaments), rocks, and gravel in the soles of the shoe may be evidence of the location from which the body was brought before it was deposited in the water (if a homicide). Should the body be impossible to identify by primary means, an examination of wear patterns on the inside of the shoe may assist in a presumptive identification. These comparisons may be necessary if the body is not immediately identified, has significantly decomposed, or is the product of a homicide or aircraft disaster in which only body parts remain. All hand, head, and foot bagging should take into consideration any possible antemortem ligature marks that might be present on the body. All evidence recovered from water should be accompanied by a sample of the bottom structure as a control for laboratory analysis. The **bottom structure sample** will allow the lab people to definitively state that any residue on a body or evidence lodged in shoes was not a product of the submersion and picked up from the bottom.

The FBI depended on fiber evidence in the conviction of Wayne Williams in Atlanta, Georgia. In that case the media reported that the bodies of many of the young men killed in the Atlanta area whose bodies were disposed of in out-of-the-way places had revealed identifiable fibers. Upon reading this, Williams began stripping the bodies of his victims, except for their undergarments, and disposing of the bodies in the river. In spite of the attempts to obliterate fiber evidence, FBI forensic technicians were nonetheless able to retrieve identifiable fibers from the submerged bodies.

An adult human body weighs approximately sixteen pounds when submerged. The weight of the body only becomes a problem once the body clears the water. Although it is only in the prototypical stage, Halcyon Corporation is making an inflatable body bag with a yoke attachable to an air tank that can slowly inflate the bag, raising it to the surface. The bag is equipped with appropriately spaced and located handles to allow lifting and transporting and net panels in the bottom that allow the water to escape once the bag clears the water. The webbing is small enough to contain most trace evidence while letting the water pass. By the time this book is published, this bag will be one more tool in the underwater investigator's toolbox.

Identification of Submerged Bodies

An investigation of unattended deaths may focus on questions of identity. Whether it was an accidental death or a homicide, the identity of an unknown decedent is important. Identification begins where and when the body is found and proceeds backward, gravitating to the individuals, activities, and places the unidentified person contacted prior to death. Evidence at the scene of where the deceased was going or had been is the pathway leading to identification.

Identification methods may be described as primary or secondary. **Primary identifications** would include friends, relatives, next of kin, DNA, dental comparisons, radiographic comparison of prior injuries and surgeries, and classifiable fingerprints. Secondary methods include all other identifiers that enable a comparison to confirm or exclude identity. Secondary methods would include jewelry, eyeglasses, birthmarks, congenital abnormalities, tattoos, scars, race, color of hair, blood type, sex, and age. The key to identification is to discover features in an unidentified person that compare to the same documented features in a missing person.

Identification through Personal Effects

Personal effects, clothing, and gross anatomical features are the first items available for examination in attempting to determine identification. In mass disasters, descriptions of clothing and personal effects are provided by next of kin. Billfolds contain driver's licenses, credit cards, and personal papers. Cell phones and pagers may still be on the body and in working condition. Jewelry is often unique and engraved. Keys are often distinctive in design and function; characterizing them as door keys, auto keys, briefcase keys, or suitcase keys, and then performing a successful unlocking, provides a tentative identification.

Case Study

A body was reported in the Houston, Texas, Ship Channel. This channel brings ocean transports from all over the world into Houston. The body was bloated and the face unidentifiable. The body was recovered by Houston Police Department underwater investigators and subjected to examination. The clothing was a mix from foreign ports, not pointing to any one place of origin. On his person among his personal effects was a key ring with but one key. The harbormaster was contacted and asked to determine if any crew were absent and unaccounted for. A Soviet vessel had lost a member of its crew, someone on the cooking staff. His loss had been reported. A fitting of the key taken from the deceased provided a presumptive identification of the body as being the lost cook. Positive identification was made by the medical examiner's office through tattoos and a removable bridge. Although the death was determined to be accidental, it is good to remember that a push is hard to distinguish from a fall.

Identification through Dental Comparisons

Teeth are resistant to decomposition and, therefore, are a common source of positive identification. The major problem associated with teeth is the care that must be taken during the recovery procedure to assure that all teeth in and around **skeletonized remains** have been found. A person's occupation or oral habits may impact the condition of teeth. Carpenters and electricians who grip nails between their teeth may have notched upper incisors. Tailors may have similar smaller notches from holding pins. Musicians who play wind instruments often clench the mouthpiece between their teeth, leaving broad worn areas on the upper teeth. Longtime pipe smokers may have developed a diamond-shaped gap between upper and lower clenched teeth. Nicotine stains can be found on the surfaces of the teeth of heavy pipe and cigarette smokers. The presence of poor oral hygiene, many decayed teeth, or swollen gums is usually indicative of low economic status.

Identification through Shoe Wear

The shod foot survives burning, decomposition, marine animal depredation, and water damage more consistently than do hands and fingers. The investigator's focus is generally on hands, fingerprints, and palm prints. Soft, unprotected tissues are the first site of marine animal depredation and are the least likely tissues to render discernable, classifiable characteristics. The feet and the shoes they bear may provide readily available identification information. Wear patterns of footwear's outer and inner soles are sufficiently unique to permit comparisons for exclusionary purposes.

POSTMORTEM CHANGES

After death, physicochemical changes occur which lead to the dissolution of all soft tissues. The importance of these changes is in their sequential nature, which can be used in arriving at an approximate time of death. Knowledge of these changes can also alert us to the destructive effects of decomposition and help us avoid confusing these changes with antemortem injuries.

Using postmortem changes as a timing mechanism is generally based in part on the physicochemical processes evident upon examination of the body, such as putrefaction (decomposition).

Putrefaction

Putrefaction is one of death's realities that underwater investigators must contend with. Attempting to raise a decomposing body by attaching lines or towing by an arm or leg will prove less than satisfactory. Decomposing bodies must be bagged in the water; the alternative is to retrieve them in bits and pieces. **Rigor mortis** of the involuntary muscles and putrefaction are often viewed as indexes of time of death. The rate of putrefaction depends on the physical environment in which the body reposes. It is generally accepted that putrefaction in air is more rapid than in water, where it is more rapid than in soil. One week in air equals two weeks in water and eight weeks in soil (Perper 1993, 32). Putrefaction of a submerged body proceeds at a slower rate than does putrefaction of a body on land. Once the body has been removed from the water, putrefaction will accelerate.

Putrefaction in seawater is slower than in freshwater because the salt retards the growth of bacteria. In stagnant waters, bacteria usually abound, and decomposition is swift.

Water temperature also affects the rate of decomposition. As water depths increase, water temperatures can be expected to decrease and the rate of decomposition will slow. In evaluating postmortem changes, it is important to consider outside temperature, temperature at the water's surface, and the temperature at the depth from which the body was recovered.

Often investigators are anxious to discover the body, and when searching proves unproductive, they begin to discuss **flotation times. Flotation** of a drowned body is dependent upon the production of gases as decomposition progresses. The bulk of these gases are made up of carbon dioxide, methane, sulfur dioxide, ammonium sulfide,

FIGURE 6-2   Decomposing body.
(*Source:* Jack Zaengle, 2004)

and hydrogen sulfide. Two characteristics of these gases that militate against post-mortem flotation are that they are all **water soluble** (dissolve in water) and that they are easily compressed (pressure increases by 14.7 pounds every 33 feet of depth). It should be axiomatic, then, that because of decreasing temperature, the decomposition rate will decrease, and because of increasing pressure resulting from additional atmospheres of depth, the production of gases will be suppressed. Also with increased depth comes a decrease in water temperature. In drownings where the water exceeds 100 feet in depth and the water temperature is less than 38°F, the body may never float. Trying to assess time to flotation is foolhardy and destined to fail.

In temperate climates, decomposition on the surface begins within twenty-four to thirty hours. In water, decomposition generally begins within forty-eight to sixty hours.

Once the body has completely decomposed and has fully skeletonized, the bones may last for centuries. Bones that have been immersed for long periods may demineralize and turn to dust upon touch.

Algor Mortis

Body cooling may provide an approximation of the postmortem interval for a specific individual in a specific environment.

- The temperature of the water at the depth of the body must be taken.
- Temperature of the body must be taken in several visceral sites.
- Four temperatures need be taken at fifteen-minute intervals (Teather 1993, 25).

Once the temperatures have been taken and recorded, the medical examiner can chart the readings and determine body-cooling rate based on those readings. Once the body-cooling rate has been determined, postmortem interval can be retroactively extrapolated. It should be noted that death might not have occurred immediately after immersion in cold water. Such an exposure could have caused hypothermia prior to death, and the **algor mortis** chart cannot be accurately extended backward to an assumed normal of 98.6°F. The algor mortis determination of postmortem interval is, at best, a rough approximation for the first twenty-four hours after death.

Rigor Mortis

Rigor is caused by chemical change in muscle cells. When a person dies, the circulatory system stops. Muscles require oxygen and need to have carbon dioxide flushed. After death, carbon dioxide builds in muscle tissue, and lactic acid is created. As the lactic acid becomes more acidic, it coagulates. Over time, increased acidification dissolves the coagulant and the muscles become flaccid again. Once this secondary flaccidity occurs, new rigor cannot. Rigor can begin as early as two hours after death and become fully established within thirty-six hours, thereafter leaving the body at a reciprocal rate.

FIGURE 6-3 Skeletal remains.
(*Source:* Jack Zaengle, 2004)

Rigor mortis is affected by heat, cold, muscle mass, and pressure. It is the best indication as to postmortem interval and is used most effectively in conjunction with other observations. Traditionally, it was thought that rigor progressed from the head to the feet. In fact, rigor affects the smallest muscles first. In recovering a body wherein rigor is present, it may be necessary to reposition the limbs. It was previously believed that moving a rigored limb would result in breaking a bone. Rigor affects muscles, not bones. If care is taken, limbs may be repositioned without skeletal damage. A body underwater will become rigid in the position it assumed shortly after death. A common position for drowning victims, because of the body's partial buoyancy (primarily from the lungs), is arms and legs slightly bent, the head down, and the back curved (**semifetal position).** This position is often maintained after rigor sets in. In fast-moving water, the position of the rigored decedent may be distorted. The rigor of the body should be consistent with the position in which it is found.

Ocular Changes

Eyes of the deceased who have died on land may exhibit the earliest postmortem changes. The changes occur to the sclera (the white portion of the eye) and the cornea (the clear covering of the eye). If the eye is exposed to air after death, a thin visible film covers the eye. It covers the cornea and the portion of the sclera not protected by the eyelid. This film may be evident moments after death occurs. If the eyelids remain closed after death or the victim is submerged at the time of death, this filming may be retarded for hours. Additionally, corneal cloudiness develops within several hours of death, giving the cornea a frosted appearance. Submergence in water may delay this process significantly. In most deaths the eyes remain partially open. If the eyes are closed, the appearance of corneal filming and clouding may be delayed for twenty-four hours or longer because of the protection of the eyelid. Often the deceased has what is known as **lazy eyelid,** where the lack of muscle rigidity after death has allowed the lid to fall halfway over the eye. An examination of the eye will reveal that the lower exposed half has developed **corneal clouding** while the upper half, still damp and protected from the air, has not. As a result of a body being immersed in water, the corneal clouding that ordinarily occurs on dry land should not be immediately

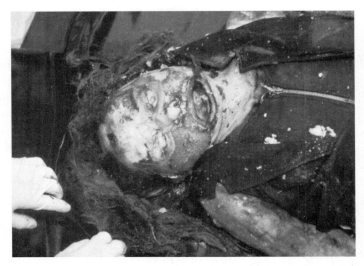

FIGURE 6-4   Corneal filming.
(*Source:* Lynn Dixon)

evident in a drowning victim. Finding corneal filming in a drowning victim is difficult to explain. The body may have floated and resubmerged as a result of the accumulation and dissipation of body gases (purged more quickly and easily on the surface where the temperature is higher and the water pressure lower). The normal flotation posture is facedown; corneal filming in drownings is indeed difficult to explain.

Livor Mortis (Postmortem Lividity)

Once the heart no longer circulates blood through the body, gravity causes blood to pool in the lower parts of the body. When this occurs, capillaries become swollen with blood. This pooling blood coagulates and imparts a purple color to the lower body parts and paleness to the upper body. Lividity occurs within four hours of death and becomes fully developed within twelve hours. **Postmortem lividity** is most apparent in bodies that have lain on land. Blood pooling can often indicate that the body discovered on land has been moved after death. If the body is placed in a position other than the position of death, an absence of lividity in the lower portions suggests the body has been moved. Bodies in water should show little evidence of lividity because of the water's buoyancy. Should lividity be prominent, death prior to submersion should be suspected. Lividity can be manufactured in fast-moving water where the current creates a gravitational pull independent of Earth's gravity. Lividity in those circumstances should be on the downstream parts of the body.

Common Errors in Interpreting Postmortem Changes

Often postmortem changes may be misinterpreted, making identification of the deceased difficult and sending investigators down a dead-end road. The following is

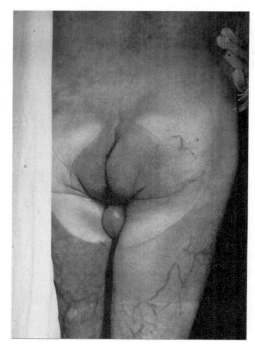

FIGURE 6-5   Lividity.
(*Source:* R. F. Becker)

a partial list of misinterpretations that may be made as a result of postmortem changes:

- Postmortem bloating of the body may create an appearance of obesity.
- Purged fluid may be mistaken for blood flow caused by an antemortem trauma. Although mouth-purged fluids are associated with drownings, they may also be present in heart attacks and drug overdoses.
- Postmortem dilatation and flaccidity of the vagina and anus may produce the appearance of a sexual attack.
- The diffusion of blood into tissues may be difficult to distinguish from antemortem bruising.
- Skin shedding may be seen as an antemortem thermal injury.
- Skin discoloration may cause erroneous racial classification.

Postmortem Interval

The problem in relying upon the results of rigor mortis and putrefaction analysis in determining time of death (more accurately, **postmortem interval,** which is at best an approximation of the time of death) is the variation in the environmental and individual characteristics that impact the determination of postmortem interval. The metabolic state of the individual plays a significant role in postmortem changes, as do the environmental characteristics in which the postmortem changes occur. Postmortem interval, therefore, can only be broadly estimated within a variable time frame. The longer the time between death and discovery, the less effective the time of death estimates and the wider the range of the time variable. Keeping in mind the shortcomings inherent in estimating time of death, the following approach is generally applied:

1. An initial determination of a wide "window of death" is established and subsequently narrowed as additional information becomes available. The window of death is defined as the time interval from positive ascertainment of life to discovery of the remains. The window of death should be established according to the most reliable testimony or evidence as to when the individual was last seen alive.

2. Using individual postmortem changes and taking into consideration temperature and physical characteristics of the deceased, a conservative window of death can be established.

DROWNING

Drowning is usually accidental. In some instances, drowning may be suicidal. Police investigators are often confronted with a body that has been placed in the water for purposes of disposal. It is the differences between antemortem and **postmortem immersion** that are the focal point for the underwater investigator. Several phases are recognized in drowning:

1. One can hold one's breath until accumulating carbon dioxide in the blood and tissues causes stimulation of the respiratory center in the brain and inhalation of water. This inhalation may be very strong and is referred to as an "agonal gasp."

2. Swallowing of water, coughing, vomiting, and rapid loss of consciousness follow.

3. Convulsions associated with gasping precede respiratory arrest, which is followed by failure of the heart, brain damage, and death.

The central question in body recovery from waterways is whether the individual was alive at the time of submersion. The scene surrounding the drowning and the deceased's clothing may provide information as to how the body came to be in the water.

Once a body has been discovered and photographs or video taken, the investigator should examine and note for the record the area around the mouth, face, and hair for the presence of vomitus. Such evidence is strongly indicative of drowning. If the condition of the body lends itself to an examination of the interior of the mouth, it, too, should be examined for silt, bottom structure, debris, or other matter that would be evidence of an agonal gasp and drowning. Whenever possible, these observations should be made while the body is in the water. If water conditions do not allow the observation to be made in the water, they should be made as soon as possible after recovery. Recording this information is an integral part of the investigation and will provide the medical examiner with information that is helpful in determining cause of death.

Case Study

A young man was found in shallow water. A short distance from the body was found an empty wine bottle. The bottle cap was screwed in place. Upon examination of the deceased, it was noted that his pants zipper was open and penis displayed. The initial impression was that the young man had been intoxicated and fell into the water while urinating. Subsequent autopsy findings confirmed that he had a blood alcohol level of 0.21. Lack of turbulence of the water in which the man was found suggested that water in the stomach was from drowning as opposed to turbulent water action. An examination of the crime scene and the deceased's clothing strongly suggested drowning as opposed to foul play. The investigators' theory was borne out by the autopsy results. Often the environment surrounding the drowning and the clothing of the deceased will reveal as much as a subsequent autopsy.

Exudate

When a drowning victim inhales water, many of the alveoli in the lungs burst, allowing blood to enter directly into the lungs. Abundant foam can be found exuding from the mouth and nostrils of many drowning victims as the pressure lessens while the body is being brought to the surface. If the **exudates** do not become visible as a result of the pressure differential, an attempt at resuscitation may apply sufficient pressure on the chest to cause the exudate to become visible. The foam is a mixture of mucus, air, blood, and water. The presence of this mixture in the airway suggests that the victim was alive at the time of submersion. As decomposition progresses, the fluid starts to smell foul and turns brown. The bloodstained exudate in many drowning victims may range from small traces to large quantities. The same kind of foam can be the result of pulmonary edema or drug overdose.

The significance of bloodstained foam in the respiratory passages of a body recovered from water was an important issue at a 1969 court hearing in Wilkes-Barre, Pennsylvania, regarding the death of **Mary Jo Kopechne.** At this hearing, arguments were heard regarding whether or not Kopechne's body should be exhumed for autopsy to determine the cause of death. The judge refused to order an exhumation based on the testimony that a large amount of pinkish foam exuded from her nose and mouth after she was recovered from the water. This finding led to the conclusion that Kopechne had to have been alive, and therefore drowned, when the car in which she was a passenger drove off a bridge at Chappaquiddick Island off the Massachusetts coast (Spitz 1969, 502).

Skin

Skin wrinkling of the hands and feet is frequently referred to as **washerwoman's skin.** Contrary to certain misconceptions, washerwoman's skin has nothing to do with drowning, but is a product of immersion. Skin wrinkling can begin as early as thirty minutes after immersion in water of 50°F. **Gloving** begins in warm waters within several hours, while in cold waters it may not begin for several days. When the skin sheds from the hands and feet, the fingernails and toenails are shed also. The shed skin may be inked to obtain fingerprints and sole prints for the purposes of identification. Both the inner and outer surfaces of shed skin will render a print. The investigator has to place his or her finger inside the deceased's gloved finger to enable the print to be inked and an impression made on a fingerprint card. If the glove is inside out, the print will be a reverse image of the natural friction ridges. A photographic negative of the print can be reversed to render an image consistent with the natural friction ridges.

Flotation

A body in fresh water sinks to the bottom unless air is trapped in the clothing (though infants may float). Gas formation generally begins in the gastrointestinal tract. The time of the reappearance of the body depends on water temperature, water depth, and antemortem diet. Gases formed are easily compressed; in cold, deep waters, gas formation may be suppressed or not occur at all. There are a number of commercial products available that allow the charting of water temperature to theoretically produce a reflotation time. The variables in postmortem gas formation are such that any estimate of reflotation time based on any theory is strictly guesswork.

ANTHROPOPHAGY (MARINE DEPREDATION)

Often postmortem injuries to the eyelids, lips, nose, and ears are mistaken for traumatic antemortem injuries. Marine scavengers focus on the body's menu of soft tissues, many of which are found on the face. A variety of algae may cover the exposed parts of the body, giving a green or black hue to those areas. A body may be so covered with algae as to give the impression that the body is covered in mud, which makes identification and time of death determination more difficult.

Anthropophagy often imparts a macabre appearance to the body. As difficult as it is for the underwater investigator to have to process a decomposing body, that physical and emotional difficulty is magnified exponentially when dealing with bodies that have been fed upon. But it is nonetheless incumbent upon the underwater investigator to record photographically and/or archivally the nature and extent of the postmortem changes, whether they occurred though putrefaction or anthropophagy. Among marine life, crustaceans have the most voracious appetite. They thrive in ocean waters and are most active in shallow and warm waters. The damage inflicted upon a body by crustaceans is more a product of their numbers than individual savagery. In concert, saltwater crustaceans may render a body a skeleton within a week. The initial site of feeding is an open wound where underlying softer tissue is readily accessible.

Clothing serves as a temporary barrier to the marauding crustaceans for the first twenty-four hours, during which they focus their activity on the exposed areas.

Anthropophagy is not limited to salt water; scavengers are found in most bodies of water. If you've sat in a cool river pool during the heat of the summer and felt minnows tickling or pulling the hair on your legs, it is actually minnows sampling the soft tissue of your legs. Virtually all freshwater and saltwater fish are capable of feeding on human remains though they are not generally scavengers. Small fish may scavenge a submerged body, but the damage is very light compared to what crustaceans do.

Maggots may be seen on a submerged body. Their presence is evidence that the body at one time after death was exposed to the air long enough for flies to lay their eggs. These eggs hatch and become maggots. If maggots are found on a submerged body, then one of the following is true:

1. The person died on land and was disposed of in the water.
2. The body refloated long enough for the maggots to hatch.

Although maggots found on a submerged body may be of little value to an entomologist in determining postmortem interval (a common use of maggots found on bodies on land), they may be useful in providing toxicological information. Medical examiners can use maggots if they are adequately preserved to determine what, if any, toxic substances may have been in the body. Putting the maggots into solution (using a blender) will allow a toxicological screen of the liquefied maggots to be conducted, yielding information about the substances in the body the maggots were feeding on.

Case Study

In April 1976 the body of a woman without head or hands was found floating in an upstate New York lake. She had a peculiar gash under the left breast. The corpse was covered with green algae. The medical examiner, who was a hospital pathologist and not a trained forensic pathologist, determined that the slim, athletic body belonged to a woman in her late twenties and that she had been dead for three weeks. Broadcasts on television and radio brought no response as to the identity of the decapitated woman.

Dr. Michael Baden, chief medical examiner for the city of New York, examined the body and determined that the woman's age was closer to fifty-five and that there had been an identifiable scar or tattoo removed from under the breast to prevent identification. Baden sent samples of the algae to a biologist who examined the algae and discovered two generations of algae. Fresh green algae had formed during the recent year, and dead algae were present from a prior year, leading to the conclusion that that the woman had been dead for at least a year and a half. Following the public announcement of the new age, time of death, and possible identifying scar, the body was promptly identified by the woman's sister, who suspected that her brother-in-law had killed his wife.

ANTEMORTEM, POSTMORTEM, AND PERIMORTEM INJURIES

There are a variety of ways in which a human body can be injured. Some may occur prior to death; these would be known as antemortem injuries. Antemortem injuries may be instrumental in determination of cause of death by the medical examiner. They may be easily confused with injuries that occurred during the recovery process (post-mortem) or injuries that were the product of anthropophagy. The possibility of post-mortem injuries inflicted during the recovery is one of the reasons the underwater investigator must examine the body before attempting to recover it, if possible. Recording all injuries existing prior to recovery will reduce any confusion as to which injuries have investigative value and which are collateral to the investigation. Bagging the body in the water also serves as "fragile packaging," which, if disturbed or damaged, will leave no doubt that the concomitant injuries to the body were a product of the recovery operation.

Postmortem injuries may have been inflicted by a malicious murderer or may have been a by-product of the body having been submerged. Bodies often refloat; when they do, they are generally in a facedown, head forward position. If a body is struck by a boat or propeller, the injuries will be on the top and back of the head and on the back. People who are alive prior to being struck by a boat generally assume an upright position in the water and attempt to fend off the pending collision or propeller contact with their hands. These wounds afflicted near the time of death (perimortem) would be on the front of the body, hands, and arms.

Defense Wounds

These wounds generally are the product of a victim's attempt to ward off an assailant using his or her hands. It is an instinctive reaction to raise the hands in a defensive "umbrella" in front of the face and between the victim and a weapon. Cuts on the palms of the hands may be antemortem defense wounds, but if their presence is not recorded prior to recovery, it will be difficult to determine whether they were caused by propeller damage during recovery or were in fact defense wounds. It should be noted that women tend to defend themselves with their strong hand while men tend to defend themselves with their weak hand, reserving the strong hand for possible counterattack (Fierro 1993). Survival wounds on the hands are not uncommon in situations where an individual has clung to an abrasive surface or object prior to drowning. These wounds differ markedly in size, depth, and location. Survival wounds may be present if a person has slid down an incline prior to drowning. These marks may be located on the forearms, elbows, chin, and forehead as well as the hands. It is not as important for an underwater investigator to know how these wounds may have occurred as it is that the wounds be recorded in notes and/or photographs. Recognizing survival wounds may assist the underwater investigator in establishing what took place that precipitated the drowning.

Case Study

A nine-year-old girl, a nonswimmer who was not wearing a flotation device, was last seen walking barefoot on a wharf at a small marina. The father missed the girl and began a search but was unable to locate the child. The state dive team was called in and, upon entering the water in the area adjacent to the wharf, found the child with little difficulty. An examination of the body revealed a serious laceration along the lower ankle about two inches from the center of the sole of the foot. An examination of the wharf revealed an exposed bolt approximately the correct height for inflicting the noted wound. The bolt was located immediately above the body's resting place. The injury was consistent with one that could have been obtained had the child tripped on the bolt during her exploration and play upon the wharf (Teather 1993, 38).

Case Study

An elderly male was attempting to step into his boat that was tied to a dock. People at the marina purchasing bait and gasoline remembered seeing him getting into his boat, which was found approximately 200 yards offshore and away from the dock. A group of recreational divers began their search for the body where the boat had been located. Their repeated dives were fruitless. The state dive team was called to the scene and began interviewing people who had last seen the elderly gentleman. They all recalled seeing him stepping into his boat but did not recall seeing him thereafter. One of the team members visually checking along the dock saw what appeared to be a body lying at the bottom of the dock against the piling closest to where the boat had reportedly been tied. A diver entered the water and was able to retrieve the body. Examination of the hands and forehead strongly suggested that the man had hit his head on the dock upon entry into the water and had tried to claw his way to the surface using the pier piling as an aid.

Travel Abrasions

The usual position for a drowning victim in the water is facedown in a semifetal position. The nature of this position may allow the forehead, nose, knuckles, knees, and tops of the feet and toes to be dragged along the bottom by waves, tides, or currents. The travel abrasions left by this motion may be mistaken for antemortem or perimortem injuries, raising the specter of homicide in what might otherwise be viewed as an accident or suicide. Travel abrasions can be readily identified, keeping in mind that the watercourse in which the body was found must have some mechanism whereby the body can be moved along the bottom. The abrasions found in the expected locations for an inverted semifetal position should be recognized as travel abrasions and not associated with cause of death.

Thermal Injuries

Vessel and aircraft fires and explosions often leave the underwater investigator with bodies and debris that have been burned and that require specific procedures in recovery and investigation. Vessel and aircraft explosions may result in fires. Aircraft crashes are often accompanied by fire. Whether the fire and explosion are the result of accident, negligence, or criminal enterprise, the investigation will focus on the underwater recovery site and the evidence obtained therefrom. Underwater investigators may mistake seriously burned bodies recovered from underwater as displaying signs of advanced putrefaction.

Approximately 70 percent of the human body is composed of water, and 25 percent is combustible organic tissue. The remaining 5 percent is noncombustible inorganic compounds, primarily salts and calcium phosphate. Vessel fires may attain temperatures high enough to burn soft tissues, but aircraft fires prior to crash and submersion are not likely to burn long enough to produce that degree of burn. Burn injury severity is directly related to the heat and duration of exposure. Most house-hold, aircraft, or shipboard fires seldom exceed temperatures of 1,300°F. At that temperature, an adult body will not burn completely.

Fire is not an effective way of disposing of a body. A crematorium must fire its chambers to 1,500°F for one and a half hours to reduce an adult body to manageable proportions. Even after that length of exposure, some large bone fragments remain and must be reduced in size before being placed in a funerary vessel.

It may be possible to determine the duration of the exposure of a burned body to heat. It takes considerable time and temperature for a fire to expose the body's bones. At 1,200°F the rib cage and facial bones are exposed simultaneously in approximately twenty minutes. Shinbones are not exposed until after twenty-five minutes, and thigh bones are not completely exposed until after thirty-five minutes (Richards 1977). Using this timetable, it may be possible to reconstruct where a vessel or aircraft fire has burned the longest, where it began, if the fire was a product of an explosion, and if accelerants were used.

The use of a flammable liquid for disposal of a body results in patchy, disproportionate burning. If a body recovered from an underwater repository has had the face charred and the teeth destroyed while the remainder of the body is less burned, it may represent an attempt to obliterate identity prior to disposal. Chemical analysis of clothing may reveal the presence of residual accelerants. Such accelerants may still be discernable after lengthy submersion. Dried, burned, uncharred skin may also reveal traces of hydrocarbons.

Teeth are highly resistant to fire. If facial soft tissues are not destroyed, the lips and the mouth may be sealed by the heat and dryness, thereby providing additional protection to the teeth. Recovery of bodies from aircraft or vessels that have been burned should include retrieval of bottom samples as a control specimen. If the remains of clothing bear traces of hydrocarbons, bottom samples will prove helpful in eliminating **background contamination** and aviation fuel as possible sources.

Identification of the Burn Victim

The rate of decomposition of a burned body decreased significantly, just as cooked meat decomposes more slowly than does uncooked meat, thereby rendering time of death determinations based on underwater decomposition inapplicable. Absence of uniformity in decomposition suggests that decomposition was caused by heat rather than time. The rigidity of a burned body found in a **pugilistic position** may be mistaken for rigor mortis; this rigidity is caused by a denaturation of muscle proteins and body fluids.

Investigation of recovered burn victims should focus on two points:

1. Identification
2. Cause of death

The usual parameters available for identification are significantly altered or no longer available in burn victims. The weight loss of a burned victim may approach 60 percent. The length of the body may be shortened by inches. Facial features are changed because of skin tightening. Fingers and hands may shrink to one-third their original size. The skin on the hands may detach, as in drowning victims, forming a glove which includes the fingernails. The glove and the underlying skin are still subject to fingerprinting. These gloves are more fragile than those obtained from the drowning victim and must be handled with care. They must be oiled gradually to replace the lost moisture, or handling will result in their destruction. Hair color may change, except that black hair remains black. Scars, birthmarks, moles, and tattoos may be altered or destroyed.

Racial identification may be impossible because of the charring unless tight clothing or shoes have kept the skin intact. Intact skin is most likely to be found under belts, brassieres, or shoes and in the armpits. Intact skin at the wrists or ankles may have been a product of bindings, and unburned skin at the neck may be indicative of ligature strangulation.

It is difficult to distinguish a skull fracture caused by heat from one caused by trauma. Cranial fractures seen in burn victims are usually above the temple on either side. The presence of such fractures does not necessarily suggest criminal enterprise.

Just as the skull may fracture as a result of heat, so may the skin split on occasion, exposing the abdominal cavity. In distinguishing skin splitting because of heat from antemortem cuts and slashes, it is good to note the direction and depth of the splits. Splits caused by heat involve only the skin, not the underlying tissue. Heat-caused splits run parallel to the muscle. Splits across a muscle are not heat-related.

As a result of the shrinkage of anal tissue or of abdominal gas buildup, the rectal wall may protrude through the anal opening. This protrusion could be mistaken for an antemortem sexual assault.

DEATH FROM EXPLOSION

The main investigatory objectives for death caused by explosion are to:

- Identify the deceased
- Reconstruct the events
- Identify the explosive mechanism

Identification of the decedent progresses as in any other death investigation except that body parts may be widely dispersed. Facial destruction requires that emphasis be placed on other means of identification. Fingers, feet, teeth, and dentures are the tools of identification in deaths where body parts are dispersed or intermingled.

Reconstruction of the event is dependent upon the location and extent of damage to the vessel, aircraft, or vehicle as well as the location and extent of injuries to the deceased. In a case involving an explosion in an automobile, on-the-scene examination by investigators determined that the explosive was not in the glove compartment or affixed to the undercarriage of the vehicle. The combined investigation by the police and the medical examiner determined:

- Which of the two occupants was the driver and which the passenger
- That the bomb was located on the floorboard between the passenger's feet
- That the passenger was holding and leaning over the bomb when it exploded
- That the bomb was being transported when it accidentally exploded (Spitz, Sopher, and DiMaio 1970, 417)

Ascertaining the materials of which a bomb is made is valuable in determining the identity of the perpetrator. Bomb fragments may be trapped in the clothing and body tissues of the bombing victim(s). In the auto bombing referred to above, X-rays of the car's occupants revealed a 1.5-volt mercury battery, a portion of a spring, several rivets, and two thin metal wires buried in the body parts of the deceased. Some of the materials removed at autopsy were identified as part of a clock mechanism that was traceable to the manufacturer.

Clothing and personal effects must be treated as repositories for traces of the explosives used in the **explosive device** as well as **microtaggants** embedded in the explosive by the manufacturer to assist in identifying the type of explosive, lot, and area of distribution. These microtaggants are microscopic, multicolored, magnetic bits implanted to facilitate discovery. Those victims closest to the epicenter of an explosion may have all their loose clothing blown off. In some instances death may result from massive lung hemorrhages, with little or no external evidence of trauma.

MASS DISASTER

Man-made mass disasters are those in which human factors are involved. The most frequent man-made disaster is an aircraft crash or train derailment. It is to these disasters that underwater investigators may be called. Aircraft crashes are most visible because of the high profile accorded them by the media, the great number of airports, the numerous aircraft, and the potential for large numbers of injured and dead. There are an estimated two thousand aviation fatalities a year. In every aircraft crash, local authorities are first on the scene, and their conduct often determines the success or failure of the accident investigation and plays an important role in the successful identification of the dead. In the absence of specific evidence to the contrary, all mass aircraft disasters should be treated as a product of criminal enterprise. The airliner crash of TWA flight 800 in 1997 off the coast of Long Island, New York, was a perfect example of the resources and technology that can be brought to bear on a submerged crash site when criminal enterprise is suspected. No less diligence should be applied at every other submerged crash site until evidence corroborating accident, such as voice and data recordings, is recovered. The perfect example of a crash site processed less effectively was the Florida ValuJet crash of 1996. There was no contingency plan, no trained recovery teams, no central command . . . the list could go on forever. The processing of the crash site began before anyone had determined whether or not it could or should be processed as a crime scene. The skills and equipment existed to do it right; all that needed to be added was a contingency plan and a trained group of underwater investigators who knew how to process this type of disaster scene. The other fallacy associated with mass disaster recovery operations is the "closure quest." Why do we risk the loss of valuable evidence and the possible loss of life in rushing to recover bodies? The reality is that in most instances there are no bodies, only pieces.

We must resist all pressure to expedite recovery operations and concentrate on doing the job correctly, which means *make haste slowly*. We must concentrate on recovering all victims and body parts, process all recovered evidence, and identify remains. Time is the variable that assists most in accomplishing these objectives.

As in explosion recoveries, the primary objectives are to recover the bodies, identify the bodies, and reconstruct the events. The objective of the first responding team is to secure the scene from any and all trespass. With any exterior crime or disaster scene, and air crashes in water are no exception, it is helpful to establish three separate zones of security, each emanating from the scene center. The closest zone should not be penetrated by anyone other than forensic specialists with specific authorization. A ledger should be kept as to who enters, time of entry, and time of departure, and a list kept of what has been removed from the scene. The second tier of security should prevent anyone not actively involved in the investigation from entry. The third tier, farthest from the center of the scene, should establish a perimeter that allows monitoring of all traffic approaching the crime scene from any direction. The opportunity for looting is most apparent in a mass disaster. A mass disaster plan should be developed, including procedures for underwater recovery operations, for every community and every department. Specific individuals should be given responsibility and authority to keep all unauthorized personnel, including unauthorized police personnel, away from the crash site.

On June 24, 1975, Eastern Airlines flight 66 crashed in New York. Police on the scene gave each body a consecutive number, removed all valuables from the bodies, and put all recovered jewelry and wallets into manila envelopes. The envelopes were then sent to the property room to prevent theft. The bodies were lined up on the tarmac and covered with sheets. All this was done before any efforts were made to use wallet contents, jewelry, or position of the bodies to identify the victims. An examination of the personal property envelopes that supposedly contained the valuables and personal effects of the passengers revealed an aircraft full of paupers (Baden 1992, 84). All valuables had been removed and lost in the handling.

Although gathering and inventorying personal effects is important, it is more important not to remove any of these materials until the entire wreck site has been searched and photographed and all remains have been photographed in relationship to debris and personal effects. The most valuable tool available in identifying bodies and body parts in an airliner crash is proximity, the position of bodies relative to other bodies or the position of body parts relative to other body parts or intact bodies.

Most underwater investigators use 35-mm cameras and color film. Video footage often reveals a perspective that may be lost in still photography. The entire underwater site should be videotaped in overlapping strips and later dubbed with narrative and then relegated to conventional 35-mm still shots, presuming water visibility allows for photography. However, it should be noted that cameras are capable of rendering discernable images in water where diver visibility may be restricted.

Recovery and identification of the passengers is generally the most time-consuming part of an air crash investigation, more so if that investigation is taking place underwater. Identification can be positive or presumptive. Positive identification is based on pre- and postmortem comparisons of dental records, fingerprints, palm prints, footprints, or DNA profiling. A positive identification removes any doubt from the identification of the body. Presumptive identifications are other means of identification that result in an identification that is less than certain. Presumptive identifications require several points of inconclusive comparisons that cumulatively establish legal identity of the body.

The easiest way to begin the underwater air crash investigation is to obtain a passenger list and seating assignments. Bodies that have been torn asunder, disfigured, or mutilated as a result of impact or deceleration often hamper the investigation.

Body parts and personal possessions may be proximate to an assigned seat, giving some clue as to the victim's identity. A body or a body part may still be belted into the seat. It may take time to obtain information necessary to begin identification, such as flight manifest, seating assignments, family members, employers, and medical and dental records.

In most cases positive identifications are made on the basis of dental comparisons. Few people today have not had dental work done on their teeth. That dental work is as individual as fingerprints. Fingerprints are the next most common method of identification. Only a single fingerprint is necessary to confirm identification when compared with the fingerprint records of passengers.

In those cases involving extensive body fragmentation, identification is more difficult. For presumptive purposes, a single finger, foot, part of a dental prosthesis, pair of eyeglasses, or jaw can identify a passenger as having died in the crash. There are around 200 bones in the body; any one of them may have specific characteristics that will allow identification when compared to antemortem X-rays. Such identification will allow a death certificate to be issued. An unidentified individual hampers the investigation and places the burden of an unsettled estate upon the person's beneficiaries.

In all crashes, the specter of a man-made explosion hovers. All clothing, personal effects, and body parts should be handled in the same fashion as for a known bombing. Any underwater searches should include a search for detonator components. Aircraft parts should be recovered and documented like any other evidence. Bodies, body parts, clothing, carpeting, seating, and fuselage parts should be examined for explosive residue. The presumption in an aircraft investigation should be that criminal intervention was involved. Even in those crashes where there is confirmation of accidental causes, those causes are best discovered and corroborated by treating the recovery operation as a criminal investigation.

With an air crash, investigators are subject to pressures to move quickly to determine cause and to forestall the clamor of relatives trying to determine if their loved ones were passengers. Those pressures should not affect the quality of the investigation. Underwater recovery is a time-consuming operation, and the public, media, and federal agencies must learn to accept that. The recovery operation is, in every sense of the term, an underwater archaeological excavation, bringing into play the panoply of underwater skills used in recovering, measuring, and processing evidence. Time, diligence, and patience are the commodities of an underwater excavation; the very same commodities are anathema to the public and the media. Once human remains have been recovered, there is little reason to hurry an investigation of an air crash.

REVIEW QUESTIONS

1. Explain the difference between traditional methods of handling drownings and an investigative approach to handling drownings.
2. What might shoes of a drowning victim reveal to an underwater investigator?
3. What does exudate have to do with drownings, and what role did it play in the Mary Jo Kopechne drowning?
4. How is washerwoman's skin caused, and what does it say about cause of death?
5. There is a common drowning position; describe it.
6. What zones of security should be established in an aircraft disaster?
7. What is the most valuable evidence in an air crash recovery operation? Why?
8. What is anthropophagy?
9. What would the presence of maggots on a submerged body mean?

REFERENCES

FIERRO, M. F. 1993. Identification of human remains. In *Spitz and Fisher's medicolegal investigation of death*, 3rd ed., ed. Werner U. Spitz, 71–117. Springfield, IL: Charles C. Thomas.

PERPER, J. S. 1993. Time of death and changes after death: Anatomical considerations. In *Spitz and Fisher's medicolegal investigation of death*, 3rd ed., ed. Werner U. Spitz, 14–49. Springfield, IL: Charles C. Thomas.

RICHARDS, N. F. 1977. Fire investigation—destruction of corpses. *Medical Science Law* 17:79.

SPITZ, W. U., I. J. SOPHER, and V. J. M. DIMAIO. 1970. Medicolegal investigation of a bomb explosion in an automobile. *Journal of Forensic Science* 15:537.

TEATHER, R. G. 1993. *Encyclopedia of underwater investigations*. Fort Collins: Concept Systems, Inc.

SUGGESTED READINGS

BASS, W. M. 1987. *Human osteology: A laboratory and field manual*, 3rd ed. Columbia, MO: Missouri Archaeological Society.

BRAY, M., J. L. LUKE, and B. D. BLACKBOURNE. 1983. Vitreous humor chemistry in deaths associated with rapid chilling and prolonged freshwater immersion. *J Forensic Sci* 28:599–593.

BRAY, M. 1984. The eye as a chemical indicator of environmental temperature at the time of death. *J Forensic Sci* 29:389–395.

BRAY, M. 1985. Chemical estimation of freshwater immersion intervals. *Am J Forensic Med Path* 6:133–139.

DAVIS, J. H. 1986. Bodies found in the water. *Am J Forensic Med Path* 78:291–297.

DiMAIO, D. J., and V. J. M. DiMAIO. 1989. Airplane crashes. In *Forensic pathology*, 285–288. New York: Elsevier.

FISHER, R. S., W. U. SPITZ, R. BREITENECKER, and J. E. ADAMS. 1965. Techniques of identification applied to 81 extremely fragmented aircraft fatalities. *J Forensic Sci* 10:121.

GIERTSEN, J. C., and I. MORILD. 1989. Seafaring bodies. *Am J Forensic Med Path* 10(1):25–27.

HENAHAN, J. F. 1980. Fire. *Science 80* 1(2):29–38.

JUNGBLUTH, W. O. 1986. Inner sole footwear comparison. *Identification News,* May: 5–13.

LUNTZ, L. L. 1967. Dental radiography and photography in identification. *Dent Radiogr Photogr* 40:83.

McCORMICK, M. M. 1980. The National Transportation Safety Board and the investigation of civil aviation and transportation accidents. *Am J Forensic Med Pathol* 1:239–243.

ROSENBLUTH, E. D. 1902. A legal identification. *Dent Cosmos* 44:1029.

SIMSON, L. R. 1980. Aircraft death investigation: A comprehensive review. In *Modern legal medicine, psychiatry and forensic science*, ed. W. J. Curran, A. L. McGarry, and C. S. Petty, 339–361. Philadelphia: Davis.

SMERECKI, C. J., and C. O. LOVEJOY. 1986. Identification via pedal morphology. *Identification News,* May: 3–5, 15.

SPITZ, W. U. 1969. Drowning. *Hosp Med* 5:8.

STAHL, C. J. III. 1993. Identification of human remains. In *Spitz and Fisher's medicolegal investigation of death*, 3rd ed., ed. Werner U. Spitz. Springfield, IL: Charles C. Thomas.

UNITED STATES NAVAL SAFETY CENTER. 1989. *The naval flight surgeon's pocket reference to aircraft mishap investigation,* 2nd ed. Norfolk: Aeromedical Division, Naval Safety Center.

WAGNER, G. N., and R. C. FROEDE. 1993. Medicolegal investigation of mass disasters. In *Spitz and Fisher's medicolegal investigation of death*, 3rd ed., ed. Werner U. Spitz, 567–584. Springfield, IL: Charles C. Thomas.

WARFEL, G. H. 1979. *Identification technologies*. Springfield, IL: Charles C. Thomas.

Chapter 7

Firearms Recovery and Investigation

NEW WORDS AND CONCEPTS

trace evidence

firearms

protocol

underwater metal detectors

hit

target

line tugs

chain of custody

semiautomatic

bottom sample

fingerprints

SS *Brother Jonathan*

pistol

ballistics

ballistics testing

rifle

Vincent Bugliosi

semiautomatic handgun

etching agent

propellant

comparison microscope

firing pin

lands

machine gun

shotgun

revolver

automatic

caliber

submachine gun

rifled

groove

gauge

breechblock

primer

jacketed bullet

cartridge case

firearms examination

Calvin Goddard

National Firearms Act of 1968

class characteristics

degree of twist

LEARNING OBJECTIVES

- Describe the characteristics of a firearm
- Describe the characteristics of cartridges
- Explain the role of the firearms examiner

INTRODUCTION

The search for a firearm most commonly occurs following a statement by the person who used it and mentioned its location. In those instances the firearm is corroborative evidence and becomes pivotal only if the person, after having led the police to the location, recants the confession. Should that occur, it is impossible to go back and treat the firearm as an important piece of evidence that may have forensic **trace evidence** in residence. **Firearms** are also often recovered with the help of a witness who saw the weapon being deposited. It is best to establish a **protocol** for the recovery of firearms irrespective of how they have been discovered and what role they may play in the courtroom. It should be remembered that the search begins in the areas that provided access and exit for the person who deposited the evidence in the water.

The criminal investigator in charge of investigating the crime in which the suspect weapon was used should provide the information necessary to determine what type of recovery is needed. The problem with that, however, is that at the time of the writing of this text, many criminal investigators have little or no appreciation for the types of forensic evidence that may be contained in and on a submerged firearm.

It is best to approach firearms recovery as though the weapon may be used in a courtroom as evidence, along with any other evidence that may be on or in the weapon. In waters of limited or zero visibility, **underwater metal detectors** may provide the eyes for the underwater investigator. A tethered diver with or without an underwater communication system will move across the bottom of the watercourse, sweeping in front as he or she progresses. The metal detector is hand-operated and monitored by headphones.

The dive tender maintains the quality of the search sweep, and all items detected are investigated by the diver (tactile examination in zero visibility). It is this tactile examination that is the first touch since the depositing of the weapon. The underwater investigator knows that this weapon has potential forensic value, so the tactile examination of a **hit** is done carefully, without haste, and minimally invasively. If the hit item is determined not to be a firearm, it can be moved an arm's distance toward the shore or diving platform to prevent a hit on the next search sweep. When the diver has found the **target,** he or she notifies the tender and support team by line pulls or verbally.

Those teams that do not have the budget for underwater metal detectors search for firearms using their sense of touch if water visibility prevents visual searching. This requires greater concentration on the part of the diver, and there is a fair possibility that the item sought may be missed in black water operations. In training of

FIGURE 7-1   Underwater metal detector.
(*Source:* R. F. Becker)

underwater investigators at Southwest Texas State University and at Chaminade University of Honolulu, the one constant for supervising divers doing hand searches in zero visibility is that they often pass over the firearms and other weapons. In fairness, it should also be said that many of the teams passing through those two institutions using hand searches for firearms are successful. Also, using an underwater metal detector is not a guarantee that the item will not be passed over in those instances of poor search line integrity or inattention on the part of the diver.

Once a diver has found a firearm, the diver should give the appropriate **line tugs** to indicate he or she has located the weapon. The diver remains with the object while noting on a slate (visibility permitting) or relating through the voice communication system the depth, time, water temperature, water conditions, and any additional reference information previously requested by the criminal investigator.

At the surface, the tender notes the amount of line that has been deployed and advises the team leader or incident commander that the weapon has been located. The archivist takes a compass bearing of the line and two other permanent landmarks (triangulation). Those bearings orient the search line, and the length of line deployed, once measured from the tethered end, gives a very good measurement for the location of the firearm. The time and location are recorded along with the identity of the tender and diver, who may be called to testify. The triangulation should take place quickly to reduce the time the diver must spend in the water. If the primary diver is reaching maximum bottom time (twenty-five minutes, including a five-minute extension), it may be necessary to replace the diver before any other measurements are taken. Should that be the case, the replacement diver will take up the position of the original diver, who has marked his or her position with a small buoy (not on but next to the firearm).

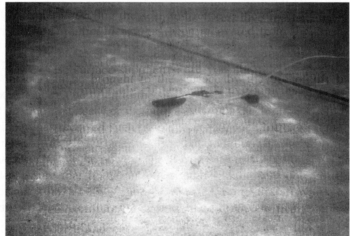

FIGURE 7-2 Submerged rifle and pistol.
(*Source:* R. F. Becker)

A more accurate measurement can be obtained by trilaterating the measurements as described in Chapter Six. The method of measurement should be selected by the criminal investigator, presuming the investigator understands the measurement methods available. If no request is made as to method of measurement, trilateration should be the method of choice. By trilaterating, any dispute as to actual location of the recovered firearm is foreclosed.

Once the firearm has been photographed (if visibility permits, and keeping in mind that cameras see better in limited light than do human eyes), measured (triangulated and/or trilaterated), packaged underwater (with Tupperware or capped PVC tubing), and brought to the surface, it must be appropriately labeled. That label is placed on the surface of the container and should contain:

- Name of recovery diver
- Date
- Time
- Location

An evidence log should be completed, recording the same information as was recorded when the item first emerged, plus:

- Who received the evidence
- From whom the evidence was received
- Date of receipt
- Time of receipt
- Location of receipt

The evidence log is used by the prosecution and the defense to establish and/or challenge the **chain of custody.** Maintaining a chain of custody is the responsibility of the state. The state must show where the evidence has been since its discovery: from the water to the criminal investigator; from the investigator to the laboratory; from the laboratory back to the investigator, who most likely will store it in the evidence room until trial or presentation to the defense for examination. The item of discovery must be accounted for. That accounting must reflect every minute of the evidence's existence from the time of discovery until the time it appears in court. The evidence log will assist in proving that chain. Failure on the part of the state to maintain and prove chain of custody will result in the evidence being excluded at the time of trial.

In dry-land crime scenes, firearms are unloaded and placed in an open slide position **(semiautomatics).** The ammunition is marked to represent its placement in the clip, magazine, or cylinder. The ammunition is packaged separately from the handgun, and the handgun is packaged in a plastic bag and labeled. This method

FIGURE 7-3 Labeled and packaged firearm.

(*Source:* SMART)

assures that the weapon is not mishandled and accidentally fired. The weapons recovered by underwater investigators are all presumed to be loaded. Whenever possible, the weapon is packaged without altering anything from its original circumstances. It does pose a hazard and must be treated accordingly. A firearm will fire underwater, will cause a lethal wound if close enough to the target, and can cause damage to the ear upon discharge even if no other injury occurs. It should be left to the dry-land investigator to determine how the weapon should be packaged, presuming that investigator understands what potential the weapon has for producing trace evidence. Absent a contravening reason, the default protocol is to leave it loaded and handle it as little as possible.

Once the firearm has been appropriately recovered, it is necessary to obtain a **bottom sample.** The bottom sample serves as a control for background contamination. If there is trace evidence on the firearm, it will be contended that the trace materials were a product of submersion and picked up off the bottom of the watercourse in which the firearm was found. In anticipation of that allegation, it is necessary to provide a bottom sample of whatever existed below the firearm at the time of recovery. Any semisterile container can be used for the bottom sample, which, once obtained, should be labeled with the same information that would be included in tagging any other type of evidence, with the additional label of "bottom sample."

The underwater investigator may be asked by the untrained dry-land investigator why the weapon has been placed in a container and why mud has been placed in another container. Alternatively, the dry-land investigator may remove the firearm and disregard the bottom sample. Not everyone receives the same training that underwater investigators do. It is frustrating to deal with these types of situations, but the best response is to tell the dry-land investigator that the report filed by the dive team will show that the weapon was turned over in a water bath with a bottom sample. The absence of either will be the responsibility of the dry-land investigator to explain at the time of trial.

Once the firearm has been removed, its location marked (buoy), and a bottom sample obtained, the area can be further searched for any evidence that might be associated with the firearm or the crime being investigated. In too many recoveries, the search is stopped once the item sought is discovered. In many instances that termination may be too soon. There may be additional evidence available. Often the cartridges and spent casings are disposed of separately but in the same area. A cursory examination of the area within a fifteen-foot radius of the point of discovery of the firearm may disclose related evidence.

The recovery of firearms is a straightforward proposition. No expensive lift equipment is necessary, and the time involved in the recovery is minimal once the firearm has been located. The location and mapping of firearms should be handled in the same fashion as for any other important submerged evidence.

The recovery method usually employed is to pick the handgun up by the barrel and swim it to the surface, where it is handed to someone who puts it in a plastic bag. Placing the weapon in a plastic bag after it is recovered is somewhat counterproductive in that the trace evidence that may have been in residence has been lost, contaminated, or destroyed. Why weapons are handled in such a cavalier fashion is demonstrative of a lack of appreciation of the effect of water on ferrous metals and of the potential transient evidence contained in every firearm.

FIREARMS INVESTIGATION

The recovery and preservation of firearms is accomplished for four purposes:

1. Medicolegal examination
2. Ballistic comparisons
3. Weapon identification
4. Fingerprint examination

Fingerprints

The likelihood of discovering **fingerprints** on a weapon that has been submerged is not as remote as may be the common impression. This year scientific divers began the recovery of the **SS *Brother Jonathan***, which was sunk in July of 1865. They expected to find gold and silver. Gold coins were recovered, although they were corroded and virtually unrecognizable. The coins were placed in the hands of a team who removed the corrosion chemically, revealing the coin beneath. The coins were in perfect condition, as if recently released by a bank. Beneath the corrosion on one coin was a human fingerprint, intact and discernable, awaiting the light of day.

Certain surface parts of a firearm are ideally designed for the placement and retrieval of fingerprints. Considering that most firearms have been cleaned, lubricated, and loaded by hand makes it likely that some remnants of that handling remain. Additionally, handguns that have been fired deposit gunpowder residue on the shooter's hand. Along with the sweat secretions from the finger's pores and the body oils collected on the finger ridges, the residue creates the ideal medium for the depositing of a latent fingerprint on the smooth surfaces of a weapon. Additionally, clips and magazines are likely to be oiled and, once handled, will retain a fingerprint.

In efforts to demonstrate the feasibility of obtaining fingerprints from firearms, the faculty of the Underwater Institute at Southwest Texas State University have submerged various firearms, clips, magazines, ammunition, and ammunition components in all types of water to determine the sustainability of fingerprints on their surfaces. In each case we have found that oiled surfaces and surfaces impressed with gunpowder residue readily retain identifiable fingerprints over time. Any shooters who have shot handguns without wearing gloves leave information behind. That experience leaves both hands covered with gunpowder residue, which is transferred among hands, **pistol,** and ammunition as the weapon is continually handled. Upon completion of the shooting day, the shooter will attempt to eliminate the gunpowder buildup on his or her hands and fingers with soap and hot water and discover how difficult that removal is. The same tenacity of evidence is apparent in the fingerprints that have been left on the firearm and expended cases (which were loaded with "dirty" hands). The only way to remove the powder from the pistol is to use a chemical solvent. Any shooter who has experienced the difficulty in removing gunpowder residue from a fired firearm recognizes that **cartridge cases** with gunpowder fingerprints will withstand immersion in water.

Ballistics Testing

A firearm retrieved from salt water after lengthy submersion may appear relatively unaffected. Once it is retrieved and subjected to the air, oxidation begins immediately and thorough rusting may progress in less than an hour, rendering **ballistics** examination impossible. It is therefore crucial to keep the weapon immersed in water until the preservation procedure can begin. When a firearm is properly retrieved and maintained, preservation techniques may allow **ballistics testing** to be conducted on the weapon and its ammunition. All firearms need to be preserved for testing, and that preservation begins with the divers who recover the weapon while keeping it immersed in water. At the time of the publication of this text, there are no evidence containers being manufactured for the preservation of underwater evidence. In most instances, handguns are placed in Tupperware containers and **rifles** are put in jury-rigged PVC tubing containers (the military has the perfect container for all submerged long guns; used U.S. Army or Navy sonobuoy tubes are watertight and reusable). The container should be opened underwater and allowed to fill with water, and the firearm (loaded or unloaded, as found) should be slid into the container and the lid secured. Whatever is on or in the weapon upon discovery is preserved using this method. It is for the forensic laboratory staff to remove any trace evidence.

Barrel Blowback

In addition to fingerprint and ballistic evidence, a firearm, especially a handgun, may contain hair, tissue, blood, and fibers. The muzzle blast of a gun fired in contact with a body and the negative pressure in the barrel following discharge may cause blood, hair, tissue fragments, and fabric to be found several inches back inside the barrel (Spitz 1993, 319).

It should be apparent that retrieving a weapon by inserting something into the barrel will only serve to dislodge and destroy any trace evidence.

The perception that a submerged firearm is bereft of any relevant forensic information is erroneous. The perception that human tissue, hair, and blood are displaced from the barrel of a firearm as a result of submersion is also erroneous. **Vincent Bugliosi,** in his book *And the Sea Will Tell* (1992), describes the testimony of an FBI serologist who testified during the trial of Buck Walker for the grisly killing of Mac and Muff Graham. The serologist testified that, after three years' submersion in the Pacific Ocean, a metal container in which it was believed that Muff Graham had been dismembered, burned, and submerged tested positive on a phenolphthalein screening test. The phenolphthalein screen is sensitive to a drop of blood in 10,000 parts of water. However, this screen only determines if the sample in question is blood, not whether the blood is human. The serologist went on to describe a second test that he

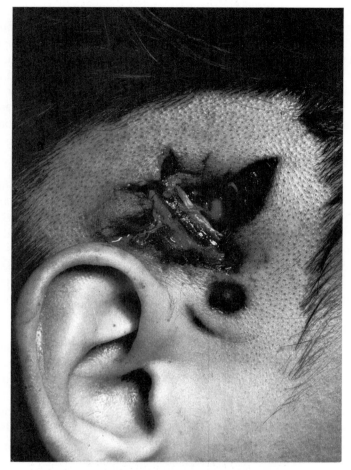

FIGURE 7-4 Picture of a contact starburst wound.
(*Source:* R. F. Becker)

performed called an Ouchterlony screen that does determine if a blood specimen is human. The serologist was able to determine that, after three years of sand, water, and marine intrusion, the cloth sample removed from the submerged case was stained with human blood (Bugliosi 1992, 279).

Presume for a moment that a **semiautomatic handgun** has been used in a homicide in which there was a contact wound to the head. The weapon now most likely has barrel blowback containing tissue, blood, hair, and bone. The murderer takes the weapon and places it his jacket pocket. Upon arriving at his automobile, he withdraws the weapon from his pocket, which now has fiber evidence attached to the sharp protrusions on the firearm (magazine release, sights, and safety), and slides it under the seat of his carpeted automobile. He drives to a river, lake, or canal and withdraws the weapon from under the seat, adding fibers to those already in residence from the jacket pocket. He walks to the water's edge, grabs the weapon by the barrel, and throws it as far as possible out into the water. The water enters the gun primarily through the barrel, forcing whatever may be in the barrel against the breech face and trapping it there. The fiber evidence that was not disturbed from the throw may also be in place, awaiting discovery. If discovered, the weapon most likely will be treated as though it has no forensic value, and as a result of its handling, it will have none. However, should it be determined that the weapon has forensic value, the underwater investigator will take pains in geographically locating the weapon and in packaging the weapon.

Serial Numbers

Every firearm is stamped with a variety of numbers. The serial number is useful in determining original ownership of the weapon. Serial numbers may be more readily apparent immediately upon discovery by the dive team than later, after mishandling and oxidation have occurred. One of the initial acts of the dive team should be to record and photograph the serial number in the water if visibility allows. Once rusting begins—and it happens very quickly—retrieval of the serial number may be difficult or impossible.

Serial numbers are usually stamped with hard metal dies. These dies strike the metal surface with a force that allows each digit to sink into the metal at a prescribed depth. Restoration of serial numbers can be accomplished because the metal crystals in the stamped zone are placed under a permanent strain that extends a short distance beneath the original numbers. When an **etching agent** is applied, the strained area dissolves at a faster rate than the underlying uncorroded metal, thus causing the underlying number pattern to appear in the form of the original numbers. The recovery of serial numbers using etching acids is governed by the extent of corrosion of the firearm. It is, therefore, readily apparent that corrosion must be confined to that existing at the time of recovery and not added to by exposing the firearm to oxidizing agents.

FIGURE 7-5   Handgun serial numbers.
(*Source:* Austin Police Department)

FIREARMS IDENTIFICATION

The identification of firearms is often incorrectly referred to as ballistics. Ballistics is the study of projectiles in motion. Ballistic studies involve four discreet regimes:

1. Interior ballistics is the study of the motion of projectiles in the gun barrel and the conversion of the chemical energy of the cartridge **propellant** into the kinetic energy of the projectile.

2. Exterior ballistics deals with projectile flight from the muzzle end to the target (taking into account air resistance, gravity, windage, and elevation).

3. Terminal ballistics is the study of the interaction of the projectile with the target.

4. Transitional ballistics deals with the transition from the projectile's passage through the gun barrel to the projectile's flight through the air.

Firearms identification is primarily concerned with the identification of firearms from their fired bullets and cartridges, and it is only tangentially related to ballistics.

National Integrated Ballistics Information Network

The National Integrated Ballistics Information Network (NIBIN) is a nationally interconnected, computer-assisted ballistics imaging system used by firearms examiners to obtain computerized images of bullets and cartridge cases. These images can be

FIGURE 7-6   Revolver (top) and semiautomatic pistol (bottom).
(*Source:* Austin Police Department)

compared with other images previously entered into the system. The system is made up of federal, state, and local law enforcement crime laboratories. The Bureau of Alcohol, Tobacco, Firearms and Explosives (ATF) has been given the responsibility for the development and deployment of the system nationally.

Prior to the creation of NIBIN, the FBI and ATF had their own computerized ballistics imaging systems. NIBIN was established to incorporate the FBI's "Drug-fire" system with the ATF's "Ceasefire" system. NIBIN uses the ATF's imaging system and the secure, high-speed telecommunications network of the FBI.

Recent bills introduced in Congress would require all manufacturers to supply spent cartridges and bullets for inclusion in the system before being allowed to sell or import firearms. This would significantly increase the ability to trace firearms that are used in crimes. Presently, the participation of federal, state, and local law enforcement agencies in NIBIN is restricted by law to the ballistics imaging of data associated with only those guns used in crimes.

Historically, comparison of bullet and cartridge case marks was accomplished by firearms examiners using **comparison microscopes.** This process was accurate but slow and labor-intensive. In the early 1990s the ballistics imaging and matching process was computerized. Digital cameras were used to photograph bullets and cartridge cases and to scan them into a computer. These images were then analyzed by a software program and stored in a database, making ballistics matching faster. When the computerized system was connected across numerous law enforcement agencies through a telecommunications system, it allowed the rapid comparison of bullets and cartridge cases used in crimes from different jurisdictions. The use of computerized images of bullets and cartridge cases streamlines chains of custody for those bullets and cartridge cases that are to be used in court.

NIBIN is a repository for images of ballistics evidence found at crime scenes and is composed of several computer-connected networks. The goal is for NIBIN data to be shared nationally. The ATF has more than eighty offices around the country that can provide a repository for the deposit and retrieval of ballistics images.

Equipment

Four different types of Integrated Ballistics Identification Systems (IBIS) make up the NIBIN network:

1. Regional server: The central data repository for the region where all images are stored and bullet and cartridge casing correlation requests are executed.

2. Digital Acquisition System (DAS) remotes: An IBIS system comprising a microscope and a computer unit that will allow image acquisition or evaluation. These systems are linked to a regional server where the images are stored and bullet and cartridge casing comparison/correlation requests are sent.

3. Rapid Brass Identification (RBI): A portable cartridge casing system that allows on-site digital capture of fired cartridge casings for transmission to a central IBIS for processing, comparison, and storage.

4. Matchpoint: A desktop computer connected to a DAS remote by LAN (local area network), allowing bullet/cartridge analysis.

IBIS technology is designed to be used without extensive computer training or sophistication. A sample that results in a hit will provide:

- Demographic information about the crime
- Images of the correlated bullet casing, which would include:
  - Breech face
  - **Firing pin**
  - Ejector marks
- Images of the correlated bullet, which would include:
  - **Lands**
  - Accidentals

If the image is captured at a DAS remote, the data is sent to the regional server for comparison. A hit results in the correlation data being returned to the DAS remote. Images captured by an RBI system are sent by telephone to the cooperating DAS remote. The images are transmitted to the regional server for comparison in the region's database. A hit results in the correlation data being returned to the cooperating DAS, and the RBI user is notified by telephone. Ejected cartridge casings found at a crime scene can be digitized right at the scene. The information can then be transmitted to a laboratory where a technician can use the system to conduct a search. If a match is found, results can be returned to the personnel at the scene while the investigation is still in progress.

The IBIS analysis system does not provide "matches," it provides "correlations," a short list of possible matches. The final analysis for a match is conducted by a firearms examiner through a comparison microscopic study.

Types of Firearms

Firearms examiners generally come into contact with five types of firearms: pistols, rifles, assault rifles, **machine guns,** and **shotguns.**

Pistols

A pistol is a firearm designed to be fired with one hand. Pistols are either single-shot, single-action **revolvers;** double-action revolvers; or self-loading pistols (commonly referred to as **automatic** pistols). If a pistol were fully automatic, it would continue to fire as long as the trigger was depressed and ammunition was still available. The pistols that are called automatics are incorrectly identified and should be referred to as semiautomatic or self-loading. Some self-loading pistols store the recoil energy of the barrel in coiled springs, then use that energy to extract the expended cartridge casing from the firing chamber, eject it from the weapon, cock the firing mechanism in preparation for firing the next round, and load a live round into the firing chamber. Self-loading pistols may also work on a blowback principle. In blowback-operated pistols, the slide and barrel are held together only by the inertia of the slide and the pressure of the recoil spring. The recoil of the cartridge provides the energy for extraction, ejection, cocking, and loading (Wilbur 1977). Revolvers may have either a single or double action. Single-action revolvers must be manually cocked before each firing. Double-action revolvers are cocked by the pull of the trigger. There is a high-powered hunting pistol that fires a single high-velocity rifle cartridge. This weapon combines the power of a rifle with the portability of a handgun. It is breech-loaded with a single cartridge and must be "broken" open to eject each round and to load each new round.

Rifles

A rifle is a weapon designed to be used with two hands and fired from a shoulder position. There are single-shot rifles, lever-action rifles (fed by magazine), bolt-operated rifles (fed by clip or magazine), semiautomatic rifles (fed by clip or magazine), and automatic rifles (fed by clip). Lever-action and bolt-action rifles use the manual manipulation of a lever or turnbolt to extract and eject each expended cartridge, cock the firing mechanism, and load a live round into the firing chamber. Semiautomatic and automatic rifles are blowback, recoil, or gas operated. Gas-operated rifles use a portion of the hot propellant gases tapped from the barrel by a gas piston to extract, cock, and load. Automatic rifles use limited-capacity magazines, while light machine guns generally fire belted ammunition.

Assault Rifles

During the two decades following World War II, the world's armies replaced their bolt-action and semiautomatic rifles with assault rifles. An assault rifle is a hand-carried, shoulder-fired semiautomatic or automatic weapon in a rifle **caliber.**

Machine Guns

Submachine guns and machine guns are fully automatic weapons. Machine guns load their ammunition from magazines or from belts. Because of the recoil, machine guns are fired from a tripod or bipod (unless you are John Wayne or Rambo). Submachine guns, which are automatic weapons designed to be fired while being held in the hands, fire pistol cartridges (Hogg 1977).

All the types of weapons discussed to this point are **rifled** firearms. Their barrels have a set of spiraling lands and **grooves** within them. The lands of the rifling are the raised ridges that bite into the surface of the bullet and give it a rotational motion as it moves down the barrel; the grooves of the rifling are the recessed areas between the lands. The rifling grips the fired bullet and engraves its surface with land and groove impressions. The microscopic imperfections of the rifling produce patterns of parallel scratches called striations (or striae). Rifled firearms may be characterized by their caliber or bore diameter. The bore diameter of a rifled barrel is

FIGURE 7-7   .223 AR 15 and .223 cal Bushmaster AR15
(*Source:* Austin Police Department)

the diameter measured from the tops of opposing lands. The caliber and bore diameters of American and British weapons are normally given in inches, while those of other weapons are given in millimeters. Many manufacturers and users express caliber in both inches and millimeters.

Shotguns

A shotgun, like a rifle, is designed to be fired from the shoulder, but a shotgun is a smooth-bore weapon, having no lands or grooves in the barrel. Unless firing a slug round, shotguns fire multiple projectiles, called pellets. Shotguns may have single or double barrels. Single-barrel shotguns may be single-shot weapons or repeaters. Repeating shotguns have magazines from which rounds are loaded into the weapon either manually with a pump action or semiautomatically (Hatcher, Jury, and Weller 1977). Shotguns are referred to by their bore diameters, which are expressed in **gauge** measurements. When all firearms fired spherical lead balls, their bore diameters or gauges were expressed as the number of such lead balls that could be made from one pound of lead (e.g., ten lead balls, having the same diameter as the interior of the barrel of a 10-gauge shotgun, should weigh one pound). The exception to this measurement scheme is the 410-gauge shotgun, which has a bore diameter of .410 inches (Nonte 1973).

The Firing Mechanism

The firearms examiner needs to know how certain components of a firearm's firing mechanism perform. The **breechblock** is the part of a firearm's action that supports

FIGURE 7-8   Tech 9 (top right), Uzi (top left), and Mac 10 (bottom).
(*Source:* Austin Police Department)

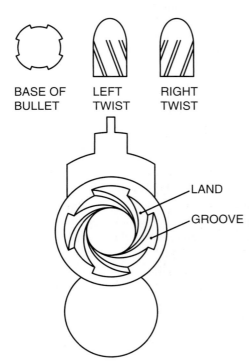

BASE OF   LEFT   RIGHT
BULLET   TWIST   TWIST

LAND

GROOVE

FIGURE 7-9   Barrel rifling.
(*Source:* Austin Police Department)

the base of the cartridge in the chamber when it is fired. The firing pin is the part of the firearm's action that strikes the cartridge **primer** in order to fire it. Breechblocks may be finished with an end mill, by turning on a lathe, or by hand filing. The breechblocks of semiautomatic pistols are usually finished by filing vertically down through the ejector slot in the slide. This gives a characteristic direction to the striations imparted to the soft metal of the primer caps of fired cartridges. Firing pins are turned on lathes or filed flat by hand (Hatcher, Jury, and Weller 1977).

AMMUNITION

Types of Bullets

The three most commonly used bullets in rifled firearms are lead-alloy bullets, semijacketed bullets, and fully **jacketed bullets.** Lead-alloy bullets are harder

FIGURE 7-10 Shotguns (top to bottom): semiautomatic, double barrel (over and under), double barrel (side by side), and pump action.
(*Source:* Austin Police Department)

than pure lead bullets and less likely to produce lead fouling of the rifling. Pure lead .22-caliber bullets may be coated with a very thin film of copper. This film has a tendency to flake off the surface of the bullet, removing the striations produced by the rifling (Mathews 1962).

FIGURE 7-11   Pistol bullets.
(*Source:* Austin Police Department)

Jacketed bullets consist of a lead core surrounded by a jacket of harder material. Jackets are commonly made of a copper-nickel alloy or mild steel. Semiautomatic pistols use fully jacketed bullets because the noses of the bullets must slide up a ramp as rounds are chambered (Nonte 1973).

A semijacketed bullet has a copper-alloy or aluminum jacket that covers only part of the bullet's surface. The jacket covers the side of the bullet, leaving the nose exposed. A semijacketed bullet is designed to mushroom on impact so that most of its kinetic energy is expended in the target. A hollow-point bullet has a hollow in the exposed lead core at the nose of the bullet. A soft-point bullet is a semijacketed bullet with a soft metal plug inserted in its nose. Both the soft metal insert and the thinner jacket facilitate bullet expansion.

Another approach to obtaining proper expansion of a semijacketed bullet is to place a hard metal insert in the nose of the bullet. Bronze-point bullets are special bullets intended for hunting. Upon impact, the bronze point is forced back into the bullet's core, causing it to mushroom.

Frangible bullets are composed of powdered iron or powdered iron with an organic binder. These bullets are used in shooting galleries and in urban law enforcement because they disintegrate on impact without the danger of a ricochet or penetration through thin walls. Steel-jacketed armor-piercing bullets have an extremely hard steel jacket surrounding a tungsten-carbide core. The hardness of the jacket generally precludes the rifling of the weapon firing such ammunition from marking it extensively. A special-purpose bullet called an accelerator cartridge has been developed by Remington. The projectile is a normal .223-caliber soft-point bullet pressed into a .30-caliber plastic grommet (sabot). Upon firing, the bullet and the sabot exit the barrel, and at some distance from the muzzle, the bullet separates from the sabot and continues along its trajectory as the sabot falls away. There would be no identifiable rifling marks on such a bullet. Bullets may have round noses, pointed noses, or flat noses. Their bases may be flat or boattailed. The shape of a bullet is dictated by a number of considerations, including aerodynamics. Boattailed bullets are designed to reduce turbulence in the wake of the bullet, thereby reducing bullet drag.

Propellants

Smokeless powders are classified as degressive-burning, neutral-burning, or progressive-burning. Degressive-burning powder grains burn from the outside in; the surface area consequently decreases along with the burning rate of the grain. Solid, uncoated powder grains burn in a degressive manner. Neutral-burning powders have perforations so that the burning of the outside of the grains is balanced by the burning on the interiors of the perforations; the net effect is that the surface area remains relatively constant, as does the burning rate. Progressive-burning powders are coated with a deterrent material that slows down the initial burning of the powder grains; once the deterrent coating is burned off, the burning rate goes up (O'Connor 1965).

The manipulation of powder burning rates through variations in grain size, shape, and coating is necessary because of the variations in caliber, barrel length, and chamber size among firearms. When a weapon is fired, the propellant begins to burn, generating hot gases. These gases expand, forcing the bullet from the cartridge casing into the barrel. Once the bullet begins to move, the volume available to the gases generated by the burning propellant increases. If the production of gases stopped immediately after the unseating of the bullet into the barrel, farther travel of the bullet down the barrel would cause the pressure behind it to fall. At the point where the pressure exerted on the bullet is balanced by the frictional force acting between the bullet and the barrel, the bullet would come to a stop. To prevent this, the powder must continue to burn as the bullet proceeds down the barrel. Burning powder after the bullet exits the barrel wastes energy because none of the energy released after the bullet exits the barrel can be converted into kinetic energy. The weight (amount), grain size, and burning rate of a cartridge's propellant must be adapted to the type of firearm used to fire it.

Primers

The centerfire cartridge is a nineteenth-century invention. Eventually, it supplanted the rimfire cartridge in all but the smallest calibers. Centerfire ammunition manufactured in the United States uses the Boxer primer (named for its inventor, E. M. Boxer, a colonel in the British army). This primer consists of a metal cup containing a small amount of primer material placed between the cup and a small metal anvil. When the weapon is fired, its firing pin crushes the primer material between the cup and anvil. The flame from the primer's explosion reaches the propellant through a large flash hole in the base of the cartridge. Centerfire cartridges manufactured outside the United States use the Berdan primer (named after its inventor, Hiram Berdan, a colonel in the Union army during the American Civil War). Cartridge cases that accept the Berdan primer have a conical anvil as an integral part of their bases. The primer cap is simply a small metal cup containing a pellet of primer compound. Two or three small holes spaced evenly around the anvil communicate the flash of the primer through the base of the casing to the propellant (Tarassuk and Blair 1979).

Beginning in 1900, primers based on potassium chlorate began to appear as replacements for mercury fulminate primers, but their residue proved as corrosive as the residue of the latter. Modern primers are exclusively nonmercurial and noncorrosive. A typical centerfire primer cap produced today will contain lead styphnate, antimony sulfide, barium nitrate, and tetracene (O'Connor 1965).

Cartridge Cases

Cartridge cases are available in a wide variety of shapes and sizes. Differently shaped cases are intended for use in different types of firearms. Revolvers fire straight, rimmed cartridges; the rims prevent the cartridges from falling through the revolver's cylinder. Self-loading pistols fire straight, rimless cartridges; since they are clip-fed, there is no need for a rim. Cartridge cases may have cannelures rolled into them near their mouths; these cannelures prevent the bullets from being inadvertently pushed back into the cases. A bullet may also be held in place by crimping the mouth of the cartridge onto the surface of the bullet.

The heads of cartridges frequently bear stampings that provide information about the maker of the cartridges. For instance, the letters *R-P* on the head of a cartridge case indicate that Remington-Peters made it. Cartridges may also carry markings identifying the nominal caliber of its bullet.

Shot Shells

Most shotgun ammunition contains pellets, although some commercially available shot shells have either a single round ball or a rifled slug. Shotgun pellets come in a variety of sizes, from 000 buckshot (0.36 inches in diameter) down to number

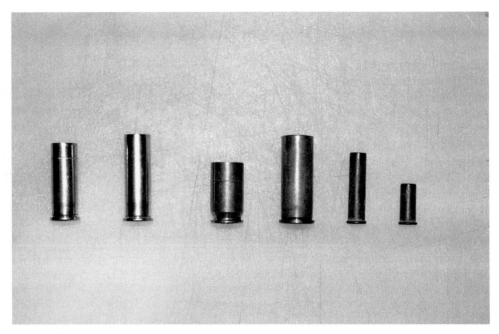

FIGURE 7-12   Types of cartridge rims.
(*Source:* Austin Police Department)

12 birdshot (0.05 inches in diameter). The larger the shot number, the smaller the shot. The number of pellets of each size making up the load of a shot shell depends on its gauge. For example, 12-gauge number 1 buckshot cartridges generally contain sixteen pellets, while a 16-gauge number 1 buckshot cartridge generally contains twelve pellets. Shotgun pellets may be lead, lead alloy, or soft steel. Concern that waterfowl might eat toxic lead pellets has begun a movement to replace all lead-based shot with the more environmentally sound, nontoxic, soft steel shot. At one time, shot shells were made completely of brass. These brass shells have disappeared and have been replaced by shells with brass bases and paper or plastic sides. The pellets in the shot shell are separated from the propellant by one or more powder wads. These wads are used to separate the propellant gases from the shot and to cushion the pellets during their acceleration up the barrel. Wadding is made of cardboard, felt, or plastic. In modern shot shells, the pellets are held in a plastic cup that prevents their deformation through contact with the interior of the shell casing. In some shell casings, the cup in some applications also serves as a wad.

FIREARMS AND FORENSICS

The Early History of the Examination of Firearms

The history of contemporary **firearms examinations** may have begun with the work of Dr. Albert Llewellyn Hall, a practicing physician in Buffalo, New York. In 1931

Hall published an article in the *Buffalo Medical Journal* titled "The Missile and the Weapon" (Hall 1931). This article concerned the possibility of matching fired bullets to the weapon that fired them based on microscopic examination of the striations on the bullets.

The first firearms case in the United States should have established the precedent for the admissibility of firearms comparison testimony. In *Commonwealth v. Best* (1902), the Supreme Judicial Court of the Commonwealth of Massachusetts permitted the introduction of the results of comparative examinations of markings on bullets. The case was ignored until rediscovered in the 1930s. The widespread acceptance of comparisons of bullet markings took nearly a quarter of a century. Courts seemed willing to allow the introduction of case comparisons but extremely reluctant to allow the admission of testimony pertaining to comparison of bullets, firing-pin impressions, or extractor marks.

The first use of firing pin impressions and extractor marks as evidence occurred during the investigation of the Brownsville massacre. On the night of August 13, 1906, unknown persons shot up downtown Brownsville, Texas, killing a local barkeep. Local civilian witnesses claimed that the shooting was carried out by black soldiers. During the ensuing Senate investigation, an Army officer and a civilian technician from the U.S. arsenal at Springfield, Massachusetts, examined the firing impressions and extractor marks on cartridges found in the streets of Brownsville the day after the shooting.

These examiners found that most of the cartridges had been fired from rifles of B Company, 25th Infantry. Being unable to fix blame on a specific soldier and believing that a conspiracy of silence existed among the personnel of the 25th Infantry, the War Department dishonorably discharged all 167 enlisted men in the battalion (Lane 1971). The readiness of courts to accept comparisons of marks on cartridges but not rifling marks on bullets may have been due to the greater visibility of the marks on cartridges and to the absence of a comparison microscope.

In 1929 **Calvin Goddard** was called to Chicago to examine the fired bullets and cartridges in the St. Valentine's Day Massacre. He was able to determine that the victims of the gangland execution had been killed with two different Thompson submachine guns, one with a 20-round magazine and the other with a 50-round drum magazine (Goddard 1930). Goddard's impressive performance led to the establishment of a private forensic laboratory in Chicago under Goddard's direction. This laboratory later became the Chicago Police Department Crime Laboratory. This was the same year that found Goddard testifying in *Evans v. Commonwealth* (1929), which became the precedent-setting case for the admissibility of comparisons of rifling marks.

Examination of Weapons

As an examination protocol, test firing is not necessarily the first step. There is a possibility that the weapon was last used in a homicide involving a contact wound. If the barrel was in contact with the body upon firing, there may be blood and tissue in the barrel as a result of barrel blowback. The weapon's bore may also have fibers from its owner's pockets. There is also a possibility that the weapon, its components,

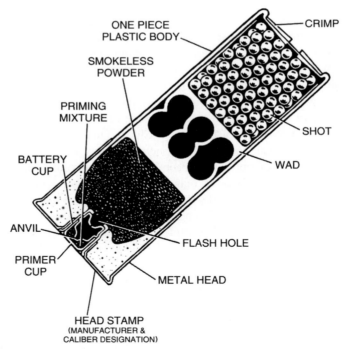

FIGURE 7-13   Shot shell components: primer, powder, wadding, and shot.
(*Source:* Austin Police Department)

and its ammunition may retain fingerprints. Once the firearm has been processed for fingerprints, a complete identification of the weapon should be made. The identification should include:

- Make or manufacturer
- Type (revolver, pistol, etc.)
- Caliber
- Serial number
- Model*
  - Number of shots
- Barrel length

> *model will include a manufacturer's identification for the particular type of firearm made, e.g., Winchester model 30-30.

The make, manufacturer, and model are determined from names, trademarks, and proof marks placed on various components of the weapon. The caliber of the weapon may be indicated by the name or by trademark information. A weapon may be modified by fitting a different caliber barrel to the weapon's frame.

The **National Firearms Act of 1968** requires retailers to record the serial number of a weapon and the name of its purchaser. Because of the importance of the serial number for tracing a firearm's owner, a criminal may remove the stamped serial number by grinding. If the grinding does not go deep enough into the metal, a stamped serial number may still be recovered by chemical etching, electrochemical etching, or ultrasonic cavitation. Many firearms have parts of the serial number stamped into internal components. Handguns often have the serial number stamped at different locations on the frame.

In a case involving an accidental firing or a firing that "accidentally" occurs during a fight, the amount of force required to pull the trigger may be important. The trigger pull may be measured by gradually increasing the amount of weight hanging from the weapon's trigger while the weapon is held vertically with the mechanism cocked. The measurement should be made with the actuating force applied to the trigger at the same spot that the finger of a person firing the weapon would be placed.

Examination of Bullets

In the absence of a suspect weapon, a firearms examination is confined to the determination of **class characteristics** of the bullets, such as caliber, direction of twist of the rifling, **degree of twist,** number of lands and grooves, and width of the lands and grooves. With this data, the firearms examiner may be able to determine the make and model of the firearm that fired the bullets. If there are two or more fired bullets that exhibit the same class characteristics, they are then examined under a comparison microscope to determine if the bullets were fired by the same weapon. Before class characteristics of bullets are determined, the bullets should be examined for the presence of trace evidence such as blood, hairs, fibers, wood splinters, glass particles, paint, concrete, or soil particles. Blood, hairs, and fibers may be picked up by a bullet as it passes through a shooting victim. Trace evidence such as wood splinters or glass particles embedded in a bullet indicates that the bullet may have passed through an intermediate object such as a door, wall, or window. Paint, concrete, or soil particles may be found if a bullet ricochets off a hard surface.

Caliber

The caliber of an undeformed fired bullet may be measured with a micrometer. The diameter of interest is the diameter across the land impressions (which on the expended bullet will be indentations made by the barrel lands). Allowance must be made for the fact that firearm calibers are merely nominal indications of the true bore diameters. A group of Colt pistols, all nominally .38-caliber weapons, were found to have bore diameters ranging from 0.348 to 0.395 inches. The caliber of an intact but badly deformed bullet may be estimated from its weight. The determination of caliber by weight will rarely allow the examiner to specify a particular caliber for the bullet, but certain calibers may be eliminated as possibilities. When the bullet is fragmented, an accurate weight can no longer be obtained. In such a case, the caliber of the bullet may be estimated by measuring the widths of a land impression and an adjacent groove impression (Mathews 1962).

In bullets recovered intact, the number of lands and grooves can be determined by counting them. In cases where bullets are badly deformed, measurement of the width of the land and groove impressions may be combined with a knowledge of the caliber of the bullet to calculate the number of lands and grooves. Because manufacturers use a specific number of grooves in their firearms and this number is generally constant for a given make and model, the number of lands and grooves is an important class characteristic (Mathews 1962).

Rifling Twists

The direction of twist of the rifling may be determined by inspection of the fired bullet if it is not badly deformed. The rifling may spiral either to the left or to the right. Left-hand twist rifling is often referred to as Colt-type rifling, and right-hand twist rifling is often referred to as Smith and Wesson–type rifling.

Land and Groove Width

The width of the land and groove impressions may also be measured using a filar micrometer, traveling microscope, or toolmaker's microscope. Measurements are made perpendicular to the axis of the bullet. Observing that the land impressions on a bullet are wider than the groove impressions allows the firearms examiner to eliminate certain makes and models of firearms. Land and groove impressions that are of a markedly different width from the other impressions on the bullet may reflect a defect in manufacture that is sufficiently rare as to be almost unique (Mathews 1962).

Bullet Comparisons

Bullet comparisons are made using a comparison microscope. A comparison micro-scope consists of two compound microscopes, each with its own objectives, stage, and focusing adjustments. The microscopes are joined by a comparison bridge, a system of prism mirrors that brings the images of the two microscopes together, so they may be compared side by side through a single ocular. The images of the two microscopes may be superimposed, or they may be viewed side by side, with the field of view divided equally between the two microscopes. The bullets to be compared are attached to short, cylindrical bullet holders. The bullet holders slip onto the shafts of the bullet-manipulating mechanisms, which in turn are attached to the microscope stages. The bullet-manipulating mechanisms are provided with universal joints so the bullets may be oriented at any desired angle. Once the bullets are mounted, the examiner begins the search for matching patterns of striations. The lim-ited expansion of jacketed bullets leads to only occasional contact with the bottoms of the grooves, and only the base may be upset sufficiently to seat well in the bar-rel's rifling. Therefore, the initial examination is most likely to discover a pattern of striations near the base of the bullet. A land impression on a test-fired bullet is com-pared successively to each land impression on the suspect bullet until a match is obtained or it is determined that no match is possible. Once a match has been made with a pair of land impressions, the bullets are rotated synchronously to see if other matching striation patterns may be observed. If both bullets were fired from the same barrel, numerous matching patterns will be readily evident. Marks other than land and groove striations, such as the following, may be observed:

- Skid marks that are caused by the bullet sliding over the beginnings of the lands at the breech end of the barrel

- Shaving marks that occur when a revolver bullet in the cylinder is not per-fectly lined up with the barrel. The bullet strikes the edge of the forcing cone (the flared opening in the revolver's frame in front of the cylinder where the fired bullet enters the barrel), and a portion of the bullet is shaved off on the side striking the forcing cone. Comparing shaved spots on a bullet may be difficult. Test firing may not always result in a similar shaving, and many shots may have to be fired before a similarly shaved bullet can be obtained.

In an effort to avoid detection, criminals may flatten, bend, or shorten the bar-rel of a firearm. Flattened barrels may by restored to round, bent barrels may be straightened, or bullets may be forced through the barrels. The marks on bullets fired through the barrel at its original length may not match the marks on bullets fired through a shortened barrel.

The examination of fired bullets may lead to any one of three conclusions:

1. The questioned bullet was fired from the suspect weapon.
2. The questioned bullet was not fired from the suspect weapon.
3. The results of the examinations are insufficient to reach a final determination.

Examination of Cartridges

In examining a fired cartridge, the examiner using a low-power microscope will note:

- Size
- Shape
- Type (rimmed, semi-rimmed, rimless, belted, rim-fire, centerfire)
- Size of firing pin impression
- Position of firing pin impression
- Location of extractor marks
- Location of ejector marks

The shape and location of the firing pin impression on the cartridges of bullets shot from a .22-caliber single-shot breech-loading rifle can serve to identify the make and model of the rifle. The relative positions of the extractor and ejector marks on cartridges from self-loading pistols allow the same determination (Mathews 1962). If a suspect firearm is available and if the class characteristics of cartridges from that weapon match those of the questioned cartridge, the examiner fires test shots with the suspect weapon in order to obtain fired cartridges for comparison purposes. The cartridges are then placed inside an iris diaphragm that attaches to the bullet-mounting devices in the comparison microscope. Comparison of the various marks on the fired cartridges begins with the firing pin impressions, firing pin drag marks, and breechblock marks. A match of these marks would show that both cartridges were fired by the same weapon.

After the examination of the above marks has been completed, the examiner compares the extractor marks, ejector marks, chambering marks, and magazine (clip) marks. A match of any of these types of marks indicates that the two cartridges have been run through the action of the same weapon but does not establish that they ever passed through the barrel.

Examination Objectives

Whenever a firearm is discharged in the commission of a crime, physical evidence is likely to be available. Such evidence in the hands of a competent firearms examiner may answer many of the following questions:

- Can the crime scene bullet or cartridge casing be linked to a suspected weapon?
- Is a recovered weapon capable of being fired?
- Can the weapon be accidentally fired?
- What is the trigger pull?
- Can the serial number be restored?
- Can the type of gun be determined from an examination of the class characteristics of a bullet or cartridge recovered at the crime scene?

Legal Aspects

A Virginia case decided in 1897, *Dean v. Commonwealth* (1897), is the first in which an appellate court approved of testimony regarding the similarity between fatal and test bullets (weight was the compared variable). Beginning with *Jack v. Commonwealth,* a Kentucky case decided in 1928, expert testimony concerning firearms identification began to receive objective appellate appraisal. A year later, this same court, in *Evans v. Commonwealth* (1929), rendered the first exhaustive opinion treating firearms identification as a science and sanctioning its use for the purpose of establishing the guilt of the accused. Today the accuracy of firearms identification is commonly accepted, and ample case law upholds the admissibility of firearms evidence when presented by a qualified expert. As with other expert testimony, the witness is permitted to testify that in his or her opinion a particular bullet was fired from a certain weapon. The expert's testimony is confined to his or her areas of special knowledge. For example, a witness whose expertise concerns only the identification of bullets through their microscopic markings would not be permitted to testify on the issue of whether a certain wound was caused by a particular weapon or whether the bullet traveled a particular trajectory prior to striking the victim. In situations where bullets are mutilated beyond identification or the suspect weapon cannot be fired, an expert may still be permitted to testify regarding other relevant matters. Even though the condition of fatal bullets may preclude an identification of the evidence weapon, an identification is permissible on the basis of cartridge case breech face imprints, firing pin impressions, or ejector and extractor marks (*Williams v. State* 1960).

Class Characteristics

A firearms expert may be able to identify only the class characteristics of a badly deformed bullet. That expert may still testify to the fact that the fatal bullets were fired from a gun having characteristics similar to those of a gun obtained from the accused and had physical characteristics like those of the bullets in the accused's gun (*State v. Bayless* 1976).

Cartridge Evidence

Identification based upon a comparison of breech face imprints, firing pin impressions, and extractor and ejector marks was recognized by the courts in *State v. Clark.* This Oregon case, decided in 1921, allowed the expert to testify that "a peculiar mark on the brass part of the primer" matched that found on a cartridge fired from the suspect weapon (*State v. Clark* 1921).

In Montana, another case was decided based upon comparative evidence (*State v. Vuckovich* 1921). The expert in this case testified that a peculiar crimp on an empty shell found at the scene of the murder was similar to a mark on shells fired from the defendant's pistol. Evidence was introduced to show that the "firing marks made by the lands and grooves of the barrel of the pistol were the same" on both the test and the fatal bullets. This decision confirmed the acceptability of using shells and bullets as comparative evidence.

Chain of Custody

As with all evidence, the chain of custody of weapons, shells, and bullets must be unbroken and documented. If it is necessary for more than one examiner to handle the evidence, that should be recorded, and the documentation should be available to the defendant upon request. Every moment of the existence of the evidence, from the time it entered into the possession of the state (through the hands of law enforcement personnel) to its introduction at the time of trial, must be accounted for and supported by the appropriate chain of custody documentation.

Long periods of time may elapse between the time shots are fired and the time the bullets or shells are collected. In *State v. Boccadoro* (1929), a bullet fired into the ground a year or two prior to the commission of the murder under investigation was recovered and identified as having been fired by the murder weapon. In *State v. Lane* (1951), shells dropped into a river during target practice months before their recovery were admitted. The time the shells spent underwater was to be considered when assigning weight to the evidence, but it was not detrimental to admissibility. In *Commonwealth v. Ellis* (1977), bullets that had been fired into an oak tree four months prior to the homicide were recovered and matched to the bullets found at the scene of the crime. The destruction of ballistics evidence before the defendant has had an opportunity to conduct his or her own tests may be a violation of a defendant's constitutional right to due process and of the confrontation assurances of the Sixth Amendment. Where the destruction is inadvertent, the courts have been unsympathetic to such claims. The state inadvertently destroyed the alleged murder weapon and bullets in the case of *People v. Triplett* (1965), and the defendant contended that this destruction denied him his right to confront the state's firearms expert with his own expert's analysis of the physical evidence. The court rejected this assertion, refusing to take an absolutist view of the confrontation clause.

Expert Testimony

The testimony of the expert does not require a concomitant introduction of the test bullets themselves. In fact, little is to be gained by entering the bullets as evidence. The expert will take photographs of the comparison microscope views and have them enlarged for courtroom use. The greater the number of comparisons of striations on bullets or casing markings on shells, the easier it will be to convince the jury that the bullets were fired from the same firearm. Photographs of the matching bullets and shells are not required; the oral testimony of the expert is considered to be sufficient to get the matter before the jury (*Commonwealth v. Ellis* 1977). It bolsters the expert's testimony for the jury to receive a detailed explanation of the comparisons upon which the expert has based his or her opinion. Additionally, photo enlargements go a long way in defusing the defendant's allegations that not enough points of comparison were ascertainable to support a positive identification.

Tests performed by firearms examiners need not be conducted in the presence of the accused (*State v. Aiken* 1967). It was held to be an error in *Johnson v. State* (1971) to admit prosecution evidence in a case where the fatal bullet was not made available for an examination by the defense. But when the bullet, shell, or weapon is made available for an examination by the defense expert, it is reasonable to condition the test upon the presence of a state expert. The court in *State v. Nutley* (1964) held that, since firearms identification is a relatively exact science with a common methodology, no prejudice to the defense is incurred by prosecution representation.

The myth associated with the recovery of submerged handguns has been that all submerged firearms are bereft of forensic value. Firearms constitute the most neglected evidentiary item recovered from water. A variety of places exist on a firearm that may retain forensic material. Unfortunately, critical evidence frequently is lost due to traditional recovery methods, expedience, and ignorance. If divers hold recovered firearms by the barrel and raise them over their heads as they surface, they drain the contents of the weapons and lose potentially crucial evidence. To avoid this, divers should package weapons in water, while in the water, and obtain a bottom sample to ensure that any fibers or other material found on the weapons are not the product of immersion.

REVIEW QUESTIONS

1. What is a scientific protocol, and how could it be applied to underwater investigations?
2. Might fingerprints be retained on a submerged firearm? If yes, how and where? If no, why not?
3. What is a bottom sample? What role does it play in underwater investigation?
4. Of what significance is the SS *Brother Jonathan* in the discussion of fingerprints?
5. Where are fingerprints most likely to be discovered on a submerged firearm?
6. How can a submerged firearm best be preserved for ballistics testing?
7. What is the difference between firearms examination and ballistics?
8. Why is a pistol that fires each time the trigger is pulled misnamed if referred to as an automatic?
9. What role do lands and grooves play in a bullet's flight and also in the examination of a suspect bullet?
10. What is the measure for expressing the size of a shotgun or a shotgun shell? How is it determined?
11. Who was Calvin Goddard, and what did he contribute to the field of firearms examination?

REFERENCES

GODDARD, C. H. 1930. St. Valentine's Day massacre: A study in ammunition tracing. *American Journal of Police Science* 1:60–78.

HALL, A. L. 1931. The missile and the weapon. *American Journal of Police Science* 2:311–321.

HATCHER, J. S., F. J. JURY, and J. WELLER. 1977. *Firearms: Investigation, identification, and evidence.* Harrisburg, PA: Stackpole.

HOGG, I. A. 1977. *The encyclopedia of infantry weapons of World War II.* New York: Thomas Y. Crowell.

LANE, A. J. 1971. *The Brownsville affair: National crisis and black reaction.* Port Washington, NY: Kennikat.

MATHEWS, J. H. 1962. *Firearms identification*, vol. 1. Springfield, IL: Charles C. Thomas.

NONTE, G. C. 1973. *Firearms encyclopedia.* New York: Harper & Row.

O'CONNOR, J. 1965. *Complete book of rifles and shotguns.* New York: Harper & Row.

SPITZ, W. U. 1993. Injury by gunfire. In *Spitz and Fisher's medicolegal investigation of death*, 3rd ed., ed. Werner U. Spitz, 311–412. Springfield, IL: Charles C. Thomas.

TARASSUK, L., and C. BLAIR. 1979. *The complete encyclopedia of arms and weapons.* New York: Simon & Schuster.

WILBUR, C. G. 1977. *Ballistic science for the police officer.* Springfield, IL: Charles C. Thomas.

TABLE OF CASES

Chapter 8

Vehicle and Small Aircraft Investigations

NEW WORDS AND CONCEPTS

emergency locator transmitters	lift points
underwater locating devices	penetration dive
debris field	lift bags
National Transportation Safety Board	STAR
gross anomalies	starburst pattern
swim around	pontoon bags

LEARNING OBJECTIVES

- Discuss the procedures associated with submerged automobile investigations
- Discuss the procedures associated with submerged aircraft investigations

AIRCRAFT RECOVERY OPERATIONS

Although the frequency of small-aircraft recoveries is less than for automobiles, there are in excess of 2,500 small-aircraft crashes each year in the United States (Teather 1993). There are similarities in the recovery processes for small aircraft and for automobiles. However, it might be good to include at this point an incident that occurred on Lake Travis in Travis County, Texas. During a small-plane recovery operation in which the crash was considered to be accidental and, therefore, not worthy of a full underwater investigation, the color and tenor of the operation changed when drugs and firearms were found some distance from the fuselage. Water visibility was approximately three to five feet. While divers were measuring and geographically

locating the submerged aircraft, a diver with a video camera that was being monitored topside was panning the bottom and came within fifty yards of the aircraft. What
could plainly be seen in the monitor was invisible to the diver aiming the camera: On
the bottom lay firearms of various descriptions that apparently had been thrown from
the plane on impact. The dive supervisor instructed the recovery team that the area
was, in fact, a crime scene. The nature of the recovery changed abruptly. The lesson
to be learned, once again, is that small-aircraft crashes should not be presumed accidental; rather, they should be treated as though they are a crime scene.

Locating the Aircraft

There are many techniques and search patterns that can be used for locating an intact
small aircraft that has crashed into the water. In most instances of airplane crashes,
little is left that resembles an aircraft. If the aircraft crashed into the water rather
than crash-landed in the water, there may be little left intact. In reality, in most
instances the search is not for an aircraft, but for remains of that aircraft. Many small
airplanes are equipped with **emergency locator transmitters.** However, even if the
pilot turned the device on prior to the crash, the signal sent by the transmitter may
not be strong enough to penetrate the water. Recognizing the shortcomings of traditional locator transmitters, some manufacturers have equipped their aircraft with
water-activated **underwater locating devices.** These signals can be received only by
a hydrophone receiver that is placed in the water. One of the most effective ways of
locating a downed aircraft is by tracking the surface fuel slick created by the downed
aircraft. A very small amount of fuel can result in a very large slick.

Measuring the Debris Field

Once the wreckage is located, the **debris field** should be marked and charted. Buoys
should mark the margins of the perimeter within which the search and recovery operations are to take place. Each piece of debris is evidence and must be treated accordingly (i.e., geographically located). We discussed measurement techniques in Chapter
Five. Those techniques will work for all recovery operations. It might prove
illustrative to point out that the U.S. Navy charted each piece of the TWA flight that
crashed off Long Island. In doing so, they accomplished a number of things:

- They knew where various parts of the aircraft landed.
- They knew where body parts were located in relationship to fuselage pieces.
- They knew that the rear part of the plane crashed before the front part.
- They knew that the airplane came apart prior to crashing.
- They knew that the front part of the plane continued flying after the rear
  portion had crashed.
- They knew something caused the plane to break in two.

All of this information was solely a product of having recorded the locations
of every body and airplane part that was recovered. The recovery was so successful

FIGURE 8-1 TWA restoration photo.
(*Source:* U.S. Navy)

FIGURE 8-2 ValuJet recovery operation.
(*Source:* R. F. Becker)

that more than 75 percent of the aircraft was recovered and reassembled. The reassembly allowed a forensic examination of the reconstructed aircraft for explosives residue, microtaggants, missile fragments, and smoke and fire damage.

Generally speaking, the Federal Aviation Administration (FAA) has jurisdiction over aircraft in the air, while the **National Transportation Safety Board** has jurisdiction over aircraft on the ground, except for small aircraft, which remain the purview of the FAA. It is representatives from these agencies who direct the recovery operations employed in a particular plane crash. They do not, however, provide the recovery divers or necessary support personnel. Local recovery divers are used unless the aircraft crashes into water governed by the U.S. Navy or Coast Guard.

Handling Evidence

The recovery of all submerged aircraft evidence (wreckage and bodies or body parts) is usually done at the direction of the on-scene designated air crash investigator. Those directions may be given with little concern for the preservation of evidence but must nonetheless be followed. Many federal air crash investigators have an agenda that is not based on the preservation of evidence. As training progresses nationally, federal agencies are becoming aware of the value of submerged evidence. In all instances of air crash recovery operations, the underwater investigators can make accurate observations and record those observations. As in all recovery operations, the best record is a photographic record whenever possible.

If the aircraft is intact, there may be **gross anomalies** that suggest crash causation. If the fuselage is intact, the engine in place, and the propeller visible, the condition of the propeller can be significant in determining the cause of the crash. If the intact propeller is bent at the tips and the bend is directly back, it may be presumed that the propeller was not under power upon impact. If, however, the intact propeller is twisted backward, it is suggestive of the craft entering the water under power. In the first instance, the presumption that the airplane ran out of fuel might be confirmed by the absence of fuel in the tanks (if intact) or the absence of fuel in the water (Teather 1983). The condition of the propeller should be discovered during the **swim around** and recorded accordingly; thereafter, a photographic record should be made.

In all air crashes, survivors are recovered first. The reality is that few survive an aircraft crash. For these victims, the procedure usually involves the recovery of intact bodies first, followed by body parts. All body parts, regardless of size, should be recovered, keeping in mind that fingers, fingertips, feet, and teeth can be instrumental in identifying occupants. All human remains should be removed from the wreckage whenever possible, bagged in the water, and lifted to the surface. The onset of wreckage recovery presumes the absence of human remains. In small-aircraft crashes wherein the fuselage remains intact, occupants may be found compacted against the back of the passenger compartment. In many instances of small-aircraft crashes, the engine is launched from its mounts and thrown some distance from the rest of the wreckage. The engine is a vital part of the recovery process. An examination of the engine or engines may reveal fire, explosion, or mechanical difficulty.

In most instances a request will be made to recover the pilot first if possible. An autopsy of the pilot may reveal information that leads to a determination as to the cause of the crash. If the pilot died prior to impact or was under the influence of alcohol or drugs, the autopsy and toxicological screen may reveal the cause or a participating factor in the air crash (Wagner and Froede 1993).

Aircraft Recovery

Prior to any efforts at recovery of a small airplane, the recovery protocol should include a swim around very similar to the one used in automobile recoveries. Again, the swim around checklist allows a diver to tactilely examine the exterior of an aircraft to determine gross anatomical features. If the aircraft is intact, the swim around

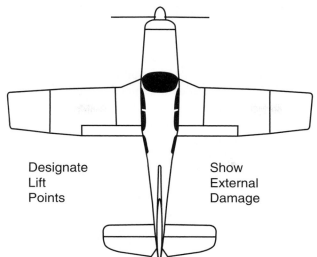

AIRPLANE SWIM AROUND CHECKLIST

Data
Time
Location
Divers

Depth
Visibility
Water Temperature
Access Point

Make
Model
Owner
Registration #

Number of Passengers

Obtained:
Cargo Manifest
Flight Plan
Bodies on Board

Designate
Lift
Points

Show
External
Damage

Show External Damage

	yes	no
Fuselage intact	yes	no
Engine separated	yes	no
Propeller bent	yes	no
Hazardous cargo	yes	no
Petroleum slick	yes	no
Wheels down	yes	no
Tires inflated	yes	no
Collision lights on	yes	no
Carburetor de-icer on	yes	no

FIGURE 8-3   Aircraft swim around checklist.

(*Source*: R. F. Becker)

will prove valuable in determining to what extent the plane is damaged, whether occupants are still in the aircraft, and potential **lift points.**

Most small aircraft are equipped with a ring or harness designed to allow lifting the aircraft. Discovery of that lift point will allow the plane to be brought to the surface with the least amount of trauma to the aircraft and its occupants. Entering a small airplane is a **penetration dive** and should be done only by divers with appropriate overhead environment training. In 2001 divers attempting to recover a downed eight-passenger aircraft attempted to penetrate the interior of the cabin. They knew that the appropriate protocol included stationing a safety diver and tender at the entryway, but they ignored the protocol and made the decision for a single police diver to enter. The diver swam over the passengers' seats on the left side to gain access to the pilot. His tanks scraped on the fuselage overhead. As the diver swam over the seat directly behind the pilot's, the seat moved from a reclining position to a fully upright position, pinning the diver to the overhead. Tugs on the line were to no avail, because the tender line leading over the seats and out the door did not allow a full pull on the line. The tender recognized that line tugs had not been forthcoming in what he judged to be a reasonable time, so he dispatched a safety diver who managed to recline the seat and retrieve the diver.

Once all evidence has been recovered from the crash site, removal of the aircraft can proceed. Wreckage recovery has been described. However, if the aircraft is intact, its recovery is a significant step in the investigative process. The aircraft, if intact, can be brought to the surface by the use of **lift bags.** Rigging submerged evidence to be lifted to the surface by air bags is a skill that requires specialized training and practice. For the purposes of this discussion, it will be presumed that the dive team has received such training, has attached lift bags, and has successfully lifted the aircraft to the surface. Once afloat, the aircraft can be towed to shore by boats with sufficient motor power. The towline needs to be longer than the depth of the water to assure that if the aircraft should sink, it will not pull the boat(s) after it. In the same vein, a buoy should be attached to the aircraft with a long enough line to assure it will float on the surface and allow discovery of the aircraft should it sink.

Large-Aircraft Recovery Operations

For a large body of water over which passenger aircraft fly, it is a matter not of if but of when a passenger aircraft will crash into that waterway. When the ValuJet crash occurred in Florida, it took days to establish police jurisdiction over the operation and equally as long to bring together the manpower, resources, and command necessary to run the operation. In comparing and contrasting the operations that took place in the TWA Long Island crash and the ValuJet Florida crash, we see the difference between preparation and lack of preparation. There was one major difference between the crashes: which entity had jurisdiction and responsibility. Having jurisdiction and responsibility does not necessarily go hand in hand with preparation.

The Florida crash occurred within waters over which the state had jurisdiction and responsibility. The lack of planning for the possibility of such an event was evident in the days and events that preceded the actual recovery of the ValuJet. Authorities originally failed to recognize that the crash site had become a biological and chemical hazard because of the aviation fluids and decomposing body parts. Searchers wading in knee-deep water were not initially provided appropriate clothing or orientation. No one was ready for the devastation that had been wreaked upon the aircraft and its occupants.

The TWA crash occurred in waters that allowed the United States Navy to participate. They brought with them their protocols, expertise, manpower, equipment, and resources. The U.S. Navy showed how an airline passenger underwater crime scene could and should be processed. They were able to locate and map body parts and debris as a part of their investigation. The attention to detail was a product of allegations that a missile had been the cause of the crash. Because of the question of criminal enterprise involved in the crash, the site was handled as a crime scene—a first for an airliner recovery operation. The U.S. Navy provided the protocol and established the working model for treating all airliner crashes as a product of criminal enterprise until proven otherwise. If the determination as to criminal causation is left until after the black boxes are found, by then the scene will have been so disturbed as to be rendered virtually worthless should it become necessary to treat it as a crime scene.

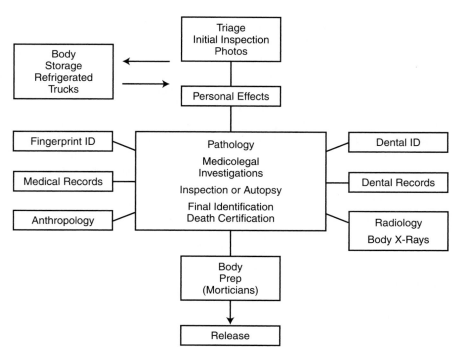

FIGURE 8-4   Aircraft disaster contingency plan flow chart.
(*Source:* R. F. Becker)

If we consider the complexity of the issues that have to be addressed in a mass disaster of this nature, it becomes apparent that a contingency plan is the foundation upon which a recovery operation must proceed—a contingency plan that must be put into place prior to the event for which it is a contingency plan. Each component of the plan must be fixed in place and subject to activation at a moment's notice. The question that often arises among police agencies is: "Who's responsible for constructing an aircraft crash contingency plan?" The answer to the question is that it is the responsibility of the local and state governments, but it is most likely not recognized as such. Waiting until an airliner crashes is the worst possible way to develop a contingency plan. It would be a safe bet to say that the Florida authorities who had responsibility for the ValuJet operation now have an airliner crash contingency plan. Having the contingency plan is an integral part of the recovery operation, as is the presumption that the precipitating cause of the crash was criminal. Together these two concepts provide a protocol for investigating aircraft crash investigations.

VEHICLE RECOVERY OPERATIONS

Much of what we know about vehicles with occupants in the water we have learned in movies. What Hollywood includes in films is sensational and, to the discerning eye, is also incorrect. Perhaps the earliest examples of moviemakers getting it wrong was in the early gangster films where revolvers were fitted with silencers (suppressors). Not having technical consultants on the set made for some high suspense but poor accuracy. Revolvers expel as much gas from the mouth of the cylinder as they do from the end of the barrel, making suppression of revolver reports highly unlikely. In the same vein, we have come to believe that people who are trapped in an automobile that is sinking under the water can breathe in a pocket of air trapped in the rear of the vehicle. Before involving ourselves in the investigation and recovery of submerged vehicles, it might serve us to have some understanding of the dynamics of a sinking vehicle. The Michigan Department of Public Safety conducted a series of test immersions of contemporary automobiles as part of a grant study entitled "Submerged Transportation Accident Research" (**STAR**) (Michigan Department of Public Safety 1992). They had built a pontoon bridge long enough to allow unmanned vehicles to attain a speed of approximately 30 mph before entering the water. Entry speed was measured on a traffic radar gun and the speed of each vehicle was recorded. Electrical systems (windshield wipers and headlights) were turned on, monitored, and filmed by police divers as the vehicle submerged. Submersion time varied, based on the type of vehicle, from a minimum of one minute and thirty seconds to five minutes. The study revealed:

- Cars sink front first.
- Cars sink with water entering the front of the vehicle through vents, in a front-down position.

- Car doors cannot be opened from the inside until the water inside the vehicle rises to the level of the water outside the vehicle.
- Cars sunk in water deeper than the length of the vehicle will land upside down.
- Electrical systems continue working long after the vehicle has submerged (allowing door locks and power windows to be opened even after the vehicle had rested on the bottom).
- All vehicles tested floated long enough for occupants to exit through the windows if they acted quickly in response to the car's entry into the water.

The last vehicle that was sent off the bridge by the MDPS was manned by two divers who rode the vehicle to the bottom. With a camera mounted inside and police divers filming on the outside, it was apparent that the vehicle filled with water from the front to the rear as it headed toward the bottom. Passengers in the front seat who had not exited the vehicle would most likely follow the air into the back of the vehicle as it continued to fill with water (accounting for the discovery in many recovered vehicles of drowned victims all packed into the rear seat, contradicting the hypothesis that they breathed a pocket of air until it dissipated). Once the water filled the passenger compartment, a large bubble of air was released from the trunk as a result of the air escaping the passenger compartment through the rear seat into the trunk and around the seals of the trunk; or, if the seals were new, the air lodged in the trunk was sufficient to displace the trunk lock, forcibly opening the trunk lid. An escape protocol was developed as a result of the STAR project:

1. Don't panic.
2. Remove the seat belt.
3. Remove the seat belts of any children.
4. Roll down the window.
5. Hand children through the window.
6. Exit the vehicle through the window.

This study was conducted in Lake Michigan. If a vehicle were to enter moving water, any efforts to escape the vehicle would have to be made considering the movement of the water. If a vehicle is not tumbled by current, exit will most easily be effected on the downstream side, leaving the upstream windows closed against the current to retard sinking.

Most vehicles entering water can be safely exited; however, exiting a school bus that has entered the water is another proposition. After studying passenger vehicles, MDPS requested and received school buses from the major manufacturers. Applying the same procedure used in the automobile study revealed drastically different sinking dynamics of all the school buses. Without exception, as the buses entered the water, the windshield was smashed back into the driver, incapacitating the driver and allowing a torrent of water to enter. The passenger door also burst open, allowing water to enter, adding to that entering from the windshield. The force of the entering water was such that all the occupants and all the contents of the bus were pushed forcibly against the rear emergency exit. Under the same test conditions that allowed passengers of vehicles flotation time to escape, all the buses entering the water would have entombed all the occupants.

In the world of recovery diving, any time a diver cannot ascend directly to the surface, that diver is said to be in an overhead environment. Entering a submerged vehicle or bus is a penetration dive and requires specialized technical training beyond that which most underwater investigators receive. Only those who have received specialized training should perform recovery operations in these environments. That said, we can continue on the presumption that any diver attempting to penetrate the interior of a vehicle of any description has been trained to do so.

Vehicle Recoveries

Stolen autos are commonly retrieved from various waterways. Thieves seem to know the deepest, darkest locations for disposing of vehicles. Stolen auto recovery is such an integral part of underwater recovery operations that it has become standard procedure to presume that a submerged vehicle is simply a stolen vehicle. This presumption presupposes that all stolen vehicles that have been used in crimes have been identified. It further presupposes that all stolen vehicles used in a crime have been placed in a computer database accessible by investigators prior to efforts by a recovery team to lift the vehicle. Consequently, these "stolen vehicles" are treated as though they have no forensic relevance.

Most agencies place a hooked cable around the axle of the submerged vehicle and have it winched to shore by a tow truck or barge. If the vehicle has filled with water, the pressure of the water within the vehicle against the windows will burst the windows. Anything within the vehicle that floats will be jettisoned with the water, including clothing, paper, bodies, plastic, or items contained in plastic, all of which may have provided information about a crime that was committed in the vehicle or with the vehicle. Most divers give the interior of a submerged vehicle a cursory examination before it is winched to the surface. The more experienced teams may roll the windows down to allow the water trapped in the vehicle to slowly escape through the windows rather than bursting the windshield and other windows.

It would seem that a basic question should be considered prior to the recovery of a submerged vehicle: Why would a vehicle be disposed of in this manner? If the vehicle was taken for a joyride, it would most likely be left close to the destination of the joyrider. Professional auto thieves steal the vehicle to be resold or for its constituent parts. That leaves:

- Those perpetrating insurance fraud.
- Those masking a crime.
- Those entombing bodies.

Any of these three possibilities would warrant more meticulous handling of the automobile.

Exterior Damage

Often exterior vehicle damage is of little evidentiary value because of the inability to determine if the damage occurred before the vehicle was submerged, during submersion, or as a result of the salvage operation. Any damage to the undercarriage and hoses must be presumed to have resulted from the salvage operation. Even in waters of minimal visibility there are some procedures that can be performed to minimize loss of trace evidence.

The most obvious indication that a vehicle has been stolen is the absence of ignition keys. Other indications of theft might include hot-wires; blocked steering wheel or gas pedal; intrusion marks on doors, windows, or trunk; and the absence of valuable accessories such as radio, tape decks, speakers, cellular phone, hubcaps, etc. Remember, however, that the trunk can be forcibly opened as a result of air escaping from the interior of the vehicle. Generally, the driver's side window will be down or driver's side door unlocked to allow for someone standing outside the vehicle to accelerate it. Should the keys be in the ignition, the probability of the vehicle having been stolen is significantly reduced. A hand search of the interior of the vehicle for ignition keys can be performed in waters of limited visibility. If the vehicle has been stolen and it has been used in the commission of a crime, there may be fruits or instrumentalities of the crime that may be lost during recovery. The license plate number and the vehicle identification number, if retrievable, may allow for a computer check to determine the status of the vehicle. In waters of limited visibility, license plate numbers and VINs can still be read through a water bath; a plastic bag filled with clear water when pressed against a license will allow a diver to place his face mask against the bag and view the plate through clear water. However, not all stolen vehicles are immediately reported, nor are the crimes that are committed using a stolen auto. It may prove the best policy to treat all vehicles to be recovered, unless otherwise certain, as vehicles that may have been used in the commission of an offense and as vehicles that contain prospective trace evidence.

Evidence Collection

There is a considerable amount of information that can be obtained from a submerged vehicle before efforts are made to raise it. If access into the vehicle is practicable and can be accomplished safely, an examination of the glove compartment can be made. All items in the glove compartment should be removed and placed in plastic bags (leave water in the bags with the contents). The floors of the vehicle can be examined, photographed, and, if anything is discovered, tagged and bagged. The most innocuous of items may prove to be useful. The underside of seats and the area behind the rear cushions should be examined and discovered items retrieved.

Swim Around

An exterior examination of the vehicle should be conducted similar to the preflight walk around conducted by pilots of small aircraft. The swim around, when conducted with and documented upon an underwater slate, can record gross anomalies on the exterior of the vehicle. Teams with underwater communication systems can allow the communications tender to verbally provide the checklist to the underwater investigator, who verbally communicates the results, which can then be recorded. The entire swim around can be conducted in zero visibility using the hands to tactilely discover any anomalies to the exterior of the vehicle.

In 1997 in Austin, Texas, two men carjacked a Volvo with two male occupants. The occupants were placed in the trunk and the vehicle driven into Lake Travis. As a result of a thorough investigation, the perpetrators were caught and charged with capital murder. The prosecution intended to seek the death penalty. The state decided that it would enter evidence during the sentencing stage of the trial demonstrating the drama and horror of the trunk of the Volvo filling from the perspective of two bound men, entombed and drowning in the trunk. The prosecutor contacted the author to assist in the reconstruction. An inquiry was made as to the condition of the trunk. It was determined that there was damage to the trunk lid. The damage to the lid was such as would affect the filling rate of the trunk compartment. It could not be determined whether the damage to the trunk had existed prior to the vehicle's recovery or was incident to that recovery. The inability to answer that crucial question denied the prosecution the opportunity to reconstruct the filling of the trunk. The point is that had a swim around been conducted, and had it been determined that there was trunk lid damage prior to recovery, then the simulation could have been presented. All exterior damage should be sketched, noted, and photographed if possible.

If the vehicle has been used in a hit and run, there will be external evidence of that episode. All windows should be assessed and described. Impact bursts on the windows may have occurred as a result of an occupant or a pedestrian striking the window. Without a written or photographic record of the **starburst pattern** on the windshield, there would be no evidence of it after recovery since the damaged window would probably burst upon raising of the vehicle. Any hair, fiber, or tissue that might have been lodged within the starburst will also be destroyed.

Lights
It is helpful to the investigation to know whether the lights were intact prior to recovery, because they too are often a casualty of the recovery operation. If the light lenses are intact prior to raising the vehicle, no false assumptions will be made as to how the lenses were broken if they should be broken during the recovery of the auto. If the lenses are not intact prior to raising the auto, a bit of evidentiary information has been obtained. If there are pieces of the lens still in place, they will probably not be in place upon recovering the vehicle. The pieces, therefore, should be photographed, bagged, and tagged prior to lifting the vehicle.

The fact that the light switch is on or off is not always indicative of whether the lights were on at the time the vehicle entered the water. In recovery operations the light switch will likely be struck by debris or bodies thrown forward as the vehicle is raised by its rear axle. The bulbs from the lights themselves can often reveal whether or not the lights were on when the vehicle entered the water. A retrieval of the lightbulbs may prove to be useful as the investigation progresses.

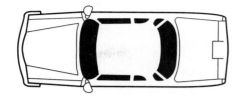

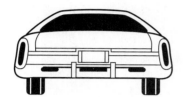

License plate number

VIN number

Windows lowered prior to lifting
yes   no

Auto swim around

Occupants
If   mf   rf
Ir   mr   rr

Windows intact

windshield	yes	no
rear	yes	no
lt. front	yes	no
lt. rear	yes	no
rt. front	yes	no
rt. rear	yes	no

Driver's window open
yes   no

Keys in ignition
yes   no

Accelerator blocked
yes   no

Headlights intact
left   right

Taillights intact

Glove compartment
content   bagged

Reported stolen
yes   no

Crime vehicle
yes   no

Owner contacted

FIGURE 8-5   Auto swim around slate.
(*Source:* R. F. Becker)

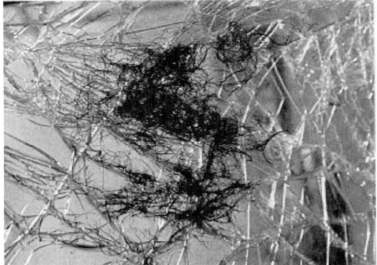

FIGURE 8-6   Windshield starburst; hair in starburst window.
(*Source:* R. F. Becker)

Filaments

Burning light filaments break upon impact in a characteristic fashion that differs from how they break when not lighted or when they simply burn out. It is important not to remove the bulbs from their housings when bulb comparisons may be necessary. Remove the entire light assembly so that damage to the bulbs and filaments is kept at a minimum. The direction of an external impact to the front or rear of the vehicle can often be ascertained by noting the direction in which the filament is distorted.

If the vehicle has been involved in an accident or a hit and run, the investigating officers will probably subject it to a vigorous examination. If there are dents, scratches, fabric, or paint on the exterior that may have been transferred from another vehicle or body, all scuba and salvage equipment will have to be eliminated as a possible source of the dent, scratch, fabric, or paint before any trace evidence can be considered useful. Therefore, the salvage operation should be done with the least possible adverse impact upon the vehicle, and all scuba and salvage equipment should be logged and specifically described to allow for exclusion of possible contamination by the dive and recovery team.

It should be remembered that all items packaged wet (i.e., in a water solution) must ultimately be removed from the plastic container and dried before they can be properly examined. Items that are recovered in the water should be completely immersed in the medium from which they were retrieved; they should not remain merely damp, because mildew will rapidly form. Turning the items over to the lab while they are still in solution will then leave the drying and preserving responsibility up to the laboratory technicians.

Recovery Checklist

What follows is a checklist for every submerged auto recovery operation:

1. Photos should be taken whenever possible from all cardinal directions and from above.
2. A swim around inventory should be done, taking in all gross features of the vehicle including windows, doors, tires, body, and trim. All impressions from the swim around should be recorded.
3. A specific examination of lights and lenses should be conducted.
4. A check for intrusion marks on the body of the vehicle should be made.
5. Divers should check for license plates, front and back.
6. Vehicle identification number should be recorded.
7. The vehicle should be examined for occupants.
8. Divers should check for evidence or contraband.
9. Contents of the glove compartment should be bagged.
10. Sun visors should be examined.
11. Remember that certain surfaces, such as glass and mirrored surfaces, will retain fingerprints even in water.

Occupant Recovery

Recovery of passengers should be conducted in the water whenever possible. Much evidentiary information will be lost if the occupants are left in the vehicle during the recovery operation. Any postmortem injuries to the body resulting from contact with the interior of the vehicle during recovery will only complicate the autopsy. If occupants cannot be removed from the vehicle, efforts should be made to assure that they are belted in to provide some protection when the vehicle is towed to the surface. If vehicle occupants are removed from a water source that has a current, it is always a good idea to place someone downstream of the recovery site to retrieve a body or body parts that may be swept from the grasp of the underwater investigators.

Auto Recovery

Although most vehicle recovery is done by tow truck, floating (lifting) vehicles with air bags is a method whereby nothing inside the vehicle is disturbed and exterior and undercarriage damage is kept to a minimum. Companies that distribute salvage equipment have **pontoon bags** that can be attached to the sides of the vehicle with a yoke that allows the diver using a topside air compressor to inflate both pontoons simultaneously.

Water, current, bottom, and vehicle conditions will dictate what type of recovery technique should be employed. Whatever method is applied, the following warnings promulgated in part by Mark Lonsdale (1989) of the Specialized Tactical Training Unit are worth remembering:

- Do a complete site survey before diving, with special attention to strong currents and debris in the water.
- The team leader must do a risk assessment, balancing the benefit and importance of the recovery with the danger to divers.
- Stay on the uphill side of the vehicle in case it should move or roll into deeper water.
- Do not enter the vehicle all the way.
- Do not enter the vehicle without a dive buddy in immediate attendance.
- Beware of strong currents.
- Withdraw from the vehicle during lifting of the vehicle.
- Foresee the possibility of straps and cables not holding.
- Know your lifting equipment and its limitations.
- Never hurry; make decisions based on sound judgment and not favorable conjecture.
- Do no harm, or, at least, keep it to a minimum.

It would seem that the best advice in all dive operations is the axiom posed by Lonsdale in the last bullet point above: "Do no harm" and all that that encompasses. The objective of every on-scene commander at every dive operation is to assure that everyone gets to go home at the end of the day.

REVIEW QUESTIONS

1. What should the presumption be in all automobile recovery operations?
2. What should the presumption be in all aircraft recovery operations?
3. What is a penetration dive? What is special about it?
4. What are lift bags, and how might they be used in a recovery operation?
5. At what point are bodies recovered from airplane wreckage?
6. What is the purpose of charting a debris field?
7. What is the NTSB?
8. What is a penetration dive?
9. What is a swim around? What is its purpose?
10. What is included in an automobile recovery checklist?

REFERENCES

LONSDALE, M. V. 1989. *SRT diver: A guide for special response teams.* Los Angeles: S.T.T.U.

MICHIGAN DEPARTMENT OF PUBLIC SAFETY. 1992. *Submerged transportation accident research.*

TEATHER, R. 1983. *The underwater investigator.* Fort Collins: Concept Systems, Inc.

WAGNER, G. L., and R. C. FROEDE. 1993. Medicolegal investigation of mass disasters. In *Spitz and Fisher's medicolegal investigation of death,* 3rd ed., ed. Werner U. Spitz, 567–584. Springfield, IL: Charles C. Thomas.

Chapter 9

Vessel Recoveries

NEW WORDS AND CONCEPTS

personal watercraft

COLREGS

boat collision

vaulting

depth penetration tables

secondary impacts

boat arson

detonating devices

incendiary evidence

arson checklist

light filaments

LEARNING OBJECTIVES

- Discuss boat accident property damage
- Discuss boat accident personal injury
- Discuss boat accident reconstruction

INTRODUCTION

In 2000, 701 people lost their lives in boating accidents in the U.S. (Hickman and Sampsel 2002). The introduction of the **personal watercraft** was one of the greatest innovations in recreational boating. The number of people able to race across the water increased with the availability of these relatively inexpensive craft. Most states had to address rules and regulations regarding personal watercraft after the fact. The boating industry preceded state governments in efforts to regulate the use of Jet Ski–type vehicles.

The injury and death toll from boating accidents of all kinds combined with increased leisure time and more people recreating on waterways than ever before to form a volatile mixture. Into the mix came law enforcement. It should be no surprise that effective enforcement of boating laws is difficult, if not impossible. The primary function of law enforcement in regard to recreational boating is to respond to boating accidents. A boating accident investigation cannot depend on skid marks for speed, direction, and right-of-way determination. It is through the examination of scratch marks, paint transfer, penetration damage, and boat and content launching, as well as through body recovery, that the investigator begins to get a picture of what happened and what caused it. Witnesses and boat wreckage provide the most valuable information in a boating accident reconstruction. The boating accident investigation should focus on witness statements whenever possible. The debris from the accident should confirm what information witnesses and victims have provided.

All boaters are subject to the rules of the sea known as the International Regulations for Preventing Collisions at Sea (**COLREGS**), but few know them. Licenses in most states are not required for recreational boating, and no test is required for boat owners or operators. In response to the number of collisions occurring in their jurisdictions, some states have passed minimum-age laws regarding the operation of recreational boats and laws pertaining to operating a boat while intoxicated, but few have required testing and licensing for those operating a boat recreationally.

NAUTICAL TERMS AND MEASUREMENTS

The investigation of a boating accident requires recording of the characteristics of the boat and debris, and of the position of passengers and bodies relative to the boat. In that regard, it is necessary to have a working knowledge of basic nautical terms. The following list is not exhaustive but contains those terms most commonly used in investigating a boating accident.

A boat has sides, a front, and a back. In describing these characteristics, the nautical terms should be used:

- Front: bow
- Back: stern
- Right side: starboard
- Left side: port

Moving to the front or back of a boat is also described nautically:

- Moving to the front: forward
- Moving to the back: aft
- Center of the boat: amidships

The width of a boat is measured at its widest point and referred to as the boat's beam. The term *abeam* means something alongside a boat at ninety degrees to the boat. Something alongside a boat but to the rear is said to be abaft. Something behind the boat is said to be astern. Most boats have a keel, which is the lowest part of the boat. The keel provides resistance through the water, allowing the boat to be steered. A sailboat keel serves the purpose of allowing steerage as well as providing weight to prevent capsizing (weighted keel). The hull of the boat keeps the water out. Two other terms that are frequently used in boating refer to points of reference inside or outside the boat. The fore and aft centerline of the boat is the reference point. Anything outside the boat is outboard; anything inside the boat is inboard.

When an accident occurs, official response begins with the arrival of law enforcement personnel. The first responding officer is faced primarily with the formidable task of establishing some form of control and protection of the scene. The officer who responds to a boating accident scene is perhaps the first forgotten and most neglected member of the investigative team. The officer who first enters the scene is responsible for maintaining the conditions of that location as they are found.

Discussions with the first responding officers, witnesses, and victims may reveal important aspects of the accident. If the boat floated long enough to allow passengers to disembark, their perspectives will be helpful in determining where to look for the sunken boat, bodies, or debris. As information is gathered, the investigator will begin to form some impressions as to:

- Type of boat(s)
- Direction of travel
- Speed of the boat(s)
- Number of passengers
- Relative position of the boat(s) upon impact
- Search or recovery coordinates

In recording the points of impact and rest, investigators use the bow of one of the involved boats as a reference point. In measuring boat resting points, debris, bodies, etc., the point of reference should be from the reference boat if possible, and angles should be measured from the bow of the reference boat, with zero being the bow and the angles progressing clockwise toward 360 degrees.

Measuring distances involves miles, feet, and inches, not nautical measures. Speeds are recorded in miles per hour, although the nautical measurement is the nautical mile per hour, or knot. Most recreational boating uses miles per hour as the method of measuring speed, so as a convenience, miles per hour should be the standard.

When relating the accident site to permanent landmarks, degrees and miles, feet, or inches should be used. When diagramming the findings, the diagram

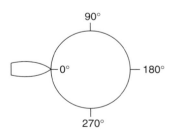

FIGURE 9-1 Degrees from the bow of the reference boat.

(*Source:* R. F. Becker)

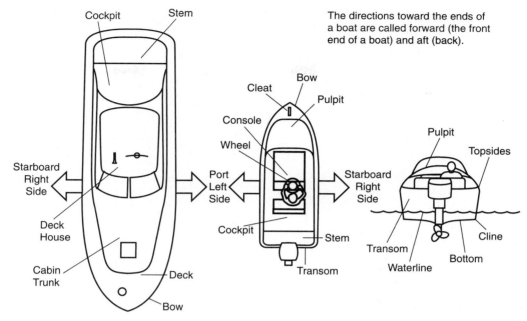

FIGURE 9-2 Standard boat terminology.
(*Source:* Dr. William Chilcott)

should have a reference rosette that commonly consists of the letter *N* with an accompanying arrow showing where north is in relationship to the items displayed in the diagram. Whenever possible, it is customary to arrange the drawing so that north is up.

BOAT ACCIDENT INVESTIGATION

Boat collisions differ markedly from auto collisions. The automobile accident reconstructionist generally deals with automobiles that remain on the ground and leave visible traces of their passage. Occasionally a vehicle will vault and become airborne, but ultimately the path of the vehicle can be traced by the marks left prior to **vaulting** and those left when the vehicle returns to the ground. The automobile accident investigator deals with two dimensions. Not so for the underwater investigator who is trying to reconstruct a boat collision. If two boats collide, one generally rides up onto the other. There are no skid marks to reveal the paths of the boats or their impact point. There are no skid marks in the traditional sense, but sunken boats have evidence of having come into contact with one another, and marks borne by the boats can reveal much about the directions of travel, impact point, and right-of-way. Keeping in mind that boat investigations involve three dimensions, some of the information that will be available to the investigator may be submerged. In fact, point of impact can be confirmed by debris left as a result of the impact. Just as in auto collisions, there is a beginning and end to the debris

FIGURE 9-3 Photo of wrecked boat.
(*Source:* Dr. William Chilcott)

left at the accident site. Finding the beginning of the debris puts the investigator very close to the point of impact. Underwater debris that can be associated with one or more of the vessels involved in a collision can assist in determining point of impact. Of what value is point of impact? In auto collisions, assessing the point of impact and the resting point of the vehicles can assist in approximating their speed at time of impact; to a lesser degree, locating the point of impact can assist in determining right-of-way and speed in boat collisions. In those witnessed collisions where the impacting boat is launched over the top of the impacted boat, determining the distance traveled by the impacting vessel can assist in determining its speed. Most boating accidents do not occur in a vacuum. Someone survives; someone witnessed the collision or the boats prior to collision. With the extensive use of recreational waterways today, there is almost always someone watching, if not video recording or photographing, in the area. Those who may be witnesses need to be identified as soon as possible and interviewed. Photographs and video footage should be examined for other observers or witnesses and for boats or automobiles in the background (Hickman and Sampsel 2002).

When boats collide, one of two patterns generally results. If the impacting boat is planing (on step), its bow will be elevated. If the collision occurs with the impacting boat's bow elevated, the boat is likely to pass over or onto the impacted boat. In those situations there will be evidence of that passing on the bottom of the impacting boat. Any scratches on the bottom of the impacting boat that are attributable to the collision will impart a direction to the impact. In addition to the damage to the impacted boat caused by the impacting boat, there may be evidence of damage or injury resulting from the propeller or bow cleat (tie down). If the impacting boat does not pass over or onto the impacted boat, damage should be to the hull of the impacted boat and to the bow of the impacting boat. The speed and weight of the

FIGURE 9-4   Photo of vaulting boat collision.
(*Source:* Dr. William Chilcott)

impacting boat will contribute to the depth of penetration in these kinds of collisions. There are no standard **depth penetration tables** that can be used based on
make and model of boats as there are for automobiles, but the depth of penetration
can partially explain what happened before, during, and after the collision.

Occasionally the dynamics of a crash can be best understood by reenacting the
crash and documenting the collision and its aftermath.

The collision may result in the destruction of a boat's tachometer and/or
speedometer. When this happens, it is reasonable to conclude that the speed or

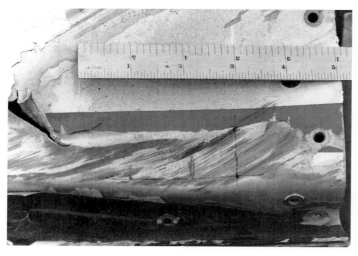

FIGURE 9-5   Photo of the bottom of the vaulting boat.
(*Source:* Dr. William Chilcott)

FIGURE 9-6   Photo of vaulted boat damage.
(*Source:* Dr. William Chilcott)

horsepower shown on in the damaged instrument reflects the speed of the boat at the time of impact. Upon impact the indicator needle of the instrument may slap the back of the gauge and lodge there, or if the needle is flourescent, the impact of the collision may leave a flourescent image on the back of the speedometer cover glass. That imprint can be viewed under ultraviolet light as in Figure 9-7.

Occupants will secondarily impact with the interior of their boats or be thrown from them. The occupant of a boat involved in a collision will be thrown in the direction opposite to the collision impact. Often these **secondary impacts** leave evidence of the change in speed during the collision. Steering wheels that are misshapen or broken and windshields that are cracked are evidence of passenger impact and can be used to ascertain speed. A similar type of steering wheel or windshield can be subjected to laboratory testing, applying force sufficient to duplicate the damage on the original item and giving some indication of the velocity necessary to create the deformation.

FIGURE 9-7   Photo of ultraviolet speedometer.
(*Source:* Dr. William Chilcott)

Propeller Injuries

Often in boating accidents, an occupant may be thrown from the boat. If the occupant is the only person on board, the vessel may begin to circle at high speed, heading back to the point at which the occupant was lost. Most boats today are equipped with safety mechanisms that turn the engine off should the driver be thrown from the boat, but many boaters fail to use this mechanism, making them subject to the high-speed turning boat.

It is not uncommon for boats to run over swimmers, snorkelers, divers, waterskiers, or other boats. In instances when injury or death arises from the incident, some conclusions may be drawn from the propeller cuts on the body. Different types of boat engines impart unique characteristics to propeller cuts. Deformities in the propeller may also be evident in the injuries produced by the propeller. In investigations involving propeller injuries or death, it is important to obtain the motor and propeller from the boat. An examination of the propeller may immediately rule out a particular boat, or tests may have to be done to determine whether the propeller in question caused the injuries or death being investigated.

The character of the wound may suggest a number of things:

- Straight cuts occur when a propeller is performing at maximum efficiency (moving rapidly in or through the water). The cuts are fairly equidistant in spacing, with substantial distance between cuts.
- Curved cuts occur when a propeller is performing at less than its maximum efficiency (moving slowly in or through the water). The slow movement of the propeller cuts and pushes tissue backward.
- Cuts close together generally indicate a propeller in reverse gear. The backward motion of the vessel is substantially reduced by gear ratios, thereby depositing numerous cuts very close to each other.

Much of what needs to be known about propeller cuts can be discovered by experimentation with limb prosthetic devices or anatomically correct dummies.

Propellers themselves can provide information about a crash, property damage, human injury, and death. A thorough examination of the propeller will reveal that it has come into contact with something. The bends and dents may be a product of general use, but serious distortion prevents the propeller from operating without shaking the boat apart. Serious distortion is a product of contact with something hard enough to damage the propeller. In cases of injury and death, it may be necessary to remove the propeller from the motor and package it so as to preserve it for laboratory examination. A gross examination of a propeller will reveal that it has been impacted, but a microscopic examination may reveal the source of the impact. Blood, tissue, hair, and fiber may cling to the propeller. Suspect boats should have propellers packaged in such a fashion as to avoid the loss or damage of trace evidence.

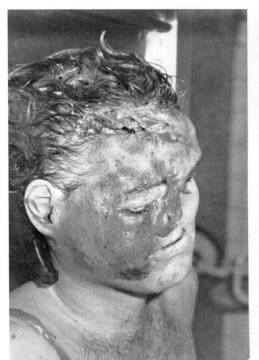
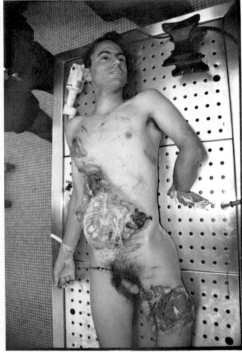
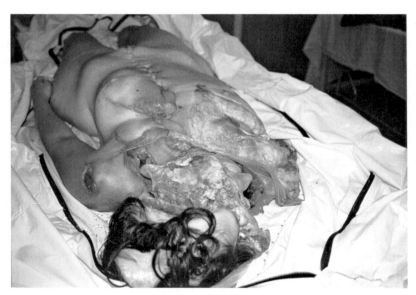

FIGURE 9-8   Photos of propeller injuries.
(*Source:* Dr. William Chilcott)

Boat data

Operator's name _____

Address _____

Owner's name _____

Address _____

Rented or owned _____

Age of operator _____

Number of persons in boat _____

Type of boat

Motorboat _____

Personal watercraft _____

Sailboat _____

Raft _____

Canoe _____

Other (specify) _____

Hull material

Wood _____

Aluminum _____

Steel _____

Fiberglass _____

Boat number _____

Boat name _____

Boat manufacturer _____

Boat model _____

Mfr. hull identification number _____

Propulsion

Outboard _____

Inboard _____

Sail _____

Paddle _____

Boat measurements

Length _____

Width abeam _____

Depth (transom to keel) _____

Year built _____

Number of engines _____

Make _____

Horsepower _____

Other (specify) _____

Accident data

Date _____

Time _____

Name of waterway _____

Location (charted and measured) _____

City, county, state _____

Weather conditions _____

Wind

Speed _____

Direction _____

Activity

Towing _____

Cruising _____

Racing _____

Rowing _____

Fishing _____

Scuba diving, swimming, etc. _____

Waterskiing _____

Other (specify) _____

FIGURE 9-9 Boat accident report.

(*Source:* Dr. William Chilcott)

continues

Water conditions _____   Narrative

Visibility _____   Accident causation

Type of accident   Alcohol/drug use _____

  Sinking _____   Right of way _____

  Capsizing _____   Speed _____

  Collision with fixed object _____   Inattention _____

  Collision with floating object _____   Other (specify) _____

  Collision with vessel _____   Operator culpability _____

  Fire or explosion _____   What happened _____

  Other (specify) _____   How it happened _____

                                                   Why it happened _____

FIGURE 9-9   Boat accident report. (*continued*)

FIRE

Fire is a natural danger of using gasoline to power a boat. During the process of taking on fuel or storing it, fuel vapor will settle to the lowest part of the boat. Many boats have bilge blowers that cleanse the fuel vapor from the air prior to starting the boat. We often forget how volatile gasoline is, and that can lead to fires and explosions. The problem in investigating fires is that often most of the boat and virtually all of the evidence have been consumed. In addition to the consumption of evidence, the boat may sink. One of the most important parts of investigating a boat fire is to determine what role arson may have played in it. Boats are susceptible to fires set for the purpose of defrauding an insurance company. **Boat arson** is one way of "unloading" a boat that has lost its appeal, has lost its resale value, or taxes the financial resources of the owner.

Arson

A fuel will interact with oxygen to produce a flame only when the fuel is in a gaseous state. This is true if the fuel feeding the flame is wood, paper, cloth, plastic, or gasoline. In the case of a liquid fuel, the temperature must be high enough to vaporize the fuel. The vapor that forms burns when it mixes with oxygen. The flash point is the lowest temperature at which a liquid gives off sufficient vapor to form a mixture with air that will support combustion. Once the flash point is reached, the fuel can be ignited by some outside source of high temperature. The ignition temperature is always higher than the flash point. With a solid fuel, the process of generating vapor is more complex. Solid fuel will burn only when it is exposed to heat that is great enough to break down the solid into a gaseous product. The chemical decomposition is called pyrolysis. Gaseous fuel and air will only burn if their composition (the fuel-air mix) lies within certain limits. If the proportion of fuel to air is too low or too high (as in a flooded auto carburetor), combustion will not occur. The mix range within which air and fuel will support combustion is called the flammable range. There are instances in which a fuel can burn without a flame. A burning cigarette and red-hot charcoal are examples of glowing combustion or smoldering. Combustion takes place on the surface of a solid fuel in the absence of heat high enough to break down the fuel into a gaseous product (pyrolyze the fuel). This same phenomenon can be seen in wood fires once all the gases have been expended; the wood continues to smolder until the entire carbonaceous residue has been consumed (Saferstein 1995).

Fires and explosions provide little information upon which an investigation can proceed. What information is available is generally circumstantial. Arson and bombings are committed with some degree of planning, and the arsonist or bomber is usually far from the scene when the crime is discovered and responded to. The extensive destruction at the scene renders most evidence unidentifiable or unusable. The laboratory can provide only limited assistance in identifying accelerants that may have been deployed or in reconstructing igniting or **detonating devices.** Although forensic scientists may be able to identify minute amounts of an accelerant in the materials provided for examination, there is no scientific test that will determine whether a particular arsonist used the accelerant, unless a suspect is taken into custody with evidence of the accelerant on his or her clothing or in a container. The cause of a fire may be readily apparent or require extensive investigation. Fires may be caused by accident or intent. One way of proving intent is by ruling out accidental causes of the fire. A final determination must take into consideration numerous factors and requires a complete and meticulous investigation. That type of investigation can be conducted only by properly trained and experienced investigators. Normally, an ordinary match will ignite fuels. However, other igniters must be considered; electrical discharges, sparks, and chemicals may provide temperatures in excess of the ignition point of most fuels.

There are two types of evidence available to the investigator:

1. **Incendiary evidence,** which includes crime scene debris, witness statements, observed burning characteristics, and an absence of evidence of accidental causation

2. Direct evidence that links the arsonist to the fire, such as eyewitness identification or motive

Incendiary Evidence

Fires tend to move upward, and, therefore, the point of origin is often the lowest point that shows intense burn characteristics. Igniter containers may be left at or near the scene. Most arson fires (except those set by vandals) are started with the use of an igniter other than a simple match. An ignition device allows the arsonist to exit the area safely and may provide ample time to secure an alibi for the time the fire was set. Igniters can be very complex or deceptively simple. The more complex the igniting device, the more likely unburned remains will exist.

Once evidence of arson has been discovered, the material should be placed in an airtight container. In order for the laboratory to run tests, three things are necessary:

1. An uncontaminated sample
2. A sufficient sample
3. A background sample (control)

Contamination is a by-product of fire and the extinguishing of the fire. Additional contamination resulting from mishandling is what must be avoided. Improper containers made of plastic or polyethylene will react with hydrocarbons and may result in the destruction of hydrocarbon vapors. When gathering material for collection, the investigator should try to preserve sizable specimens using airtight, unused paint cans as containers. The point of origin should produce a gallon of porous material, soot, and debris and any other substances thought to contain accelerant residue. It is important that all materials suspected of containing volatile liquids be accompanied by a thorough sampling of similar but relatively clean control specimens from an area of the fire in which accelerants are thought to have been absent. The laboratory scientists will check the control materials to ensure that they are free of flammable residues, thereby removing cleaning solvents or other household hydrocarbons as possible sources of contamination. Any empty or partially filled containers that may contain flammable substances should be collected and placed in sealed containers. Because a container is empty does not mean there are no traces of the contents left.

The search for igniters should begin once the point of origin has been discovered. If a match was used, the fire will likely have consumed it, but this is not always the case. Something as insignificant as a match, ammunition, firearm, a Molotov cocktail (a bottle of gasoline with a gasoline-soaked rag as a wick), a cigarette, or a matchbook may be the key to the investigation. The match or cigarette may come from a matchbook or a pack of cigarettes found on a suspect (a rare event but not unknown). The match can be identified as coming from a particular matchbook through comparison microscopy. The broken glass of a Molotov cocktail may bear fingerprints, or its wick may be matched to the cloth from which it was torn. If a suspect is in custody, his or her clothing should be examined for accelerants, and each article of clothing should be placed in a separate airtight container (Saferstein 1995).

For the investigator, the main task in boat fires is the same as in land fires: to determine if a fire or an explosion was incendiary (arson) or accidental. To aid in the investigation, dive team members examining a submerged burned boat must have some idea of what type of incendiary evidence to look for. If the hull is intact, they can do a visual examination aimed at locating portions of the vessel that are charred and portions that are left unscathed. A detailed photographic log should be made, visibility permitting, describing burn characteristics and any evidence discovered. Each piece of evidence to be recovered should be photographed in its original place and condition, visibility permitting. The scene sketch should show the location of each piece of evidence within the search site.

Fires burn in boats in the same fashion that they do in buildings: from the ignition point upward. The probable point of origin will most likely be located close to the lowest point that shows the most intense burn characteristics. The surface of charred wood exhibits a pattern of crevices similar in appearance to the skin of an alligator. The probable point of origin is in the area where the smallest pieces in the alligator pattern and the deepest charring are found. An ice pick pushed into the charred area may prove helpful in measuring the depth of charring. It is in this area that physical evidence of criminal design is most likely to be discovered, and wood samples should be taken from this area for laboratory examination for hydrocarbons (accelerants). Nothing should be touched or moved before measurements and photographs have been taken and sketches made. The presence of hydrocarbon containers should be noted. In most arsons an incendiary or detonation device of some type is employed to allow the arsonist to depart the scene and possibly establish an alibi. Such devices may be as complex as a remote-control detonator or as simple as a candle bedded in gasoline. Remnants of delay devices may be discovered near the point of origin. In the case of explosions, a larger area should be searched with the goal of discovering incendiary or detonation devices or their remains. Unburned fabric may retain measurable amounts of hydrocarbons. If the interior of the boat was splashed with diesel fuel, kerosene, or gasoline, any unburned, porous material may retain traces of the accelerant. If streamers were used to aid in acceleration, unburned remains may be found. Cloth generally does not completely burn and, if used as a streamer, may still retain accelerant traces. Hydrocarbons dissipate more slowly in water. It is imperative that any pieces of evidence discovered underwater, which may have hydrocarbon traces, be packaged in water in watertight containers for delivery to the laboratory.

Case Study

Dr. William Chilcott, a boat accident reconstructionist living in Sweetgrass, California, was involved in an investigation in Alaska that involved the death of a child and his mother in a boat fire. The father reported an accidental fire that began at the engines, with smoke from the engine area so thick as to be impenetrable. He reported high seas that prevented him from assisting his family. During the course of the investigation by local police, the father stated that he had had time to retrieve an exposure suit and two dogs and escape into a twenty-four-foot twin-engine boat he was towing as a safety boat. He motored to shore as the boat burned to the waterline. He went to his accountant's home, which was close by, to report the accident.

A check on the insurance of the boat revealed that the boat had been heavily insured and was described as a fifty-foot Hatteras. The Coast Guard arrived on the scene to film the last few minutes of the burning prior to the boat's sinking. Chilcott was called in as an expert witness to examine the film footage. He first determined that the location of the swim hatch was on the wrong side of the boat to be a Hatteras and that the two burned spots on the swim step flew in the face of the father's testimony that the seas were heavy. If seas had been heavy, in Chilcott's opinion, the steps should not have burned. Based on the misrepresentation to the insurance company of the make of the boat, its being heavily insured, and the burns on the swim step, it was Chilcott's opinion that the boat was set on fire and that the deaths may have been a homicide. He recognized his responsibility to contact the FBI to report a homicide on international waterways.

The FBI, U.S. Navy, and the state of Alaska assisted in the recovery of the boat. The Coast Guard was able to locate the point at which the sinking took place, and the Navy, using submersibles, found the sunken boat, which was a forty-eight-foot Meridian, not a fifty-foot Hatteras as described and insured. Using barges and cranes, the boat was rigged around the engines to be lifted to the surface. However, bottom suction prevented the lifting of the boat, and the cranes pulled the two motors free. The motors were recovered and examined. A nine-millimeter bullet casing was found in the motor as well as a melted metal plate on the top of the motor. The bottoms of the engines were unscathed, contradicting the father's statement that the fire had started at the engines. Based on the investigation's findings, the father was charged with murder and arson.

Prior to trial the man was involved in a high-speed collision and rendered a quadriplegic. The state of Alaska, having no facilities for handling the medical needs of a quadriplegic, relegated him to house arrest with an ankle-monitoring device. Prior to trial his body was discovered, still in his wheelchair, in five feet of water at the end of the pier at his home.

Chilcott's expertise and help allowed the FBI and the state of Alaska to complete an investigation into the deaths of the woman and child. It was Chilcott's understanding of fire, burning dynamics, and arson that allowed the investigation to progress to a successful conclusion.

Insurance companies are anxious to cooperate with arson investigations, especially in those instances where the vessel was insured. The American Insurance Association in New York City has established a twenty-four-hour Property Insurance Loss Reporting System. This is a computerized system designed to detect patterns of arson and insurance fraud nationwide. Arsonists who change geographical location or insurance companies may be apprehended with the assistance of the Property Insurance Loss Reporting System.

On pages 187–188 is an **arson checklist** of data that should be included in the report of a suspected arson or detonation.

The major objective of every search and investigation is the recovery of evidence that will help resolve questions regarding the incident. Often special evidence technicians are available to assist in evidence collection in land investigations. Generally, evidence technicians, arson investigators, explosive specialists, forensic scientists, criminalists, and forensic investigators have yet to get their feet wet. It is, therefore, incumbent upon the underwater investigator to be aware of possible evidence sites in order to preserve available evidence for laboratory examination.

- General data
    1. Owner's name
    2. Insurer's name
    3. Date and time of fire
    4. Last user's name
    5. Time and date of last use
- Owner data
    1. Financial condition of owner
    2. Prior loss history
    3. Prior criminal history
    4. Name of the insured
    5. Name of the insurer
    6. Claims history
    7. Other boat ownership, past and present
    8. Other insurers, past and present
    9. Owner vessel
    10. Property distribution (divorce or partner dissolution)
- Vessel data
    1. Vessel condition prior to fire
    2. Value of the property
    3. Insured value of the property
    4. Payment history on boat mortgage
    5. Vessel furnishings (description of furnishings will be important in the chemical analysis of evidence)
    6. Condition and location of electrical wiring prior to fire
    7. Condition and location of diesel and gas lines prior to fire
    8. Condition and location of propane lines to galley stoves prior to fire
    9. Storage of flammable fluids (based on information provided by the owner)
    10. Types of fuels used
    11. Presence of ignition keys

FIGURE 9-10 Arson checklist.

(*Source:* R. F. Becker)

- Fire assessment
  1. Name of party reporting the fire
  2. Name of party discovering the fire
  3. Time interval between discovery and reporting
  4. Names of witnesses to the fire
  5. Witnesses to explosion (if any)
  6. Speed of travel of the fire
  7. Direction of spread of the fire
  8. Location of the vessel when the fire was reported
- Fire investigation
  1. Search site
  2. Recovery site
  3. Point of origin of the fire
  4. Evidence of accelerants
  5. Evidence of incendiary devices
  6. Evidence of explosive devices
  7. Evidence of igniters or detonators
  8. Burn characteristics (describe)
  9. Recovered evidence, its location, and manner of packaging
  10. Valuable items missing (e.g., telemetry system, television, stereo, speakers, backup engine, dinghy)
  11. Insured's explanation of fire (the explanation should be consistent with the examination of the remains, specifically as to cause of fire, point of origin, type of smoke, and speed and direction of spread)

FIGURE 9-10   Arson checklist. (*continued*)

VESSEL EXPLOSIONS

The steps employed in the investigation of an explosion are generally the same as for arson, but there are several additional considerations. The chances of finding a large amount of trace evidence are remote. Like fire, an explosion is the product of combustion accompanied by the creation of gases and heat. It is the sudden buildup of expanding gas pressure at the point of detonation that produces the disruption of the explosion. Chemical explosions can be classified on the basis of the velocity of energy waves transmitted upon detonation.

Low-order explosives involve a relatively slow rate of conversion to a gaseous state. The energy wave generated travels at a speed of less than 1,000 meters per second. The most widely used explosives in the low-order group are black powder and smokeless powder. Low-order explosives can be ignited by heat and are usually ignited with a lit fuse.

High-order explosives change rapidly to a gaseous state upon ignition. The energy wave created travels at a rate between 1,000 and 9,000 meters per second. Dynamite is the most common high-order explosive, although composition C-4 (made of RDX, the most popular and powerful of the military explosives) is also used.

Unlike low-order explosives, an initiating device must detonate high-order explosives. The most common initiator is a blasting cap. However, the ignition switch on a boat can be used to provide the spark necessary to detonate high-order explosives.

The search should focus on locating the site of the device and identifying the type of explosive used. The point of detonation will often leave a gaping hole surrounded by scorching. The type of explosive used may be determined by inspecting the residue at the scene. Wood, metal, and fiberglass samples surrounding the detonation point should have sufficient residue to allow identification of the explosive. The entire area must be systematically searched to recover any trace of a detonating mechanism. Particles of explosives will be embedded in the pipe cap or threads of a pipe bomb. All materials gathered from the site of an explosion must be packaged in separate containers and be labeled with all pertinent information. The type of search used and the degree of particularity for what is sought may be dependent upon depth, current, visibility, temperature, and visibility. The decision to search at all must be predicated on those same considerations.

Many manufacturers of dynamite include magnetic microtaggants in each stick. These fluorescent, color-coded, multilayered particles identify the residue as dynamite and indicate the source of manufacture. The color should make the microtaggants visible to ultraviolet light, and their magnetism should make them susceptible to a magnet. Electric shunts from blasting caps, clock mechanisms, batteries, and pieces of wrapper may survive the explosion and concomitant fire. In those instances where humans have been the victims of a vessel explosion, their remains should be bagged. Their clothing should not be removed.

LIGHT FILAMENTS

Lighting can be an important factor in determining the cause of a boating accident. The same understanding of lightbulb filaments that is employed in automobile accident reconstruction can be helpful in determining if the colliding boats were rigged with the appropriate array of lights and, during nighttime boating, if those lights were on. Considering the immense areas of operation available to boats, it is absolutely imperative at night that boats be visible to other boaters. When the underwater investigator is gathering evidence, lights, bulbs, and filaments should be considered. The fact that the light switch is on or off is not always indicative of whether the lights were on at the time of the collision. During impact or recovery, debris or persons thrown about the boat will likely strike the light switch. The bulbs from the lights themselves can often reveal whether the lights were on when the accident occurred. A retrieval of the lightbulbs may prove to be useful as the investigation progresses (Becker 1995).

As we saw in Chapter Eight on automobile recoveries, filaments break in one highly characteristic fashion when warm and in a different fashion when cold. That understanding should apply to boat accidents and recoveries as well. Additionally, if **light filaments** don't break, they may bend in the opposite direction of the impact, providing information on direction of travel and direction of impact.

It should be remembered that all items recovered from a boat that are wet, other than lights and bodies, must be completely immersed in the medium from which they were retrieved. The laboratory will dry any wet materials before subjecting them to laboratory testing.

REVIEW QUESTIONS

1. What restrictions exist in your community on the use of personal watercraft (such as a Jet Ski)?
2. In your opinion, what restrictions should exist for the use of personal watercraft?
3. What are COLREGS? What do they have to do with boat accidents?
4. What is vaulting in a boating accident?
5. What evidence might there be of vaulting in a boat accident?
6. What are depth penetration tables, and how do they assist in boat accident investigations?
7. What is a secondary impact in regard to a boat collision?
8. What evidence might there be of a secondary impact in a boat collision?
9. What types of incendiary evidence might be available in a boat arson?
10. What would you include in a boat accident report?
11. What would you include in an arson checklist?
12. What information might boat light filaments provide the investigator?

REFERENCES

BECKER, R. F. 1995. *The underwater crime scene: Underwater crime investigative techniques.* Springfield, IL: Charles C. Thomas.

HICKMAN, R. S., and M. M. SAMPSEL. 2002. *Boat accident reconstruction and litigation,* 2nd ed. Tucson: Lawyers & Judges Publishing Company, Inc.

SAFERSTEIN, R. 1995. *Criminalistics: An introduction to forensic science.* Englewood Cliffs, NJ: Prentice Hall.

Chapter 10

Equipping the Team

NEW WORDS AND CONCEPTS

wet suit	search lines
basic recreational package	tethered diver
dry suit	BCD
buoyancy	airlifting
full-face mask	default dress
positive pressure	alternative air supply
helmet with neck dam	surface air consumption rate
communication system	dry suit seals
demand full-face mask	tether harness
gill	weight harness

LEARNING OBJECTIVES

- Describe public safety diving equipment
- Discuss equipment acquisition
- Discuss equipment training

INTRODUCTION

Often when we talk about equipping a public safety dive team we find the subject of a "basic equipment list" to be bit more controversial than we might otherwise think. In discussions with various teams in an effort to determine what equipment should be considered to be basic, we have discovered a lack of unanimity in such lists. The author has found that perhaps the question might be more easily addressed if it were first determined what it is a particular public safety dive team does. As discussed in prior chapters, there appears to be a dichotomy in function among public safety dive teams, and you should recall that this dichotomy is accompanied by certain political considerations based upon whether a dive team has search, rescue, or search and rescue responsibility. We can reduce the complexity of this issue by confining our study to police recovery (underwater investigation) operations. It should be relatively easy to see that the basic equipment list for a rescue team would be different from that for a recovery team. Since the teams of interest to us are evidence recovery teams, it would seem a simple process to poll various agencies and various teams for equipment lists. Again, however, this process does not get us what we want because various teams have different functions and/or limitations upon which the purchase of team equipment is based. It would seem that it is best to determine what it is the team intends to do and where it intends to do it. All dive recovery teams recover submerged evidence. Standard operation and procedures manuals should state under what conditions recoveries should be made. Will the team:

- Dive deep?
- Be surface-supplied?
- Dive in highly contaminated environments?
- Airlift large evidentiary items to the surface?
- Be shore-based and/or platform (boat)-based?
- Dive at night?
- Dive in fast-moving water?
- Dive in confined spaces?
- Dive in cold water?
- Dive under ice?
- Perform hull searches?
- Provide a combat function?

The answers to these questions will allow standards and procedures to be developed for each type of diver contingency, and those standards will dictate what type of equipment a team should have.

Equipment issues are inseparable from training issues. Training issues are inseparable from practice. In real estate, the three most important things to know about a piece of property are location, location, and location. In underwater investigation, the three most important things to know about recovery operations and equipment are practice, practice, and practice. Initial training wears thin quickly. The only way to assure that training sticks is to practice what has been learned in training.

Let us presume that a dive team (special response team, underwater investigation team, etc.) dedicated to recovery diving with no responsibility for rescue operations is attempting to equip itself. Presuming further that they have completed all preliminary training set out in the SOP manual, are physically and psychologically fit, and have a thorough understanding of theory and the underwater investigator's function, we can begin to consider equipment. That consideration should begin with the questions "What is it the team is going to do?" and, by inference, "What is it the team is not going to do?"

All underwater investigation teams investigate underwater. It is axiomatic, then, that what is needed to survive in an aquatic environment should top the list. For recreational scuba divers, the basic list is fairly simple:

- Face mask
- Snorkel
- Fins
- **Wet suit**
- Weights and belt
- Buoyancy compensator
- Regulators
- Gauges
- Gas cylinders

FIGURE 10-1   Basic recreational package.
(*Source:* R. F. Becker)

Many teams historically began with the **basic recreational package,** which is understandable in light of the fact that most dive teams had their genesis among those within the agency who were recreational divers. Our collective understanding of the underwater recovery business was woefully inadequate, but it was the place from which we began. Recreational divers with recreational equipment were our first underwater recovery teams. Northern teams had greater demands on them than did the teams in the South. The teams in the North were often called upon to perform recoveries in very cold water and, in some instances, under ice. Along with specialized equipment came the training necessary to perform cold-water and under-ice operations. Much of what they learned was through trial and error. Divers were injured and killed, but the teams learned. They passed on their experiences and training to other teams, and regional training programs began sprouting up. It was the unique demands of winter diving that began to affect the way we viewed Northern recovery dive teams and the equipment and training they received. The recreational dive gear used in the Caribbean and warm Southern waters was inadequate for Northern diving. New regulators had to be developed that wouldn't freeze in the open position and "free flow." Dive suits that could withstand immersion in close-to-freezing water had to be developed, and protocols had to be written, learned, and practiced for entering a world that did not give direct exit overhead. Each of these concerns was answered by manufacturers and divers. The manufacturers sought input from divers who worked in extreme environments in an effort to provide a line of equipment unique to those extreme environments. Divers began to recognize the special considerations of diving safely in those environments.

As recovery teams became wiser about the risks associated with underwater investigations, they looked to specialized dive operations for equipment ideas. They began to look to the commercial and military dive communities to see how they operated in the underwater world. Teams using recreational equipment became aware of the array of specialized equipment that was available to the military and commercial divers with an eye toward its applicability to underwater investigation. Equipment started to be upgraded in connection with the information disseminated through various educational forums describing risks associated with public safety diving. As information became more available to those providing dive recovery services, questions were raised as to the suitability of recreational scuba equipment for the underwater recovery operation. Educational programs recognizing risks unique to underwater investigations began to cull from Northern diver equipment, military equipment, and commercial diver equipment bits and pieces of gear that would reduce risks inherent in the use of recreational scuba equipment in dive recovery operations.

In Chapter Three we discussed contaminated water and the fact that all surface water in the United States is contaminated to some degree (i.e., nonpotable). There are operations wherein the contamination of the water is not an issue. Oceans and lakes generally do not pose a problem of contamination. The recreational wet suit can be used in some of the environments in which underwater investigations occur, but its general applicability has diminished over time. The standard dress for underwater investigators should be the **dry suit.** Even in water of 80°F, body temperature is slowly diminished as the body adjusts to the ambient temperature. Remember that a single degree loss in core body temperature may have severe repercussions. It should be evident that extended dive times (twenty-five minutes), even in temperate or tropical waters, can affect core temperature. One should also keep in mind that divers may be placed back in the lineup depending on how many divers have made it to the scene. We all know there are few things as uncomfortable as putting on a soggy wet suit. To address the need for warmth in dive dress, the dry suit is without question the option of choice. In underwater operations, even a dry suit may be inadequate to the task, and a suit that circulates surface-supplied warm water may be necessary. Whatever the case, the recreational wet suit has limited use in the world of the professional diver and the underwater investigator.

Wet suits keep a diver warm by trapping water between the body and the material of the suit, allowing the water to be warmed by body heat. With a wet suit, a hood is an integral part of the dress; without it, body heat loss is accelerated through the head. The thicker the wet suit, the greater the insulation value. The wet suit is depressed as depth increases, affording less insulating warmth than at the surface. Also, as a diver increases depth, water temperature decreases and pressure increases. It would seem that the use of wet suits is limited to relatively shallow, warm-water diving.

The wet suit has drawbacks as a choice of diver dress in its inability to provide sufficient warmth and to protect the diver from contaminated water that may contain chemicals that break down the neoprene of the wet suit to the point of rendering it useless. In body recoveries, the wet suit may absorb body fluids and tissues from corpses, imparting a unique texture and odor to the wet suit (Hendrick, Zaferes, and Nelson 2000, 68).

Most knowledgeable agencies fielding underwater investigation teams have moved away from wet suits as their default dive dress and have adopted dry suits. If a team is just starting, has not evolved through the recreational equipment phase of development, and has the budget to afford standard dive dress for all dive personnel and the concomitant training associated with its use, it is to the dry suit that they should turn. At the time of this writing, professional dry suits cost in the vicinity of $2,000 per suit along with some incidental costs associated with ankle weights and boot-accommodating fins. The ankle weights are needed in addition to the weights used to defeat positive **buoyancy** and are necessary to prevent the air in the dry suit that provides insulation, buoyancy, and operating room from ending up in the boots and inverting the diver. It may be humorous to watch a dry-suited diver flounder around on the surface in an inverted position, but it reflects poor training and leads to potentially dangerous consequences. Once a diver is inverted, it is almost impossible to correct the position without assistance. The good news is that your head is underwater and you won't hear the tenders laughing.

Another source of amusement for tenders is to watch divers suit up in a dry suit, gear up, and enter the water without first "burping" the collar of the suit. That makes the diver look much like the Pillsbury Doughboy. The air trapped in the dry suit during dressing must be released prior to entering the water. By squatting and opening the tightly fitting neck seals, air is released from the suit, making descent possible.

DIVE EQUIPMENT

Dry Suits

A dry suit can enshroud the diver in a material that is almost impervious to most contaminants. The neck and wrist seals keep air in and water out. The dry suits of choice have built-in booties, so there are no ankle seals. Inside the suit, the diver is surrounded with warm air that stays dry. Depending on the temperature of the water, the diver can elect to wear insulated undergarments. Those undergarments vary from thin to thick, depending on the need for additional insulation.

A number of dry suits are being marketed that are to be worn without the use of insulated undergarments. These are called shell dry suits. They provide little insulation but great protection and can be used in warmer water.

The air in the dry suit performs three functions:

1. Insulation and heat
2. Room to move comfortably
3. Prevents dry suit squeeze (the water pressing on the material and pushing it into the joints, which is very uncomfortable)

The air in a dry suit should be regulated based on these three considerations, not on buoyancy. Even with a dry suit that allows air to be admitted into the interior, that function should not be used to regulate buoyancy. The dry-suited diver should wear a buoyancy control device and use that to regulate buoyancy. If a diver were to depend on the inflator of the dry suit to admit air for buoyancy, should the dry suit be breached, the suit might not be able to contain enough air to offset the water that has been taken on.

Many dry suits come with a hood. Hoods help reduce the rate of body heat loss through the head but are primarily used to assure that the diver is insulated from any contaminants in the water. Some dry suits have built-in hoods that fit tightly around the head, leaving only the face open to the water. This would allow the diver to wear a **full-face mask** and be further insulated from the water in which he or she is immersed from head to toe. It should be noted that the degree of contamination of the water in which the team is to dive will determine the appropriate dress for the dive. Hoods and full-face masks may be used in lightly contaminated water, such as water containing light oil and gas emissions from an auto or recreational watercraft, but would be completely unacceptable for diving in seriously contaminated water. The full-face mask, even though it maintains **positive pressure** inside the mask (no demand regulator but a constant stream of air from the tank), may still leak. If it is necessary to protect the diver from all exposure to the water, then dive helmets are the option. Some water can be so corrosive that the rubber on the helmet and the material on the dry suit may be affected. Before diving in seriously contaminated water, it is important to determine the type and amount of contaminants present, and that cannot be done by simply looking at the water. Hunter's dry suits and Trelleborg's Viking dry suits have been tested to determine what their suits can withstand while still protecting the diver. Their Web sites (www.hunter-diving.com and www.trelleborg.com) keep this information available and updated. If the team is diving with a particular brand and type (e.g., rubber or laminate) of suit, it is the diver's and the team's responsibility to assure that they know the limitations of the suit and any headgear to be used.

In order to use a dry suit in contaminated water, there must be an accompanying full-face mask or **helmet with neck dam** (neck seal), hood, and sleeve-sealed gloves. The diver must be completely insulated from the contaminated water. When properly worn, the dry suit provides the diver a greater diversity of environments in which to operate, including cold water or contaminated water. It is easy to don and rolls up once dried to be carried in a duffel bag.

FIGURE 10-2   Vulcanized rubber suit and hood.

(*Source:* Hunter Diving)

A dry suit may be made of neoprene, trilaminate, or vulcanized rubber. Neoprene provides excellent insulation and is used mostly in the North. Neoprene has less resistance to waterborne hazardous materials, and it is for this reason that most agencies choose the vulcanized or trilaminated dry suit. Whatever dry suit is used, it should not be employed in the water until appropriate training has been provided. Upon receipt of a new piece of equipment, everyone is excited about getting it into the water. It is dangerous to presume that the device can be figured out as it is being used. Computers have conditioned us to avoid manuals at all costs and to stumble through on our own. Video games have reinforced that notion, especially after we have played a few games and realize that all games are just a variation on a theme as far as the controllers are concerned. That is not so with diving equipment. Some equipment is supplied with supporting information; generally that information deals with maintenance of the product. Use of the product is presumed to be the responsibility of the end user. There are warnings on all dive equipment to the effect that the equipment in question should be used only by qualified users, and not without proper training. We read the word *qualified* and think *certified* and presume that refers to basic recreational certification, and come to the conclusion that we are ready to use the equipment. *Qualified* means *trained*—trained specifically in the use of dry suits. We spend thousands of dollars equipping a dive team and forget to allocate anything in the budget for the training to use the equipment. It would be wiser not to have the equipment than to employ it without first receiving training in its use.

Dry suits require a bit more maintenance than do wet suits. There are seals and zippers that must be attended to in order to ensure the longevity of the suit. The seals can be difficult to pull over hands and head (some people's voices rise an octave because of the pressure the neck seal places on the throat), and cornstarch may help. Talcum powder has too many additives for odor and texture that may have a chemical effect on the rubber, causing dry rot. There are numerous preparations for keeping zippers zipping. Most are costly and tend to be sticky, defeating the ultimate purpose for their use. Paraffin drawn across the zipper when it is in the closed position facilitates opening and closing of the zipper. Storing a dry suit is usually accomplished by drying it, powdering the seals, waxing the zippers, and placing it in a duffel. The dry suit can absorb moisture from sweating and can develop an odor; this can be avoided by hanging the dry suit by the boot heels using commercially made hangers. The undergarments should be laundered after each use. Despite the temperature of the water, the working diver is going to sweat. In that regard, it may be that the best place for a suited diver who is a primary or 90 percent backup diver is in the water, especially on hot days. Overheating is a genuine concern for all suited divers, but more so for those in dry suits.

Dive Helmets

The full-face mask has found a niche in the world of underwater investigation. Most teams aspire to equip their members with full-face masks and the communication equipment with which many of them operate.

FIGURE 10-3   Kirby Morgan EXO
full-face mask.

(*Source:* Kirby Morgan Dive Systems, Inc.)

Use of a full-face mask or diving helmet with a dry suit allows divers to be deployed in the most severe of dive situations. Full-face masks allow for a **communication system** to be employed. There is a transceiver built into some brands of full-face mask that allows voice communication between divers and, when connected to a topside communication console, allows the dive team supervisor and other authorized team members to monitor communications between divers and to communicate with divers. The helmets currently used by dive teams have no built-in transceivers but have the necessary electrical connections to allow the dive helmet to be hardwired to the same topside communication system. For surface-supplied operations, air supplied to divers from the surface must be monitored. Some manufacturers make a surface module that combines a communication system with a surface air supply monitor.

FIGURE 10-4   Communication console.

(*Source:* R. F. Becker.)

The problem with diving helmets in the underwater investigation business is that they are heavy. The diving helmet is a product of commercial dive operations and has been adopted by many recovery teams to be used in situations different from the original design intent. Most commercial work is done with the diver standing upright and the helmet balanced on the shoulders. In underwater investigations the diver usually lies horizontal, parallel to the bottom. The helmet must be held up with the strength of the neck muscles. This is very tiring for the diver. Although the dive helmet has great applicability, it is not the first choice for dive operations. In most instances it is reserved for diving in seriously contaminated water, leaving the full-face mask with communication capabilities as the default choice. Full-face masks come in two general varieties:

1. Demand
2. Constant pressure

The **demand full-face mask** is very much like the demand regulator; it supplies gas (air) only upon demand (inhalation). The constant-pressure full-face mask provides gas throughout the dive without concern for inhalation. Upon each inhalation, the mask adds more air; in this way, the pressure inside the mask remains constant. Most constant-pressure full-face masks leak a little around the silicon skirt. It is this air loss that some teams attempt to avoid by going to a demand full-face mask. The constant-pressure mask (positive pressure) is the preferred choice. Whatever air leaks is made up for by the fact that the diver can be assured that no water will leak in. This characteristic becomes most significant when diving in contaminated water. Assuring proper fit by adjusting the topmost strap of the mask last will generally reduce air loss. Full-face masks may be equipped with a **gill** (vent) that allows the backup diver to wear the mask without drawing on his or her air supply. The gill is closed prior to descent.

Full-face masks require more maintenance, training, and practice than do recreational dive masks, but they are worth the effort. If a team cannot train regularly with the mask, including practice with out-of-air transitions from mask to pony bottle (a redundant air supply), the best choice is to keep it simple and stay with a conventional dive mask. It is through maintenance and practice that the efficacy of the full-face mask is realized.

Under certain conditions divers may choose to wear a lightweight plastic helmet for head protection along with their usual scuba equipment. Although this text does not address swift-water recoveries, teams that do swift-water work often wear such a helmet. Overhead environments and swift-water operations need additional head protection, and though both are specialized diving activities, it is worth mentioning that in addition to the training necessary to conduct these types of operations, headgear should be a consideration. Cave divers have borrowed equipment from their dry-land spelunker brethren that includes a lightweight plastic helmet that they adapt for recovery purposes. Mounted with a light, it protects the head and frees the hands from having to carry a light. Most underwater investigation takes place without the benefit of lights, but there are exceptions.

Harnesses

A diver performs search patterns with the assistance of a dive tender at the surface end of a **search line.** There is a controversy surrounding the method whereby the search line is attached to the diver. Many teams, fearing diver entanglement, refuse to consider any other method than holding onto the working end of the search line by hand. Many divers tie a loop in the end of the rope and loosely wear it around their wrist. This method reduces the diver's effectiveness by 50 percent in that the hand and arm that are used to maintain the search line cannot be used in the search. A search conducted with a metal detector is very difficult to perform with one hand. A search conducted by hand usually is done with both hands sweeping in opposing directions in front of the searching diver; having the search line fastened to one hand limits the scope of each arm sweep. Should a diver who is not tethered become entangled and drop the search line, there is no way for the backup diver to follow the line to the diver in an effort to render assistance. It is fallacious to presume that a backup diver will be able to follow air bubbles to the distressed diver. Air bubbles can be most difficult to detect in agitated or moving water. Also, if the diver needing assistance is one who is running or has run out of air, bubbles may be of little assistance in locating the diver. The main tool for locating a submerged diver is the search line, which, once dropped, places the diver in greater danger.

In most situations where a diver needs assistance, it is the backup diver (safety diver) who provides this service. The backup diver wears a contingency strap on his or her harness that allows the diver to place a carabiner (latched metal ring) onto the search line and use the line as a road to the troubled diver. The contingency strap has a breakaway function that allows the backup diver to separate from the line upon reaching the troubled diver. A backup diver using a contingency strap to descend to the primary diver has both hands free, allowing the diver to easily equalize pressure, adjust buoyancy, and descend without unnecessary trauma to the search line and, therefore, to the distressed primary diver. The contingency strap, with its quick-release mechanism, allows the backup diver to escape the search line and avoid becoming entangled in whatever the distressed diver may be entangled in or being grabbed in a panicked embrace by the distressed diver. A backup diver should never attach him- or herself to someone or something without having a way to disengage (Hendrick, Zaferes, and Nelson 2000).

As the backup diver approaches the distressed diver, the team's entanglement signals direct the backup diver to the general area of the primary diver's distress. Once disengaged from the contingency strap, the backup diver can then use both hands to free an entangled diver or lend any other assistance that might be required. A team can use a set of distressed-diver communications that might include the following:

- If the diver is in a situation where running low on air is a concern, the signal could be for the distressed diver to take the hand of the backup diver and beat it on his or her chest.
- If the diver is out of air, the signal could be for the distressed diver to take the hand of the backup diver and draw it across his or her throat.

- If the diver is entangled, the distressed diver can take the hand of the backup diver and make a circle, indicating entanglement, and point in the direction of the entanglement.
- Once the situation has been addressed, the backup diver can place a circled thumb and forefinger into the palm of the primary diver, making an OK sign.
- Should it be necessary to surface, the backup diver can place a fist with thumb extended in the hand of the primary diver.

It should be recognized that the level of competence required in emergency situations cannot be acquired on the spot. Training should include diver rescue scenarios. The only rescue business that underwater investigators are involved in is their own.

FIGURE 10-5   Harness with contingency strap.
(*Source:* Lifeguard Systems)

The use of a handheld search line lends to inefficient searches and question-able search integrity. It is the author's opinion that it poses a greater risk to the diver than does tethered diving. However, handheld search lines are a method of under-water searching that has been with us for a long time. The most efficient way of attaching a diver to a search line is by the use of a harness and a carabiner. A **teth-ered diver** is free to use both hands to conduct a search, move across the bottom, handle a metal detector, and deal with any contingencies that are encountered. A har-ness allows a diver to maintain a taut search line, using his or her whole body in opposition to the pull of the tender and any current present, thereby promoting search integrity. It is also easier to feel line tugs through the harness than it is through a handheld search line. In spite of the continued resistance to tethered diving, there are no reported incidents of tethered divers being at greater risk than divers who search without being tethered. Nonetheless, resistance remains to the notion of teth-ered diving. It is the author's belief that tethered diving will become the standard in the industry for all the reasons mentioned, but mostly because divers like having both hands available to them underwater.

A tethered diver is secured to a search line with a carabiner tied to the end of the search line with a figure-eight knot. The carabiner should be of the type that screws closed rather than the type that is pressure-opened, to prevent accidental open-ing of the carabiner and loss of the search line. The tether point should be slightly off center in the front of the harness. Placing the tether point in the center of the harness causes the search line to go between the legs of the diver at each turn (Hendrick, Zaferes, and Nelson 2000). Some divers wrap duct tape over the carabiner lock to assure that it does not accidentally come open as it is rolled across the bottom of the water column.

In an effort to avoid the hip and lower-back fatigue associated with recreational lead-weighted belts, recovery divers are experimenting with harnesses that have a tether point and also house the weights necessary to counteract buoyancy. Instead of the weights being placed on a weight belt, these harnesses allow the weights to be dis-tributed in pockets on the lower edge of the harness, thereby distributing the weights higher and relieving some of the back strain associated with wearing weights on a belt.

Many manufacturers are trying to cash in on the public safety diver boom. Recently there has been more interest directed at public safety diving than ever before. Historically, manufacturers' answer to requests for diving equipment that would meet the needs of the underwater investigator was to color their recreational equipment black, give it a macho name, and declare it fit for public safety diving. Recently, some of the recreational and technical manufacturers have been attempt-ing to create a line of equipment for the public safety diver and market it as such. The endurance of their new equipment is better; the lift capacities of their buoyancy compensators have been increased; and most now carry a line of dry suits and full-face masks. Unfortunately, the trend in recreational and technical buoyancy control devices (**BCDs**) is toward integrated weight systems. BCDs with an integrated weight system have side pockets that empty from the bottom when one activates the "dump pulls." Although the idea to free the back and hips from the trauma of weight

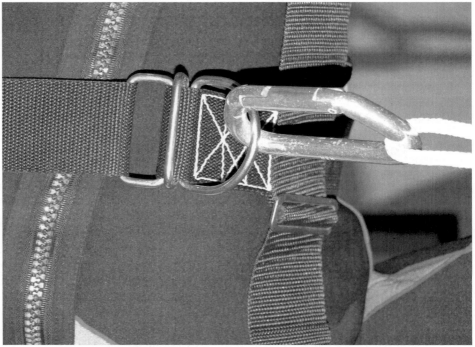

FIGURE 10-6   Tethered diver; tether point.
(*Source:* R. F. Becker)

belts is a good one, the integrated design is fraught with danger. Unless everyone on the team is using the same type of integrated system (the team should be using the same type of equipment, but seldom is), the backup diver attempting to rescue a distressed primary diver may not recognize that the BCD is an integral weight design or may be unable to release the weights because the diver is lying horizontally. Weight dumps work best when the diver is upright in the water. Since most commercial BCDs today come with integrated weighting systems, the best approach to using them is to not put all the weight in the BCD pockets but rather to wear a weight belt carrying about half of the total weight needed for working on the bottom. Most divers remember when they tried an emergency ascent while working toward their recreational certification, but most have not practiced it since. We know that a commonality in most scuba deaths is an in-place weight belt. It would seem logical that we would, therefore, incorporate ditching the weight belt and emergency ascents in our pool practice, but we do not. Without practice, a distressed public safety diver is no more likely to remember to remove the weight belt to enhance buoyancy than are recreational divers who drown wearing their weights.

Many team divers using their own recreational equipment have not upgraded their gear in a number of years. It is not uncommon to find public safety divers who are overweight wearing wet suits, BCDs, and weight belts that fit when they were fifty pounds lighter. During the training sessions at Southwest Texas State University, in an effort to convince trainees of the need for physical conditioning, exercises were designed to place divers in situations where their physical condition became apparent to them. It is easy to deny what we see in a mirror, and most people are too polite to comment on someone's weight. By requiring participants to swim relatively short distances wearing their wet suits, we brought home to many that this business is not for the unfit. Some trainees required the administration of oxygen upon removal of wet suits that were four sizes too small. Slowly, teams began requiring physical tests and basic fitness for participation on the team. Unfortunately, there are still too many overweight divers on too many teams. Wet suits should fit properly. Weight belts should fit correctly, with weights locked in place to prevent sliding and the tails of the belt left dangling. The excess allows the belt to be donned more easily, but more importantly, it allows the belt to be removed by another diver more easily. Floundering around in black water looking for the tag end of the weight belt so the assisting diver can enhance the distressed diver's ascent is difficult under the best of circumstances. It becomes even more difficult with the added adrenalin and fear associated with an assisted ascent. Additional length on the end of the weight belt makes it easy enough to find but not so long as to be an encumbrance for the diver or to pose a danger of entanglement. When placing weights, the primary consideration seems to be to distribute the weight so as to fit as much of it as possible on the belt.

Public safety divers are notoriously overweighted, and that's a product of not taking the time to find out what the minimum weight could be. Since dive dress may change from watercourse to watercourse, most divers do not keep a weight log to assist them in keeping track of how much weight is required or desired with various dive dress. Instead, a universal sum is sought and then the issue is never revisited.

If we work toward determining the minimum amount of weight necessary to conduct a particular search, we will always be adding or removing weights. Four things that should be borne in mind when deciding how much to overweight are:

1. It's heavy.
2. It's dangerous.
3. It's tiring.
4. How much lift is the BCD capable of?

In the water, wherever the weight is worn, the strain is all transferred to the small of the back. Fatigue sets in quickly, and recovery time can be substantial after carrying around twenty-five pounds of weight pulling on the back. That fatigue can begin to affect the integrity of the search when the diver's attention is more focused on back discomfort than the search. How high in the water a diver will float may depend upon the lift capacity of the BCD in relationship to the amount of weight being carried. Should the diver wish to carry an object from the bottom to the surface, that effort may be thwarted by having exceeded the lift capacity of the BCD. However, anything on the bottom that needs to be carried to the surface can be made buoyant and usually should not be carried.

In time, as you dive recreationally, you will notice that overweighting is not solely the province of the underwater investigator. Everyone seems to do it; that may be the foundation for the overweighting problem to begin with. Everyone wants to descend as quickly as possible. They have paid a substantial sum for their equipment and training for the opportunity to dive at memorable dive sites. They do not want to spend any more time on the surface than is necessary. Consequently, they generally do not take the time to empty their BCDs sufficiently to descend. They end up only partially emptying the BCD and have sufficient additional weight to overcome the buoyancy of the air still in the BCD, believing that they need twenty-five pounds of lead to get down. That perspective begins early, and there is no reason to presume it is absent in underwater investigation. Few divers *need* twenty pounds to descend; they *want* twenty pounds to descend as soon and as fast as they wish to. They carry that perspective with them wherever they end up diving. Navy divers in salt water with full wet suits wear twelve pounds of lead. Recreational divers pile it on upwards of twenty pounds.

The starting place for determining how much weight is enough weight is in the swimming pool. Each diver should check his or her buoyancy prior to each training session. The goal should be to discover the least amount of added weight that is necessary to allow descent and then to add an additional two to four pounds of weight to help resist the pull on the search line. Each training dive must be logged, or, for legal purposes, it didn't happen. The logging of training dives should begin with the amount of weight carried and its distribution around the body. As all experienced divers know, weights can be locked in place by twisting the belt before inserting the end into the weight and drawing it tight. The placement of the weight is as important as the amount being carried. Divers in limited-visibility water, crawling around on the bottom, searching with their hands or a metal detector, do not need their weights pulling them sideways. That pull will occur if the weights are not placed in exact proportion and in opposition to each other on either side of the body. The belt must be pulled tight enough to keep the weights from shifting downward. A downward shift of the weights and the belt has the diver fighting to keep from being turned on his or her side. One last point regarding buoyancy: If we continue to strive for the least amount of weight necessary to take us down and keep us there, we will discover on occasion that what worked yesterday does not seem to work today. When dealing with a pound or two of weight, we may try to combat our descent by inflating our lungs too often or too much, which happens when we are cold, excited, or frightened (perhaps, for easily bruised egos, we should say anxious). Our psychology can be reflected in our breathing. Until we have our breathing under control, a descent should not be attempted. Part of the psychology of having the backup diver become the primary diver is to address the issue of preparedness. The backup diver should be calm and adjusted to the water temperature, thereby making the transition from backup diver to primary diver smooth. The anxiety associated with low-visibility diving can manifest itself in hyperventilation or inability to equalize pressure. In any case, the backup diver should be better prepared to deal with these considerations than anyone else at the scene.

It is a common sight to see partially dressed divers walking around a dive site wearing their weight belts. This is a recognizable safety hazard but one so common that it tends to be ignored until someone falls into the water—weighted. I have seen tenders carrying weights on belts slung across their shoulders, as well as carrying integrated weighted BCDs to the dive site by wearing them—again, an accident waiting to happen. We often look for the easiest way to carry things without considering the consequence of an accidental fall into the water. The only people at a dive site wearing a BCD, weights, harness, or weight belt should be the divers who are in the process of dressing. It should be a simple matter of protocol that before a diver exits the water, the weight belt is removed and handed to a tender.

Buoyancy Control Devices

The buoyancy control device is a product of the recreational industry. There was a time when divers journeyed into the depths with a back plate to which was secured an air tank. Since the problem with diving was too much buoyancy, the issue of increasing buoyancy did not arise until it became apparent that controlling buoyancy on and under the water could be a tricky business. Buoyancy under the water was a function of the amount of weight and lung capacity. In most instances, divers were heavy in the water and used their legs to convey themselves upon, in, and under the water. Military divers needed a device that would allow them to float on the surface for extended periods while awaiting pickup. They wore a horse collar inflatable device (Mae West) that provided surface buoyancy. Technology ultimately wedded the horse collar to the back plate that supports the gas cylinder. That technology has significantly advanced in the past twenty-five years. Today a variety of BCDs are available depending on what it is the diver wishes to accomplish in the water. The basic idea of a BCD is to allow a diver to control his or her buoyancy at any place within the water column. Most BCDs today are of the jacket variety, but some provide wings and rear flotation. Considering the need for upright presentation on the surface, it would seem that the jacket-type BCD designed for presenting the diver upright on the surface would be the BCD of choice. One reason militating against that choice is that the jacket BCD inflates around the body, pressing inward. In those instances where only partial inflation of the BCD is required to reach the surface, the jacket works well. If the BCD is adjusted to fit snugly on the surface, it will be very uncomfortable for the diver to completely inflate the BCD. The winged device allows the air to be added behind the diver, posing no immediate discomfort; it does, however, force the diver's face into the water when inflated on the surface. Additionally, underwater investigators carry a number of tools on their person, in pockets around the jacket-type BCD. That option is not available to the winged-BCD wearer.

Some of the recent evolutions of BCDs made for the public safety diver sector have anywhere from forty to one hundred pounds of lift capacity. Too much lift power can be a danger. There is usually little in the water that has to be physically

FIGURE 10-7   Winged BCD.
(*Source:* R. F. Becker)

lifted to the surface (we will address using air to lift shortly). Suffice it to say that the thing an underwater investigator is most likely to carry to the surface is a body. The adult dead body weighs from eight to sixteen pounds in the water, which requires a BCD that will lift the diver to the surface carrying sixteen pounds along with the lead added to facilitate descent (in the event of even a seriously over-weighted diver, between twenty and twenty-five pounds). The total lifting capacity need not exceed forty pounds.

The material that early BCDs were made of did not stand up to use by under-water investigators. Most recreational divers strive for neutral buoyancy and have little contact with reefs, coral, or the bottom (not on purpose, anyway). Conversely, the underwater investigator is a bottom-feeder (deal with it; we all hear it often). The bottom is strewn with things that are bad for divers and the equipment they wear. Fishhooks and monofilament line are intimate associates of all public safety divers. Needless to say, recreational materials are not designed for the environment that underwater investigators operate in. New BCDs are being made of hardier stuff than the recreational variety. The only shortcomings of most commercial BCDs are the following:

- Lack of enough pockets
- Lack of high-visibility colors (Do you really want a black BCD if you're entangled in zero-visibility water?)
- Absence of a bail-out bottle (pony) pocket
- Excess D-rings attached to give it a more macho look

The good news is that Lifeguard Systems makes a BCD that is ideal for the public safety diver.

No matter how many pockets a BCD has, it will not be enough, but the access (size of opening) and location of the pockets on most commercial products leave a lot to be desired. If I am diving in low-visibility water, I want a fluorescent pink BCD. I do not care what others may think of it or me. I want to maximize my vis-ibility so someone doesn't have to tell my next of kin, "We couldn't find him in time." Most commercial BCDs have not even begun to consider pony bottles, let alone provide a pocket for one. The name of the game in underwater investigation is "nothing hangs." Anything not held close to the body is a potential entanglement. Additional rings upon which additional toys can hang are dangerous and should be removed even if they are not being used; they will catch on something. The move toward lots of D-rings emanates from technical diving. Although we have borrowed heavily from technical divers, we do not need to share their penchant for hanging things from their BCD. Dry suit inflator hoses should be passed under the arm as opposed to over the shoulder to reduce the number of things that can entangle the diver overhead. The air and pressure gauges should likewise be brought under the arm and secured to the BCD and not allowed to hang freely. Many of the new BCDs have crotch straps to keep the device from rising above the head while at the surface. They should be removed, but if they are worn, they should be worn under the weight belt to allow emergency removal of the weight belt. The BCDs that are being made for public safety divers share some long-overdue characteristics:

- They are open at the front to allow access to dry suit inflators.
- They are open at the front to allow attachment to a diver's tether.
- They are open at the front to allow emergency removal of weight belts.
- They have hardback back plates (soft backs are buoyant).
- They are available in forty- to fifty-pound lift capacities.

All BCDs have an inflator. The inflator hose connects to the gas (air) supply. The BCD aids in floating, neutral buoyancy, and light lifting. Many manufacturers install a mouthpiece on the end of the inflator, called a "safe second," allowing it to double as an "octopus," a second regulator for out-of-air emergencies. For underwater investigations, an octopus is unnecessary and, in fact, an impediment. It is something else that can be entangled and has no value to the entangled or out-of-air diver. A safety diver responding to a low-air situation cannot resolve the situation by providing an octopus so that now the distressed and rescue diver can breathe from the tank together. Underwater investigators carry pony bottles to lend additional bottom time in out-of-air situations. The backup diver has a contingency tank (full-rigged aluminum 80 with regulator in place) that is weighted sufficiently to be neutrally buoyant and available on a moment's notice for deployment in out-of-air situations. Should a diver become entangled, the first priority is to alleviate anxiety about air while the diver is being unencumbered. If there is not sufficient air in the entangled diver's tank to allow the backup diver to disentangle him or her, the backup diver will leave a pony bottle and surface to retrieve the contingency tank. Once the contingency tank has arrived, the out-of-air concerns of both divers can be placed on the back burner while the backup diver considers the best method of extracting the primary diver. It should be readily apparent that an octopus has no role in the world of the underwater investigator. As a practical matter, the safe second attached to the inflator hose is poorly situated for bottom-feeding underwater investigators. It is a magnet for mud, sand, vegetation, and other assorted trash from the bottom structure.

Buoyancy

In third-century B.C. Greece, there was a very wealthy king. The king wore a crown as a symbol of his authority. The king suspected that his goldsmith and crown maker was living beyond his means and further suspected that the goldsmith was using the king's gold to finance his lifestyle. The king believed that the goldsmith was preparing the crowns with a cheaper alloy, using a silver-gold mix rather than pure gold. No one knew how to prove or disprove the king's suspicions.

The problem of determining the gold content of the royal crown was given to Archimedes, the Greek mathematician and philosopher. Archimedes knew that silver was less dense than gold, but did not know any way of determining the relative density (mass/volume) of an irregularly shaped crown. The weight could be determined using a balance or scale, but the only way known to determine volume, using the geometry of the day, was to beat the crown into a solid sphere or cube. The king had made it clear that the crown was not to be damaged. While in the public baths, Archimedes observed that the level of water rose in the tub when he entered the bath. He realized this was the solution to his problem. He demonstrated to the king and his court how the amount of water overflowing a tub could be used to measure a volume. His calculations indicated that the goldsmith was, indeed, an embezzler. Archimedes' observation has been formalized into Archimedes' principle:

> An object partially or wholly immersed in a fluid is buoyed up by a force equal to the weight of the fluid displaced by the object.

In other words, objects denser than water, such as gold, will sink; objects less dense than water, such as wood, will float; objects of the same density as water will remain at the same level and neither sink nor float (human bodies sometimes attain this state as a result of the production of decomposition gases). Objects that sink are frequently termed negatively buoyant. Objects that float are termed positively buoyant. Objects that stay stationary at depth are said to be neutrally buoyant.

Buoyancy is most easily understood by the application of vectors. Vectors are mathematical constructs that have magnitude (such as mass) and direction (toward or away from the surface). Weight is a downward force (gravity acting on mass); buoyancy is an upward force. If these two forces are balanced, then neutral buoyancy is achieved. If they are not balanced, the object immersed will either sink or float. Divers commonly misuse the term *buoyancy.* Scientifically, buoyancy is defined as an upward force directed against the force of weight. Although commonly used in the diving community, the terms *neutrally buoyant* and *negatively buoyant* are scientifically improper, and the term *positively buoyant* is redundant. Buoyancy is much easier to understand if we only consider balancing an upward force (buoyancy) and a downward force (weight). In this scheme, there is no positive or negative. If weight is greater than buoyancy, the object sinks. If buoyancy is greater than weight, the object rises. If weight and buoyancy are identical, then the object hovers.

Most buoyancy issues can be understood by simply determining the relationship between forces acting either up or down. Buoyancy-type problems involve three factors:

1. The weight of the object submerged
2. The volume of the object submerged
3. The density of the liquid into which the object is submerged

Any two of these factors can be used to determine the third.

BUOYANCY EXERCISE 1: What is the buoyancy in seawater of a piece of wood that weighs 2,000 pounds and measures 6 feet by 2 feet by 3 feet?

ANSWER:

a.   The weight of the wood = 2000 lb
b.   The volume of wood = 6 ft $\times$ 2 ft $\times$ 3 ft = 36 ft^3
c.   The corresponding weight of an equal volume of seawater (density 64 lb/ft^3) is 36 ft^3 $\times$ 64 lb/ft^3 = 2304 lb

At this point, we know that the wood object weighs less than the corresponding volume of water that would be displaced if the entire object were to be submerged. Therefore, the object will float with a buoyant force of 304 pounds. In order for the object to sink, it would have to weigh more than an additional 304 pounds without changing volume. This is the amount of "push" you would have to exert on this log for it to sink.

BUOYANCY EXERCISE 2: A fully suited diver weighs 200 pounds. This diver displaces a volume of 3.0 cubic feet of seawater. Will the diver float or sink?

ANSWER:

a.   The weight of an equal volume of seawater = 3.0 ft^3 $\times$ 64 lb/ft^3 = 192 lb
b.   The diver will sink. This diver weighs eight pounds in the water and is severely overweighted. Removal of eight pounds will allow the diver to hover (which means the diver will have to do less work while diving).

BUOYANCY EXERCISE 3: A fully geared diver in a wet suit weighs 210 pounds. In freshwater, this diver with a scuba cylinder containing 500 psig needs to use eighteen pounds of lead in order to hover. How much lead will this diver need to hover when diving in a wet suit in seawater?

ANSWER:

a.   Weight of the diver = 200 lb
b.   Weight of weights = 18 lb
c.   Total weight = 218 lb

For the diver to be neutrally buoyant, the volume of water displaced by the diver must exert a buoyant force upward equal to the total weight of the diver plus gear (downward force). This is the buoyant force exerted by a volume of freshwater (density = 62.4 lb/ft^3) that weighs 228 pounds.

Determine volume of diver:

$$density = mass/volume$$

Rearrange:

$$volume = mass/density$$

Substitute:

$$\text{volume} = \frac{228\ \text{lb}}{62.4\ \text{lb/ft}^3} = 3.65\ \text{ft}^3$$

Now that we know the volume of the diver (assuming the volume of the weight belt is negligible), we can determine the buoyant force from the seawater (density 64 lb/ft^3) the diver would displace:

$$3.65\ \text{ft}^3 \times 64\ \text{lb/ft}^3 = 233.6\ \text{lb}$$

Buoyant force of seawater:	234 lb (rounded to the nearest pound)
Combined weight of diver and gear:	210 lb
Force of water:	24 lb

The diver who was comfortable with eighteen pounds of lead on the weight belt in freshwater must add six more pounds on the weight belt, for a total of twenty-four pounds, to dive in seawater.

Divers wearing wet or dry suits have an additional factor to consider. Within the wet suit are trapped bubbles of gas; a dry suit diver has air spaces between the diver and the suit. This gas (in fact, all air spaces) is subject to changes in volume as a result of changes in pressure. This means that as the diver moves up or down in the water column, the volumes of these gas spaces change. This change in gas volume affects the diver's buoyancy. As a diver descends, the volume of the gas decreases, less water is displaced, and the diver is less buoyant and sinks. On ascent, the pressure on the diver decreases, and the gas expands and occupies a larger volume. This displaces more water and increases the buoyant force. Archimedes' principle points out that if we are not neutrally buoyant, we are floating (moving up) or sinking. So unless our buoyancy and weight are equal, we must expend energy to hover in the water column.

Lifting Buoyancy
The lift associated with air spaces can be used to raise objects from the bottom. Since air weighs very little compared to the weight of the displaced water, it can be assumed that the lifting capacity is equal to the weight of the volume of water that is displaced by the air volume of the lifting device.

LIFTING EXERCISE 1: You wish to lift a 300-pound anchor from the bottom of a lake bed. The bottom is hard and flat, so no excess lift will be needed to overcome the suction associated with being immersed in the bottom muck. You have access to 55-gallon drums, weighing 20 pounds each, that have been fitted with over-expansion vents. How many 55-gallon drums will it take to lift the anchor?

ANSWER:

Determine weight of water displaced:

$$\text{weight} = \text{density} \times \text{volume}$$

Lake implies freshwater: density $= 62.4$ lb/ft^3

$$\text{weight} = 55 \text{ gal} \times \frac{0.134 \text{ ft}^3}{\text{gal}} \times \frac{62.4 \text{ lb}}{\text{ft}^3} = 459.9 \text{ lb}$$

Weight of displaced water $= 460$ lb (rounded off to the nearest pound)

Weight of drum $= 20$ lb (subtract from weight of displaced water)

Net force $= 440$ lb

Since the object to be lifted weighs less than the 440-pound lifting capacity of a 55-gallon drum, a single drum should be sufficient to lift the 300-pound anchor. In practice, large lifting objects such as a 55-gallon drum have a large surface area and will generate considerable drag, which decreases lifting capacity. As a rule of thumb, it is reasonable to assume about 0.75 of the calculated lifting capacity for the lifting device in an actual lifting operation. This exercise is provided to introduce the subject of **airlifting** objects to the surface. The calculations are correct for whatever item is to be lifted; however, the inclusion of this mental exercise should not be construed to suggest that anyone reading this material is prepared to lift something using these calculations. Lifting is a specialized skill and requires training in rigging and lift mechanisms in addition to the calculations associated with lifting the item. Using air to lift something from the bottom of a water column can be done safely, but not by a novice without training, practice, and experience. Attempting to bypass the training and practice relegates this activity to the very dangerous category. No one should attempt to use air to lift something from the bottom of a water column without having had training in the full array of associated skills.

Alternative Air Supply

Many public safety diving agencies have adopted full-face masks as part of their **default dress.** This raises an interesting question regarding the use of an **alternative air supply** in the form of a pony bottle. A pony bottle with a regulator is a backup air supply in case there is a malfunction, loss, or depletion of the primary air supply (back-borne tanks). Bottles come in various capacities, but the two most commonly used are the eighteen-cubic-foot tank and the thirty-cubic-foot tank. Tank size is determined by dive depth; the deeper the dive, the larger the bottle. When a diver wearing a face mask and using an air supply with a regulator in his or her mouth needs to revert to the backup air system, the pony bottle can be retrieved, the regulator removed from the mouth, and the pony bottle regulator put into place, allowing access to the emergency air supply. As simple as this process sounds, it is one that does not come automatically. As with all other equipment, pony bottles need to be used both in pool training exercises and in recovery scenarios in simulated black water. Activating a pony bottle in a swimming pool with excellent visibility is not the environment in which the bottle will be used. It is important that once the pony bottle is strapped in place, it not be forgotten. An out-of-air diver has about two minutes to find and activate the pony bottle, and any delay will have dire consequences. Practice and training can make those consequences less likely.

The role of the pony bottle raises another question as to the best place to stow the bottle during those periods when it is not in use. There are a number of options available, and teams around the country employ all three:

1. Attached to the main tank
2. In a special pocket on the BCD
3. Hanging from the front of the BCD

Whenever underwater investigators come together, they argue the benefits and disadvantages of each. In line with keeping things simple, the teams that hang their pony bottles off the front of their BCDs employ the method that is used by cave divers to facilitate a safe penetration into the depths of an underwater cave. The obvious shortcoming is the entanglement potential. The advantage is in the ease with which the bottle can be accessed. Three points that bear remembering regarding the placement of pony bottles are the following:

1. All team members should wear their pony bottles the same way.
2. All team members should use the same mask and regulator configuration.
3. Pony bottle use and activation should be part of every training scenario.

Underwater, in waters of limited or no visibility, is not the place to be looking for a pony bottle. There should be no hesitation in finding it. If assistance arrives before air is depleted, the safety diver may need to return to the surface. That can best be accomplished by knowing that all divers wear their pony bottles in the same place and in the same way. A pony bottle is an independent air supply. In order to use it, a diver with a regulator in his or her mouth simply replaces the regulator from the main tank with the one on the pony bottle. A diver with a full-face mask would have to take off the mask to use a backup regulator connected to a pony bottle. This is the reason all team members should wear the same mask and regulator configuration. Some teams use full-face masks. When the face mask is removed, the diver has no visibility and no regulator. How, then, does this diver access the pony bottle and use it?

Teams using full-face masks have dealt with the pony bottle issue in one of two ways:

1. Team members carry a face mask in a BCD pocket that can be deployed if it becomes necessary to remove the full-face mask.
2. Each diver has a manifold system that can be reached conveniently from the front and that activates the pony bottle without removal of the full-face mask.

The teams using a face mask as the backup for a full-face mask are breaching their operating procedures when removing the full-face mask, thereby exposing the diver's face to the water. One of the reasons the team has selected full-face masks is the protection it and dry suits provide against contaminated water. By removing the full-face mask, the diver's face, mouth, nose, and ears are exposed to the water. Once the mask has been replaced, the regulator of the pony bottle must be put into the mouth, subjecting the diver to the ingestion of contaminated water. To avoid these possibilities, those teams that employ full-face masks as standard equipment for all diving, including and perhaps particularly in contaminated water, must employ a "switching block" that allows air to be directed from the pony bottle directly into the full-face mask. Full-face masks and pony bottles with blocks raise the question of how a donor bottle or tank can be added to the configuration. The connections to the full-face mask and the pony bottle must allow for the in-line employment of a donor pony bottle or backup scuba tank.

Pony bottles have a limited air capacity. They are used to address immediate out-of-air situations until the diver can reach the surface or be provided with a contingency air supply. When air depletion is the issue, entanglement is not the paramount concern. Once the diver is provided with an enduring air supply, the entanglement can be addressed. The safety diver carries a pony bottle, and the underwater investigator carries a pony bottle. These two backup air supplies should be more than sufficient to allow the safety diver to return to the surface and retrieve a backup scuba cylinder that has been prepared for just such an event. Some teams use a backup tank that has been placed into a BCD with regulator attached. The BCD is weighted to offset the buoyancy of the tank. Another approach to the backup tank is to have the tank rigged with a regulator to a backboard, to be employed without a BCD. The author finds the tank and backboard easier to handle and to get in the water and down to the diver faster.

Face Masks

The single most common problem with face masks is that they do not fit. Many agencies buy face masks, fins, and regulators in bulk to cut costs. Face masks have an individual fit and require some consideration before purchase. Each diver should be fitted separately for a face mask. Requesting wide-fitting neoprene mask straps and assuring proper fit will make the journey underwater more comfortable. Mask fitting is not a difficult science, and a good fit can be accomplished easily by placing the mask against the face. Without the use of the strap, a light inhalation by the wearer should seal the mask sufficiently to the face so that it will stay in place on the face without the assistance of the hands. Pulling a vacuum identifies the properly fitting mask. That mask should not be used by any other diver. Of the entire set of dive equipment used by the team, the face mask is one that should be an individual possession.

Most underwater investigation takes place in black water and waters of limited visibility. It would seem on the face of it that defogging a face mask would be an unnecessary task for the diver. However, when the diver surfaces, his or her first action will be to look for the shore or dive platform. If the mask is fogged, the diver is likely to remove it. The default protocol for exiting the water should be with mask and equipment in place. Using a defog compound will assure that the diver does not remove the face mask upon completion of the dive circuit.

In recreational diving, the face mask is intimately associated with a snorkel. Often the snorkel is seen as a piece of safety equipment for the recreational diver. The snorkel loses its value in underwater recovery operations. It becomes one more piece of equipment hanging off the body that can get entangled or result in the mask being pulled from the diver's face. Most teams have removed snorkels from their equipment lists as unnecessary and dangerous. Remember that the idea is to streamline the body-borne equipment to present the least amount of resistance to the water and to reduce the probability of entanglement. Entanglement is going to occur; the hope is that it is minimal and allows for self-extraction without loss of time or search integrity, or a need to deploy the backup diver. Efforts to minimize the potential for entanglement include the removal of all unnecessary equipment, especially that which hangs off the body.

Regulators, Gauges, and Computers

Most teams use whatever regulators each member has. It would be nice to see all public safety dive teams with interchangeable, standardized equipment with the latest cold-water regulators, but that's generally not the way it works. Should the team have the advantage of researching regulators before purchase in order to have all team members with the same regulator, the bottom line should be a regulator that is reliable, is an industry standard, has an abundance of replacement parts available, is easy to maintain and clean, and can be sealed environmentally. Should a team be involved in cold-water operations, the latter should be a consideration in the selection of regulators.

Gauges are also a fairly straightforward proposition. Most recreational gauges provide the necessary information as to air pressure and depth. The problem, however, is that in black water gauges are indecipherable. It is to this end that **surface air consumption rates** (SAC rates) must be calculated for each diver. To find a diver's SAC rate, the following procedure may be used:

1. Descend to a depth of no less than twenty-five feet and no deeper than thirty-three feet.
2. Record the air pressure in the cylinder at that depth and at that time.
3. Record the time the air pressure was recorded.
4. Swim at that depth for ten minutes.
5. Record the air pressure at that time and depth.

Upon surfacing, the following calculations can be made:

1. Subtract the air pressure at the end of the ten-minute period from the air pressure recorded at the beginning of the ten-minute period.
2. Divide this figure by the number of atmospheres absolute (ata) (25 to 30 ft = 2 ata).
3. Divide this figure by the recorded bottom time (ten minutes).

Mathematically, this is what it looks like:

$$SAC = \frac{\text{total gas consumed (psig)}}{\text{depth (ata)} \times \text{time (in minutes)}}$$

Consider a dive of 25 feet for 20 minutes with an 80-cubic-foot cylinder. Air pressure at the beginning of the dive is 3,000 psig, and air pressure at the end of the dive is 1,100 psig.

Step 1: Calculate how much pressure was used in the dive:

$$3{,}000 \text{ psig} - 1{,}100 \text{ psig} = 1{,}900 \text{ psig consumed}$$

Step 2: Dividing the 1,900 psig of consumed pressure by the length of the dive will tell us how many psig were consumed each minute:

$$\frac{1{,}900 \text{ psig consumed pressure}}{20 \text{ min dive time}} = 95 \text{ psig/min consumed}$$

Step 3: The 95 psig/min consumption rate is the rate at 25 feet. It is necessary to determine what the consumption rate would have been at the surface. This calculation requires that we determine depth in terms of atmospheres of pressure:

$$\frac{25 \text{ ft} + 1 \text{ atm}}{33 \text{ ft}} + 1 \text{ atm} = \text{ata}$$

$$0.757 \qquad + 1 \quad = \text{ata}$$

$$1.757 \qquad\qquad = \text{ata}$$

We can determine how much air would have been used at the surface by dividing the psig/min consumed by the ata:

$$\frac{95 \text{ psig consumed}}{1.757 \text{ ata}} = 54.0 \text{ psig/min surface consumption}$$

Step 4: To calculate the actual volume of air used, we must convert the surface psig/min to cubic feet of air used at the surface. We do that by determining how many cubic feet are used for each psi, arriving at a conversion factor for that particular tank:

$$\frac{\text{tank size in ft}^3}{\text{tank's working pressure in psig}} = \text{conversion factor}$$

$$\frac{80 \text{ ft}^3}{3{,}000 \text{ psig}} = 0.027 \text{ ft}^3$$

Step 5: We now must find out how many cubic feet of air were used for each minute of the dive. We can convert psi to cubic feet by multiplying psi by the conversion factor:

$$54.0 \text{ psig consumed at the } _{\text{surface}} \times 0.027 \text{ ft}^3$$
$$= 1.458 \text{ ft}^3/\text{min}_{\text{consumed at the surface}}$$

At this consumption rate of 1.458 ft^3/min, 29.16 ft^3 would be consumed in 20 minutes at the surface.

Step 6: It is possible to determine how long a cylinder will last at depth or on the surface for a particular diver and that diver's SAC rate. To calculate the potential at the surface in minutes, divide the capacity of the tank by the SAC rate. Given a 28-ft^3 pony bottle and the SAC rate calculated above, the result would be:

$$\frac{18\text{-ft}^3 \text{ pony}}{1.458 \text{ ft}^3 \text{ SAC}} = 12.3 \text{ min}$$

Using SAC rate to calculate the longevity of a tank at any depth dive by ata:

$$\frac{12.3 \text{ min}}{1.757 \text{ ata}} = 8.5 \text{ min}$$

With a SAC rate of 1.458 ft^3/min, an 18-ft^3 pony bottle will last 8.5 minutes at a depth of 25 feet (Somers 2000).

There is a circular slide rule (SAC rate calculator) based on the above mathematics that is available from several different scuba-training agencies that makes obtaining these calculations painless. The diver monitors depth, pressure used, and time and plugs these values into the circular scale, and a SAC rate is provided. It should be remembered that SAC rates are a tool to assist in planning dive operations and should not be solely relied upon for determining air consumption for any dive or diver. They are an index that can provide information about a diver or a dive as it progresses, but they are no substitute for periodic gauge readings. If water is so dark as to prohibit visual reading of gauges, surfacing at specified intervals and upon demand can assure that readings remain within safe parameters.

Equipping a team is an expensive proposition at best. The equipment discussed along with fins, lights, gloves, and other necessary materials may be prohibitive for many teams. However, the question that should be addressed when discussing organizing and equipping a team is "Can we afford to do it right?" because, frankly, it is more expensive in the long run to do it wrong. Equipment purchases require appropriate training in areas that are not included in recreational certification. Training requires exercises that include the use of all the equipment. The goal for a team should be to obtain the equipment, train in its use, employ it in regular exercises, and standardize equipment for the entire team. Considering that many teams start by using personal equipment, standardization may seem a long way off. Rather than say that teams should not be deployed at all unless trained and equipped in a standardized fashion, standardization should be made an early goal. Once the team has equipped itself with whatever scuba equipment is available, it must address some safety issues in prioritizing new purchases, i.e., personal flotation devices for support personnel, bailout bottles for divers, a contingency tank. So equipped, the team will begin its sojourn into the world of underwater investigation. However, over time the team and its leaders will recognize the deficiencies that exist in the recreational equipment that serves as the beginning inventory for most dive teams. A crusade will begin to upgrade and supplement equipment, seeking funds from the agency or the public through contributions to the team. Often a team will ask, "What should we buy first?" In prioritizing equipment purchases, the author's recommendations would include (along with the appropriate training):

- Full-face mask (positive pressure)
- Dry suit
- Communication system

Perhaps this would be a good time to provide a list of the types of materials a team will need to work efficiently and safely in underwater operations:

Diver (from top to bottom):

- Face mask (full-face mask recommended)
- Face mask hose
- Gill (breathing vent for the face mask at the surface)
- Manifold transfer block (transfer from main cylinder to bailout bottle)
- Hoses for transfer block (quick-release rigged)
- Hood (allow head to be completely protected from the water)
- Dry suit (preferably of vulcanized rubber)
- Insulated undergarments
- **Dry suit seals** (and a spare set)
- Main tank regulator
- Bailout regulator
- Contingency tank regulator
- 80-ft^3 tank (two per diver and two contingency tanks)
- Bailout bottles (one 18–30-ft^3 tank per diver)
- Gauge console (one per diver)
- **Tether harness** (one per diver)
- Weight belt (one per diver who is not using a **weight harness**)
- Assorted weights
- Weight harness (may be used in place of weight belt)
- BCD (with sufficient flotation)
- Cutting tools (scissors and knife on harness or BCD)

- Ankle weights
- Fins (one pair per diver)

Support personnel:

- Personal flotation device (one per support person)
- Throw bags (rescue ropes in a deployable bag)
- Search lines (100-foot ropes for underwater searches)
- Commo line (communication lines)
- Assorted carabiners (you can never have enough)

Most teams have a boat or have access to one. The most common boat for dive teams is a RIB (rubber inflatable boat) with a motor. This is an inexpensive and efficient way to get divers to and from the dive site.

In any discussion involving equipment, the first questions that have to be addressed are those that were raised at the beginning of this chapter. Any equipment list can start with the kinds of basic gear described in the above list, but specialized operations and unique environmental conditions will dictate the types of equipment used and will add a host of specialized gear to the already lengthy list of standard equipment. It should be apparent that equipping a dive team is not an inexpensive proposition. An investment of the nature required to properly equip a team should not be made lightly. It might be good to end this chapter with a reiteration of an earlier concept: It is better not to have a team than to equip that team improperly or inadequately. The decision to have at team entails a number of considerations:

- Is a team needed?
- Can we find/train personnel to make up the team?
- Can we adequately equip and train a team?
- Can we keep training current?
- What is it we want a team to do?

REVIEW QUESTIONS

1. Most public safety dive teams begin with recreational equipment. Is this sufficient to do the job safely? If not, why not?
2. What function does a dive team's standard operation and procedures manual serve?
3. Why is a wet suit not the preferred choice of scuba dress for the underwater investigator?
4. What advantages does a dry suit have over a wet suit?
5. How can a diver be equipped for diving in contaminated water?
6. What special maintenance is required for dry suits?
7. What types of dry suits are available? What are their special uses?

8. What is the advantage of a positive pressure full-face mask over a demand full-face mask?
9. How does someone using a full-face mask use an alternative air supply?
10. What is a gill, and what does it do?
11. Discuss the benefits of tethered versus nontethered diving.
12. How is surface air consumption rate calculated?
13. What is the purpose for calculating surface air consumption rate?
14. In what order of priority should equipment be purchased?
15. How is the amount of air necessary to lift something to the surface calculated?

REFERENCES

HENDRICK, W., A. ZAFERES, and C. NELSON. 2000. *Public safety diving*. Saddle Brook, NJ: Fire Engineering.

SOMERS, L. H. 2000. *Open water scuba diver*. Miami Shores: IANTD.

Chapter 11

Using Recovered Evidence in the Courtroom

NEW WORDS AND CONCEPTS

venire person	identification
peremptorily struck	multiple predicates
voir dire	trier of fact
damage control	affirmative defense
chain of custody	hostile witness
jurisdiction	suppression hearing
venue	element of the offense
directed verdict of acquittal	transcript
authentication	exculpatory evidence
predicate for admissibility	culpability

LEARNING OBJECTIVES

- Describe the criminal trial process
- Describe how evidence is employed in the criminal trial process

INTRODUCTION

An investigator who intends to participate in the satisfaction of successful prosecutions must excel at two things: documentation and testifying (writing and speaking). Often students in the author's criminal justice classes become adamant when they are penalized for composition errors or required to make oral reports. They believe because they have selected law enforcement as a career field, they need not know how to write well or how to speak in front of a group of people. It serves no purpose for the best of investigators to take the witness stand without adequate documentation in support of the investigation. Trials often occur months, if not years, after the investigation has been completed. The only reliable record of the investigation is the documentation prepared by the investigator. If that documentation is sparse, inaccurate, or lacking in basic composition skills, the testifying investigator's credibility is at risk in his or her attempt to remedy those shortcomings on the witness stand.

The usual catastrophe begins with the officer testifying to facts not included in the documentation. Such testimony is a gift to the defense.

Defense: Are you a trained underwater investigator?

Investigator: Yes.

Defense: Would you describe the training provided you in that regard?

Investigator: I am a certified recreational diver, open-water diver, search-and-rescue diver, dive master, dive instructor, and underwater investigator.

Defense: Being an underwater investigator, you are required to write reports, are you not?

Investigator: Yes.

Defense: Did your course as an underwater investigator stress the importance of accurate report writing?

Investigator: Yes.

Defense: Did your course as an underwater investigator stress the importance of complete report writing?

Investigator: Yes.

Defense: You are also a police officer, are you not?

Investigator: Yes, I am.

Defense: During the course of your training as a police officer, did you take courses in report writing?

Investigator: Yes.

Defense: Did you take courses wherein the importance of accurate report writing was emphasized?

Investigator: Yes.

Defense: And in those courses did they emphasize the importance of a complete report?

Investigator: Yes.

Defense: If the testimony you just gave is important enough to tell the jury, then why was it not included in the original report?

Investigator: [blank stare]

Remember the cardinal rule of documentation: If it isn't written in the report, it didn't happen.

A failing memory that recovers in time for trial is also risky. If the report was made close to the recovery operation, would not the documentation be a more accurate rendition of the facts than an uncorroborated recollection months or years later? Obviously, a contemporaneous recording of significant events is more reliable than an uncorroborated recollection months or years later, and any suggestion to the contrary would be viewed as suspect.

Good trial lawyers are not born; they learn. Competent police witnesses are not born; they, too, are a product of:

- Potential
- Training
- Experience
- Preparation

A superb, unprepared trial lawyer will lose to an average, prepared trial lawyer—every time. That adage is applicable to any witness who enters the gladiatorial arena of the law.

Preparation is reflected in the quality of the testimony. The quality of preparation is based upon the quality of the documentation that has been completed by the investigating officers, the time spent in studying that documentation, and the sources from which that documentation stems.

A police officer who testifies well will assist the prosecutor in obtaining guilty verdicts. A police officer who can reliably testify will be seen by the prosecutor as an asset to cultivate. If the prosecutor accepts cases from an officer he or she has learned to have confidence in, that officer's conviction rate will soar. A sustained rate of convictions for any police officer cannot hurt career prospects.

A testifying police investigator can be a defense lawyer's ally or worst nightmare. In selecting the jury, defense lawyers inquire into the **venire person's** (prospective juror) occupational background. Anyone with police relatives or police friends will most likely be struck from a jury. These prospective jurors will be asked if they believe that a police officer is any more believable that any other witness. They will be asked if they are of the opinion that police officers do not make mistakes. They will be asked if they are of the opinion that police officers do not lie. Anyone answering yes to these questions will be subject to being **peremptorily** (without reason) **struck** from the jury.

Why does the defense counsel place so much emphasis on the police officer? He or she knows that the entire case may rest on the testimony of the police and the investigation they performed. The counsel also knows that each officer is bestowed with an invisible "shroud of veracity" by virtue of the esteem with which police are generally held in the community.

People believe and want to believe that police officers are honest and lack deceit. The whole jury has anticipated, since the **voir dire** (jury selection), the moment the testifying officer is called by the bailiff as a witness. That officer is scrutinized from head to foot the moment he or she steps through the door and enters the courtroom. If the officer walks confidently, is dressed professionally, and has personal pride in his or her appearance, the jury will extend the courtesy of belief. That believability cannot be damaged by anything that the defense may have done or attempts to do, but it can be stripped away by incompetent, insincere, or dishonest testimony.

For any other witness, the penalty for false testimony is to be labeled a perjurer and to be forgotten. The penalty for a police officer who is incompetent or dishonest is a verdict of acquittal for the defendant and a prosecutor who may not prosecute that officer's cases in the future.

Preparing for Trial

Habit is a tool or a vice. If from habit all investigations are conducted with the same meticulousness, a habit aimed at success is established. That habit is difficult to cultivate because police know that the majority of investigations leading to arrest never got to trial. If the case is not likely to be tried, why invest time and effort writing reports? Presuming cases will not got to trial or that another officer will do the writing assures embarrassment or dishonesty when that presumption fails. The only foolproof way to avoid falling victim to the "plea bargain" presumption is to prepare every case as though it were going to trial. It may be tedious, but even if there is no trial, the preparation process certainly provides good practice. After all, practice makes a defense lawyer's life more difficult.

The author was appointed to represent a defendant in a capital murder trial. He defended his client professionally and zealously, but the fact of the matter was that his "brilliant" defense had little to do with the jury's acquittal. The early breakthrough in the case came from a misdemeanor arrest that gave rise to information regarding the murder. The misdemeanor was handled badly, laying a constitutionally suspect foundation for the remainder of the investigation. Once it became apparent that the case had been mishandled from the beginning of the investigation, the investigators and prosecutor sought to do **damage control** on the witness stand. They fell victim to bad habits and an angry jury that did not appreciate being lied to. The author received no personal satisfaction from that victory, and it was the last criminal trial he ever participated in. He believes, all things being equal, that if the prosecution and police do as thorough a job in preparing and presenting criminal cases as prepared defense lawyers do, juries will convict.

The easiest way for a prosecutor to obtain a plea bargain from a knowledgeable defense lawyer is to convince that lawyer that the case is ready to try and that the prosecutor is confident of the outcome. Much of the paperwork generated as part of the investigation is discoverable by the defense. If a competent defense lawyer discovers shoddy and inaccurate data included in the police investigation, why plead his or her client out?

An officer with experience testifying will not wait until the day of trial to review the case. It is prudent to examine the paperwork, evidence, logs, photographs, diagrams, sketches, and charts that will be admitted through the officer's testimony before the trial. Review the condition of all evidence, including markings, labels, and **chain of custody.**

Identification

Before a witness may testify, it is necessary to describe who the witness is, what that individual can contribute to the case in question, and why that person should be allowed to testify. In determining why the person should be allowed to testify, the court must determine the relevance and the scope of the prospective testimony. The predicate (foundation that allows police testimony) for a police officer would include the following types of questions:

State:	Will you state your name, please?
Investigator:	[Respond with full legal name.]
State:	What is your occupation?
Investigator:	[Give specific function and organization and team.]
State:	To be a police officer in the state of [insert state], is it necessary to be certified?
Investigator:	Yes.
State:	What is required by your department for an officer to become certified?
Investigator:	[Relate the number of weeks of academy training, field training, etc.]
State:	What are your duties as an underwater investigator?
Investigator:	To respond to requests for underwater recovery operations mediated through a protocol.
State:	Is there any special training or certification required for officers working as underwater investigators?
Investigator:	[Provide a description of all dive training and certification required and obtained.]
State:	Were you working on the day of [date in question]?
Investigator:	Yes.
State:	Were you dispatched to a particular location at approximately [time at issue]?
Investigator:	Yes.
State:	What was that location?
Investigator:	[Describe the area of operations.]
State:	What were you asked to do?
Investigator:	Process an underwater crime scene.

The witness has now been qualified as an "expert" and the area of expertise has been demonstrated.

Once the witness has been qualified, the prosecutor will have proven that the state has **jurisdiction** over the place in question and the specific court is the appropriate place **(venue)** for the case to be tried. Failure to prove either of these two elements may result in a **directed verdict of acquittal** for the defendant. Police have little difficulty in understanding that specific offenses have particular elements, but are often ignorant of the jurisdictional and venue requirements in every case. The investigating officer is the most likely source for soliciting this information. Be prepared for the questions; they are not as innocuous as they may sound. Ideally, the prosecutor and prospective police witnesses should meet before the trial to cover the testimony and the evidence.

As a result of that meeting, a trial blueprint should be constructed containing an overview of the testimony necessary to "prove up" all evidence. Many prosecutors assume that you already know what testimony is expected, and hence they will devote little time to pretrial discussions. Another possibility is that a new prosecutor may not be sure of what his or her responsibility is, let alone try to prepare police officers for their testimonial load. It is the inexperienced prosecutor who will find a knowledgeable police witness invaluable. Making yourself invaluable is not a bad career move.

Chain of Custody

Under the common law, a chain of custody must be shown from the moment evidence was discovered until it appears in the courtroom, so the court can be satisfied that what the prosecutor is attempting to have entered into evidence is the same thing that was discovered by the police and has not been altered. Evidence should be handled only by people with a need to handle it. That need should be predicated on something other than curiosity.

The officer who recovered a particular item of evidence is responsible for testifying to what has happened to the evidence after it was recovered at the search site. Other than packaging, storing, and testing, the best thing that can happen to evidence is nothing. Every time the evidence is removed from storage, it should be recorded. If persons other than the testifying officer have handled the evidence, they may then be called by the defense to testify. They will be asked the purpose of removal; the procedures of removal; where the evidence was taken; what was done to it; and, most important, if there is any way to be sure that the item labeled as a specific bit of evidence has not been inadvertently substituted with another similar item or altered so dramatically as to cease to have evidentiary value. It avoids unnecessary testimony, confusion, and innuendo if the officer who is to prove up the evidence retrieves it and brings it to the courtroom.

Most evidence tags contain hearsay evidence, but it is a mistake to anticipate an objection and remove evidence tags prior to trial. The evidence tags can be removed at the time of trial once they have been identified for the record. Chain-of-custody testimony is basically the same for all evidence. Chain of custody is not proven until the evidence has been appropriately identified. **Authentication** is a process separate from establishing the chain of custody and varies depending on the specific evidence to be entered. This authentication is often referred to as a **predicate for admissibility.**

Officers often flounder around after being asked a question that should have been recognized as part of a chain-of-custody predicate. It is the responsibility of the testifying officers to understand the rules of evidence sufficiently to enable them to testify competently. In every situation in which evidence is to be admitted, the testifying officer should anticipate chain-of-custody inquiries. The chain of custody is proven by a series of questions containing the following or similar queries:

State: I show you what has been marked as State's Exhibit Number 1, and ask you if you have seen it before.

Investigator: [Do not identify what is being proffered at this point; simply answer "yes."]

State: What is it?

Investigator: [This is a request for a brief generic description, not a detailed description. A more detailed characterization will be solicited once the chain of custody has been established. Simply answer, for example, "a pistol."]

State: When and where did you first see it?

Investigator: [A specific date, time, and location will answer this question satisfactorily.]

State: What did you do with State's Exhibit Number 1 when you saw it?

Investigator: I located it geographically and temporally and bagged and tagged it.

State: How do you know that State's Exhibit Number 1 is the same [generic description of evidence, such as pistol, rifle, shirt, etc.]?

Investigator: [This question is designed to allow the officer to testify to the marks placed on the evidence by the investigator or the signed tape used to seal containers in which evidence not subject to marking has been placed.]

State: Other than the addition of the Identifying Mark and State's Exhibit stickers, has it been altered in any way?

Investigator: [Obviously, if the evidence has been subjected to testing, it has probably been altered. The nature of the alteration should be explained, including how the item was transported to the testing facilities and returned from those facilities. The evidence tag and ledger should contain all testing information including time out, destination, purpose, handlers, time in, and a description of how it was stored while out of the evidence room. Much of that information will be testified to by the persons receiving and testing the evidence. It may take a number of witnesses to prove an adequate chain of custody.]

State: Is it in the same or similar condition as when your first saw it?

Investigator: [The answer to this question is usually a simple "yes"; however, testing may severely alter the item. If it has been altered, the appropriate answer is to describe the alterations and attest that it is in substantially the same or similar condition but for those alterations.]

State:	How did State's Exhibit Number 1 get to the courtroom today?
Investigator:	[The best answer is for the testifying officer to have transported it.]

In some states, prior to the completed testimony the defense is allowed to cross-examine the witness regarding the evidence and its discovery, handling, packaging, transportation, and storage. This cross-examination is referred to as a voir dire of a witness as opposed to a voir dire of a jury panel. The request to voir dire a witness can be made at two junctures during the prosecution's direct examination of a witness: during chain-of-custody determination and when qualifying an expert witness. The request by the defense is simply an attempt to develop testimony that will allow the defense to challenge the chain of custody or the qualifications of an expert witness.

Authentication

Once the witness has been identified and the chain of custody has been established, the evidence will require authentication before the court will admit the exhibit into evidence. Chain-of-custody testimony evolved to assure that an item that a lawyer attempts to admit into evidence has not been altered while in police custody. Authentication evolved to assist in establishing that items that are not self-authenticating and that a lawyer attempts to admit into evidence are what the lawyer claims them to be. A self-authenticating item is one that requires no additional proof to establish its authenticity. A certified copy of a birth certificate requires no elaborate protocol to establish that it is in fact a certified birth certificate. Self-authenticating items are usually set out in state and federal rules of evidence. If the item is not self-authenticating, then a predicate of admissibility must be laid.

Various types of exhibits must be authenticated by someone with knowledge of how the item came into the possession of the police and what it is. Generally the same person establishing chain of custody will authenticate the exhibit.

Photographs

State:	I hand you what has been marked as State's Exhibit Number 1 and ask you if you recognize it.
Investigator:	I do.
State:	What is it?
Investigator:	A photograph.
State:	Do you recognize the scene portrayed in the photograph?
Investigator:	Yes.
State:	How did you come to recognize that scene?
Investigator:	I was there the day of the investigation, which was the date of the taking of the photograph.
State:	Does the photograph fairly and accurately represent the scene as you recall it?
Investigator:	Yes.

At this point the state offers the exhibit into evidence. An evidence offer usually begins with the prosecutor tendering the exhibit to the defense for any objections. If the defense objects (and the likelihood of objections increases directly in proportion to the importance of the exhibit to the prosecution's case), the defense may choose to voir dire the witness as to the authenticity of the exhibit. If the judge sustains any defense objections, it may be necessary for the state to attempt to address those objections by laying a further predicate. Having listened to the objection and the discussion pertaining to that objection, the testifying officer should have a good idea of what additional predicate needs to be laid and, therefore, have prepared an answer for the state's attorney addressing those issues. Once the matter of the defense objections has been satisfactorily resolved, the exhibit will be accepted by the judge as evidence. The prosecutor may now ask questions that will allow a description of the contents of the photograph and the significance of those contents to the state's case.

Diagrams, Maps, Plats

State:	Did you participate in the preparation of the diagram that has been identified as State's Exhibit Number 2?
Investigator:	Yes.
State:	Are you personally familiar with the objects and locations contained in the diagram?
Investigator:	Yes.
State:	Is this diagram a fair and accurate representation of the [search site, recovery site, location of found evidence, etc.] as you recall it?
Investigator:	Yes.
State:	Is this diagram drawn to scale?
Investigator:	No.

Generally, it is easier to testify about a diagram that is not drawn to scale. Defense lawyers may focus on minuscule measurement errors to undermine the credibility of the entire diagram. If all underwater measurements are linked to a permanent landmark that was located on the diagram with the aid of surveying instruments, having a scale drawing may not be a problem. Reasonable approximations are much easier to defend.

Considerable time will be taken to explain the map and plats of an underwater operation once they have been authenticated. Original notes from which the measurements were taken may prove helpful during trial. Everything that was noted during the underwater operation may not have been included on the site map. If the defense begins asking technical questions pertaining to measurement procedures, the field notes may assist in refreshing recollection.

A caveat must be offered whenever field notes are retained and used on the witness stand. If field notes are used on the witness stand to refresh memory or as a resource, those notes must be made available to the defense upon request. Anything written in or on the notes must be relinquished. The witness does not have the right to remove anything from the notes to which he or she has referred; they must be turned over immediately to the defense for examination.

Occasionally, embarrassing material is contained in a field notebook. This is material that may not be relevant to the trial. If it is in the notebook, it is discoverable by the defendant. Although irrelevant, if it can be used to discredit a police witness, it will be allowed. To the uninitiated, the idea of using irrelevant material or issues to attack the credibility of police witnesses may seem inherently unfair. The rules of evidence allow the character of a witness, especially a police witness, to be attacked on grounds of credibility. Anything that may be used to raise an issue as to a police officer's credibility, whether relevant to the case or not, is admissible. A police officer not only testifies to information and evidence, but also brings the officer's entire police history to the witness stand every time he or she testifies. We all know that and, accordingly, live our lives and conduct ourselves professionally. It is no surprise that Mark Fuhrman in the O.J. Simpson case was challenged on his use of racist vocabulary. He was asked a question from which it was impossible to recover: A yes answer would make him a racist; a no answer would open him to any instance in which it could be proven he lied. An investigator's stock in trade is his or her reputation and word.

Another rule allows the defense access to any written materials that the witness has used to prepare for court. Anticipate this question and be ready to produce any material that was instrumental in trail preparation.

Video Recordings

Today's investigator relies on photography to record the crime scene. Underwater crime scenes lend themselves, visibility permitting, to video recording as well as to still photography. The predicate for video recordings is often confused with the predicate for audio recordings. The appropriate predicate combines the audio recording and still photograph predicates.

State:	Was the videotape you have described as State's Exhibit Number 3 prepared on a recording device capable of making an accurate recording?
Investigator:	Yes.

No technical data need be supplied. However, if the witness is a competent video technician, a brief technical description may ensue. However, technical understanding is required neither to use videotape equipment nor to establish the predicate for admissibility.

State:	Who was the operator?
Investigator:	[State the name of the video operator.]

It is not necessary to have actually filmed the video to be able to prove it up. All that is required is that the testifying officer has viewed the scene prior to filming, has viewed the film, and verifies that the film is an accurate reflection of the scene.

State:	Have you viewed the tape?
Investigator:	Yes.
State:	Has the videotape been altered in any way?
Investigator:	No.

Some agencies will record a voice-over on a tape to provide for a more understandable viewing of the video images. Obviously, the voice-over is hearsay if the person testifying is not the narrator, and is probably inadmissible. If the defense objects to the voice-over, the sound can simply be turned off. It may be necessary to testify that the recording has been altered by the addition of a soundtrack but that the addition has not altered the video images.

State:	When was the tape made?
Investigator:	[Provide time and date.]
State:	Do the scenes and events contained in the video fairly and accurately reflect the scene as you recall it?
Investigator:	Yes.

The tape may now be offered to the opposition for objections and, once those have been addressed, offered into evidence.

Physical Evidence

Every investigation involves physical evidence, and every investigation should anticipate the need for authenticating each item discovered. Authentication of physical evidence is fairly standard and should pose no admissibility problems for the testifying officer. Occasionally, defense lawyers will stipulate to the authenticity of large quantities of evidence when they are convinced that the testifying witness is competent in establishing the appropriate predicate. This stipulation avoids the dramatic effect of the prosecution focusing on each piece of evidence.

State:	I hand you what has been marked as State's Exhibit Number 4 and ask if you recognize it.
Investigator:	Yes.
State:	What is it?
Investigator:	[Describe the item generically as a gun, knife, pipe, etc.]
State:	When and where did you first encounter this [generic item]?
Investigator:	[Provide the time, date, and location.]
State:	How do you know this is the same [generic item]?
Investigator:	[Describe any identifying marks placed on it or evidence labels attached thereto.]
State:	Is the [generic item] in substantially the same condition that it was in when it was found?
Investigator:	Yes. [Describe any alterations including any **identification** marks or etchings placed on the evidence.]

Multiple Predicates

Often it will take more than one witness to lay the complete predicate for a piece of evidence. For example, an underwater investigator recovers a handgun and, after proper measuring and handling, gives it to the on-scene commander, who turns it over to the homicide investigator in charge of the case. The firearm ends up in the hands of an evidence technician who checks for latent prints on the firearm and the ammunition contained within it. The technician discovers latent prints on the magazine and a thumb print on a cartridge, and manages to develop and lift both. A suspect has an inked fingerprint impression taken. The latent print and the inked impression are forwarded to the fingerprint laboratory for comparison. It will take the testimony of four witnesses **(multiple predicates)** before the laboratory analysis can be admitted as evidence:

1. The underwater investigator who discovered the handgun will identify the weapon and attest to the fact that it is the one found, describe the method of discovery and recovery, and testify that it has not been altered in any way since its discovery.

2. The forensic technician who lifted the latent prints will extend the custody chain, identify the weapon, identify the latent prints, describe the method whereby a latent print can be developed and lifted, and attest that the print lifts have not been altered in any way.

3. The officer taking the inked impression of the suspect will identify the inked impression, identify the defendant from whom the impression was taken, and attest that it has not been altered in any way.

4. The laboratory personnel who compared the latent print lifts to the inked impression will extend the custody chain for both the inked and latent prints, identify both, and express an opinion regarding the laboratory comparison that was made.

As each witness testifies, the prosecutor will request that provisional admissibility be allowed for the exhibit pending the anticipated cumulative testimony of all four witnesses. After all four witnesses have testified, the prosecutor should have overcome any objections as to the authenticity of the exhibit offered, and the court should allow the exhibit to be entered into evidence.

The Underwater Investigator as an Expert Witness

One cannot testify as an expert witness unless it can be demonstrated, to the satisfaction of the court, that the prospective expert has some special skill or knowledge that will assist the **trier of fact** (judge or jury) in understanding the facts in issue. It is, therefore, incumbent upon the judge to determine whether the prospective expert has such specialized knowledge that will in fact assist in furthering the judge's or the jury's understanding of any issues in question. It is the purpose of a qualifying hearing to allow the adversaries to establish the credentials of and need for a prospective expert. This hearing takes place during the normal course of trial and is virtually indistinguishable from the rest of the trial to the layperson. It appears to be a direct examination of a witness with an emphasis on background and specialization.

Since the hearing takes place during the course of trial, it is seldom viewed as a hearing but rather as part of the normal trial process. The scope of the hearing is restricted to the qualifications of the witness and the need for the expert's assistance. Often the credentials of the expert go unchallenged by the opposition and the direct examination of the witness begins without hesitation. However, should there be some question as to the competence of the expert or the need for such testimony, the opposition will interrupt the "expert offer" after qualifying questions have been asked, and request that the court allow the witness to be subjected to a voir dire as to competence and necessity. In many courts, after qualifying questions have been asked and answered, the party calling the witness will make a request of the court that the witness be accepted as an expert witness in the field in which the witness had just been qualified. This is referred to as "offering the witness." It is good practice to make the expert offer in that it tells the jury something special has just happened, and it conveys to the opposition that the offer of proof pertaining to the witness's expertise is complete and the time for requesting an opportunity to voir dire the expert has arrived.

Underwater investigators are a relatively new phenomenon, and qualifying such an expert poses some unique questions. It is impossible today to obtain formal education in underwater criminalistics, so one cannot use college credentials in a direct fashion. Experience, training, and education are the road to qualification for the underwater expert. That is rapidly changing. As this is being written, community colleges around the country are beginning to apply the principles outlined in this text and are offering courses in underwater investigation. Often police and fire department divers identify themselves on the witness stand as certified divers and give testimony about the training and operations they have been involved in as a way of qualifying themselves as "experts." For underwater criminalists, courts will grow to expect a substantial background of education, training, and service for expert qualification because as the field grows, so will the competence and credentials of those providing such services.

Scientific Evidence

Scientific evidence can come before the jury only from the mouth of an expert witness. Occasionally, controversy surrounds a particular scientific or pseudoscientific practice, bringing into question whether such a practice or procedure is in fact scientific. The United States Court of Appeals set forth a rule that has been followed for years, known as the Frye test. The Frye test simply postulates that scientific evidence should not be admitted until it has gained general acceptance in the particular field to which it belongs (*Frye v. United States* 1923). It is this test that has been used in determining the scientific validity of hypnosis, polygraphs, battered women's syndrome, DNA printing, and other types of evidence. Many courts have paid little attention to the Frye standard and have employed individual judicial discretion in the determination of what is scientific and what is not. The United States Supreme Court has decided that Federal Rule of Evidence 702 supersedes the Frye test (*Daubert v. Merrell-Dow Pharmaceuticals, Inc.* 1993). Rule 702 deals with the admissibility of expert testimony and provides that "if scientific, technical, or other specialized knowledge will assist the trier of fact to understand the evidence or to determine a fact in issue, a witness qualified as an expert by knowledge, skill, experience, training, or education may testify thereto in the form of an opinion or otherwise." If Frye is no longer the standard, then what standard is to apply? That Frye was replaced by the Federal Rules of Evidence does not imply that there are no restrictions on scientific testimony. Under the rules, the trial judge must ensure that any and all scientific testimony or evidence admitted is not only relevant, but also reliable (*Daubert v. Merrell-Dow Pharmaceuticals, Inc.* 1993). The trial judge must consider whether the technique employed is replicable and has been subjected to peer review and publication, and to what extent the technique has been accepted by the scientific community.

The standards set forth by Ian McCormick in his law journal article entitled "Scientific Evidence: Defining a New Approach to Admissibility" would provide greater guidance in determining the probative value of proffered scientific evidence. McCormick offers eleven factors to be considered in a probative analysis of scientific evidence:

1. The potential error rate in using the technique
2. The existence and maintenance of standards governing its use
3. Presence of safeguards in the application of the technique
4. Analogy to other scientific techniques whose results are admissible
5. The extent to which the technique has been accepted by scientists in the field involved
6. The nature and breadth of the inference adduced
7. The clarity and simplicity with which the technique can be described and its results explained
8. The extent to which the basic data is verifiable by the court and jury
9. The availability of other experts to test and evaluate the technique
10. The probative significance of the evidence in the circumstances of the case
11. The care with which the technique is employed in the case (McCormick 1982)

The underwater investigator may be called as an expert witness. The methods employed in an underwater investigation may fall within the purview of expert testimony:

- Dive briefings
- Interview process
- Interrogation procedure
- Search site selection
- Search methodology

- Photographing the evidence
- Measuring the evidence
- Handling and packaging of evidence
- Transporting evidence
- Dive debriefings

The simplest test to apply to any suggested scientific or expert procedure is the replicability of the procedure and the opportunity to test the validity of the results. Applying such standards will reduce the arbitrary discretion of trial courts in admitting things like astrological and junk-food influences on defendants' behavior.

DEFENSE LAWYERS, PROSECUTORS, AND INVESTIGATORS

The following is adapted from *Criminal Investigation* by the author (Becker 2002).

The Defense

All states require lawyers to adhere to a code of professional responsibility. Each code demands maintenance of client confidentiality and provision of the best possible defense allowed by law and propriety. The conventional wisdom is that if the defense does its job, the prosecution does its job, and the police do their job, a just verdict will result. On the condition that all participants in the legal process act competently, the only consolation a defense lawyer has in defending a client he or she believes to be guilty is that justice will be done.

A defense lawyer does not inquire into a client's guilt or innocence. It is not in the client's best interest to confess guilt, and most clients do not. On the other hand, it could injure the quality of a defense lawyer's preparation of the defendant's case if he or she relies heavily on the defendant's protestations of innocence. Believing in the defendant's innocence may prevent the lawyer from examining certain evidence or interviewing witnesses and, thus, revealing conflicts best discovered before trial. It is virtually an axiom of criminal law that you should not assume your client has told you the whole truth. Valuable information may be lost to an attorney who places too much confidence in the statements of a criminal client.

Defensive Burden

The legal burden generally borne by the defendant can be summed up succinctly: none. It is the responsibility of the defense lawyer to ensure that the defendant receives a fair trial and that neither the prosecution nor the court trespasses upon the due process rights of the defendant. There are certain defenses that require a preliminary showing of the applicability of the defensive position to the offense. These defenses are referred to as **affirmative defenses.**

Affirmative Defenses

The state generally has the responsibility to carry the burden of proof. It always has the responsibility to carry the burden of persuasion. In specific situations enumerated by statutes (codes of criminal procedure), the defense has the responsibility to put forth certain defenses, the most common being self-defense. The list of affirmative defenses is not a long one. It varies from state to state but typically includes the following:

- Insanity
- Incompetence
- Self-defense
- Coercion
- Entrapment

In most states, the defense must notify the prosecution in writing before trial that it intends to put forth an affirmative defense and must specify which defense it will proffer. One common result of an affirmative defense is that a new and separate procedure is required, such as a competency hearing. The purpose of a competency hearing is to determine the state of mind of the defendant at the time of trial, whereas the purpose of an insanity hearing is to determine the state of mind of the defendant at the time of the crime. If found by the court to be incompetent, the defendant will be remanded to a mental institution until his competency has been restored. Once it has been restored, the defendant will be required to stand trial for the offense charged. In a competency hearing, the burden is upon the defendant to produce clear and convincing proof that he or she (1) does not understand the nature of the proceeding against him or her and (2) is unable to assist in his or her own defense. A defense of incompetence is an affirmative defense and shifts the burden of proof to the defendant. It is the defense lawyer's job to put forth all applicable defenses and to attempt to impeach the credibility of all witnesses and attack the admissibility of all evidence.

Defense Strategies

There are basically three ways the defense can win a criminal trial:

1. By impeaching the evidence
2. By impeaching the police
3. By creating confusion and delay

Impeaching the Police

Closely tied to the issue of inadmissible evidence is the question of the competence and credibility of the police. Obviously, an attack on the training, education, and experience of the officers involved would be one way to try to discredit the evidence, a main defense objective. This strategy is sometimes referred to as striking the evidence over the shoulder of the police. If training, education, and experience issues can be raised, they may affect a jury's view of the credibility of the testifying witness and everything that witness has touched in the course of the investigation. If even one small bit of evidentiary procedure is wanting in the conduct of the investigating team, the whole team will be viewed more skeptically. A discredited police officer brings discredit to the entire investigative team and the investigative process.

Police are subject to greater personal scrutiny than any other type of witness. An officer's entire personnel record, job performance, and personal life, as well as any complaints made against the officer, will be examined prior to trial, and anything that can be used to undermine the officer's testimony will be admissible on the grounds of challenging the officer's competence and credibility.

Suppose a prosecutor discovers for the first time at trial that the chief investigator in a racially charged case is a racist. The options confronting the prosecution are fairly straightforward: Call the witness or do not call the witness. If the prosecution decides to call the witness, it must be prepared to deal with the racial issue. No purpose is served by the prosecution attempting to distance itself from its own witness. In the law, it is understood that the party calling a witness, in effect, vouches for that witness. A questionable prosecution witness can only reflect badly upon the prosecution.

The questions the prosecution has to ask in deciding to call a questionable witness are the following:

- Is the witness vital to the prosecution's case?
- Is there sufficient evidence absent this witness to win a conviction? If the witness is vital to the prosecution's case, two further questions need to be asked:
  - Can the witness's questionable qualities (e.g., racism) be presented in such a way that they will not alienate the jury?
  - If the qualities cannot be so presented, what impact will they have on the jury?

If sufficient evidence exists to win a conviction absent this witness, other questions arise:

- Will the defense call the witness?
- If so, what impact will this witness have when called by the defense as a **hostile witness** (a witness who is favorable to the other side)?

When the analysis of the situation has been completed, the prosecution must decide whether to go forward with its case or dismiss it. No matter how odious the crime, insufficient evidence and impeachable witnesses (persons whose veracity is open to question) undermine not only the case in question, but also the criminal justice system as a whole. It is too late to ask the necessary questions at the time of trial.

Impeachment Impact
Dismissing a case because of tainted evidence or unreliable witnesses is the remedy that should be employed by the prosecutor when egregious errors have been

made. Unfortunately, police, investigators, and prosecutors sometimes compound the problem by attempting to engage in damage control. That is a fatal mistake. Sometimes prosecutors become so emotionally involved in a case that they cannot distance themselves enough to assess objectively the impact of potentially damaging evidence or testimony. They want a conviction so badly that they lose sight of their professional duty, which is to see that justice is done. When objectivity is lost, the decision to dismiss a case that should be dismissed is avoided, and disaster looms. The trial then becomes a series of damage-control skirmishes that ultimately will sink the prosecution's case and undermine the judicial system.

Confusion and Delay

There is an old legal defense axiom: If you can't win on the facts, argue the law; if you can't win on the law, argue the facts; if you can't win on either, delay. The U.S. Constitution guarantees a defendant a "speedy trial." The truth is that most defendants do not want a speedy trial. As long as the trial is not held, a verdict of guilty is not rendered. As long as a trial is not held, the defendant (if bonded) remains free. The longer the trial is delayed, the greater the chance the state will lose a witness and the dimmer memories will grow. Most defendants do not benefit by rushing to the courthouse and have everything to gain by waiting.

There are competing components of the U.S. Constitution that come into play in getting a defendant to trial. The United States Supreme Court has handed down many decisions dealing with proper legal representation and efforts put forth in preparing a defense. The defendant's right to have sufficient time to prepare a defense militates against a speedy trial. The nature of the U.S. criminal justice system also influences how soon a defendant comes to trial. Most judges and prosecutors face a crowded criminal trial docket and, therefore, do not oppose postponing criminal trial proceedings except in the instance of a high-profile case. While the wheels of justice slowly turn, police witnesses change agencies and eyewitnesses move, their memories wane, or they die. A speedy trial is virtually a mythical beast in today's judicial forums.

Another old defense axiom is that a good defense lawyer can make the simplest of cases complex. Many cases today involve forensic evidence and complicated expert testimony. The more difficult the testimony is to understand, the more room the defense has to sow confusion. Trials in which DNA testimony occurs are so convoluted that even people who understand DNA typing often lose track of the testimony and its significance. Instead of discussing forensic aspects of blood and its genetic composition, the defense attorney, in cross-examination, might bring up allele frequency, population statistics, laboratory procedures, and other matters of little relevance to the question of who left blood at the crime scene. This approach uses two defense principles: impeach the evidence and confuse the jury. Without actually impeaching the evidence, the defense attorney so obscures the forensic procedures that a jury member might mistake confusion for a reasonable doubt. All testifying witnesses must have the ability to make the difficult easy to comprehend and must understand what they are testifying to so well that they can provide clear answers to questions intended to obfuscate. A cross-examination conducted by a competent defense attorney is a fearsome thing and should not be underestimated by the witness or the prosecution.

Suppression Hearings

More cases are lost in **suppression hearings** than by a verdict of acquittal. Indeed, investigators spend more time in these hearings than they do testifying at trial, for it is in these hearings that most of the important judicial decisions regarding evidence, confessions, and police conduct (or misconduct) are raised and resolved. A suppression hearing gives defendants an opportunity to see what kind of case the prosecution has and what caliber of witnesses they are facing. In most instances, if a defendant's motion to suppress illegally obtained evidence and statements is granted, the prosecution dismisses the case for lack of evidence. It is important to remember that the prosecution's burden is to prove the offense beyond a reasonable doubt, which represents a 40 percent increase over the burden of proof police need to make an arrest.

Motions to suppress are heard long before a jury is picked or a trial date set. The defense need not worry about the impression the jury will get from harsh treatment of the testifying witnesses. Investigating officers can be made to feel like criminals through vigorous and vehement cross-examination. The defense wants to see what will "play" and uses the suppression hearing to feel out the opposition.

The best way to avoid a suppression hearing is to ensure that all police conduct is above question. An investigator should presume that any investigation will end up at trial and at a motion to suppress. It might not be true, but no one is able to distinguish beforehand between investigations that will lead to a trial and those that will not. The investigation that has taken evidentiary shortcuts is almost certainly doomed, but it may be years before the trial reveals that to the investigating team. In professional golf, there are no "quit shots" (shots delivered without hope of success and with little effort); likewise, in the realm of criminal investigation, there are no quit cases, slam dunks, or unimportant pieces of evidence.

The two most commonly litigated issues in criminal cases are (1) illegal searches and seizures and (2) illegally obtained statements. Given the quantity of time and effort that goes into training criminal investigative teams, one would think that they would know the difference between a legal and an illegal search, a legal and an illegal arrest, and a legally and an illegally obtained confession. The rate of suppressed evidence strongly suggests that the performance of many police officers is deficient. Either the training they received was inadequate or they have chosen to ignore the training and model their actions on television portrayals of what police do and how they do it.

The Prosecution

In a trial, the prosecution has the burden to prove the following:

- Jurisdiction
- Venue

- Identification
- Elements of the offense

Each criminal trial is a competition involving these four issues. Although a trial may take a day, week, month, or even longer to complete, the basic objective of the prosecution is to prove beyond a reasonable doubt each and every **element of the offense** with which the defendant has been charged. The prosecution must also establish that the court trying the matter has jurisdiction over the case, that the venue is proper, and that the person standing trial today is the one arrested for the offense.

Jurisdiction

Each state has a tiered system of trial courts, ranging from small claims courts to courts like those featured on television to courts of last review (often referred to as supreme courts). Trial courts are granted authority to hear cases based on their subject matter and/or the amount of money at stake. Criminal courts are generally divided into two categories: courts handling serious crimes (felonies) and courts handling less serious offenses (misdemeanors). Court jurisdiction has nothing to do with geography; it has to do with statutory authority. It should not be confused with police jurisdiction. Police jurisdiction is geographic in nature, for it sets the territorial boundaries within which police may act. Court jurisdiction in a criminal case is determined by the type of offense. If it is a felony case, it is heard in district court; if it is a misdemeanor case, it is heard in a lesser court. Lesser courts are referred to as courts of limited jurisdiction. It is necessary to show the court in which a case is being tried that the offense charged is covered by the court's statutory authority. Proof of the court's appropriateness is generally accomplished through the testimony of the criminal investigator. Such proof is most crucial in states that determine the seriousness of theft offenses based on the sum stolen. If stealing something that has a value of more than $750 is a felony, there must be testimony offered by the state proving the value of the item stolen in order to establish for the record that the offense was in fact a felony over which the court has felony jurisdiction. Absent that showing, the state has failed to prove an essential ingredient of its case and may be subject to a motion for a directed verdict of acquittal when the defense raises the issue to the judge. Upon a motion for a directed verdict, the court will direct the court reporter to examine the record for any testimony pertaining to the value of the item stolen. Should that testimony not be there, the defendant's motion may be granted, resulting in a dismissal of the case. The **transcript** typed by the court stenographer is the official record of what has taken place during the course of the trial. Upon appeal, the only issues that are reviewed by the court are those raised at the time of trial and memorialized in the transcript.

Venue

The geographical area over which a court presides is called its venue. (The concept of a court's venue can be understood by comparing venue to police jurisdiction.) The prosecutor has the responsibility to establish through competent testimony that the crime with which the defendant is charged has occurred in an area over which the court has authority. It is through police testimony that this element of the state's case is generally proven. The Sixth Amendment to the U.S. Constitution requires that the defendant be tried in the geographical area in which the offense was committed. An investigator must testify that the crime occurred in the state, county, and city over which the court has authority. Failure to do so will result in a motion by the defendant for a directed verdict of acquittal. It should be noted that double jeopardy attaches once the jury has been sworn in, so a dismissal prejudices the prosecution from refiling the case and the defendant goes free.

In-Court Identification

In every criminal case, the prosecution must assure the court that the individual in court is the same person arrested for and charged with the offense of which he or she stands accused. The entertainment media has conditioned us to think that the in-court identification of the defendant is a cursory affair that can be handled in a cavalier fashion:

Q: Officer, is the man whom you saw leaving the scene of the crime and whom you arrested for the crime in the courtroom today?

A: Yes.

The prosecutor then tells the judge, "Let the record reflect that the witness is pointing to the defendant." It is not only the judge who must be satisfied that the defendant has been identified as the perpetrator. On appeal, the reviewing court will look to the trial transcript in determining whether the identification was made acceptably. The problem with letting the "record reflect" is that the record reflects only words and conduct. It is the testimony of the prosecutor that establishes the identity of the defendant, but the prosecutor is not a competent witness, and what he or she says is not evidence. It should be apparent that this method of identifying the defendant does not meet legal requirements. Lawyers, like police, can be affected by watching too much television. It helps if the witness and the prosecutor know what is required for making a proper in-court identification of the defendant. The following protocol is one that has withstood appellate review:

Q: Officer, is the man whom you saw leaving the scene of the crime and whom you arrested for the crime in the courtroom today?

A: Yes.

Q: Where is he sitting?

A: In front of the bar at the defense counsel table with his attorney.

Q: Would you describe what he is wearing?

A: He is wearing a blue sport coat, gray pants, a white shirt, and a red tie.

It is unnecessary to use the dramatic Hollywood gesture of a pointed finger. The record now does reflect an appropriate in-court identification. It is axiomatic that the record only reflects what the record in fact reflects.

Elements of the Offense

That the burden of the prosecution is to prove the elements of an offense may seem self-evident, but proving this is not always as simple as it may sound. The prosecution and the testifying investigator have the responsibility of knowing what the elements of an offense are and which facts to be admitted into evidence support each and every element of the offense. Many investigators have a superb familiarity with the penal code of their state and can quote line and verse in discussing various arrests and prosecutions that they have been involved in. Yet it is a whole other skill to be able to recognize from a labyrinth of information and facts exactly what crime has been committed and what can be charged. Relying on the state penal code will always leave a gap in an investigator's understanding of the legal elements of various offenses. Applicable case law helps in interpreting code provisions when ambiguity arises. It has been said that the existence of the plethora of criminal laws is a product of the endless attempts by individuals to circumvent the ten basic laws known as the Ten Commandments. Be that as it may, there are a number of relevant cases that accompany every section and offense enumerated in the penal code. The well-prepared investigator has an annotated version of the penal code that assists in fully understanding the elements of an offense.

For example, according to most penal codes, burglary of a habitation occurs when a person enters or remains on the premises of another, without effective consent of the owner, for the purpose of committing theft or another felony. By this definition, can a person burglarize her own home? It would seem not. If a person, seeing an open window, pushes a pole through the window and lifts up and removes a purse resting on the table without any part of his person entering the dwelling, has a burglary been committed? Not if we literally apply the penal definition. Or if a person, seeing an open window and a purse on a table, sends in a trained monkey to retrieve the purse, has a burglary been committed? The answer to this question as well will not be determinable without annotated cases interpreting the code. A well-trained investigator knows not only the codified elements of an offense, but also where to find the cases to assist in interpreting the codes when an element of human ambiguity enters the fray. (For the curious, yes, a person can burglarize her own home, and using a pole device or trained animal has been seen by the courts as extending the human arm and, thus, constitutes burglary.) A failure to prove jurisdiction, venue, in-court identification, and the elements of the offense charged will result in a verdict for the defendant and a loss for the prosecution. Remember, the prosecution is part of the criminal investigation team, and when the prosecution loses, the investigator and the investigation lose.

Testimonial Devices to Avoid the Truth

There are numerous opportunities during the course of a criminal investigation for things to go wrong. Conducting an error-free investigation is impossible, and what is done to address the errors that occur will often determine the outcome of the investigation and the trial. Once an error has been made, there are three ways of dealing with it:

1. Deny it ever occurred (denial).
2. Blame someone else for the error (scapegoating).
3. Admit the error, and examine various ways to address it (growth).

Scapegoating

We have grown accustomed to referring to automobile collisions as "accidents." Accidents are considered to occur by chance. In truth, chance has little to do with most traffic collisions. Speed, tailgating, intoxication, and lack of attention are the precipitating causes of collisions, not fortune, chance, or fate. Evidently, if we all agree to call automobile collisions "accidents," we can avoid the mantle of irresponsibility worn by one or more participants in a collision. Having a "traffic accident" is a lot like dying of "complications" in a hospital or during surgery. A surgeon might claim that an operation was a success but that the patient died of complications. This way of putting the matter seems to remove the surgeon and the hospital from the chain of responsibility for the death. Police euphemistically say that a defendant "got off on a technicality." In such instances the police probably failed to do their job or failed to do it correctly. There are no technicalities upon which a defendant may be released. Only police misconduct of constitutional dimensions can result in the defendant being released on a "technicality." Is coercing a confession a technicality? Some police believe it is. Is searching a person or his home or effects without probable cause a technicality? Some police believe it is. By reducing an infringement of the U.S. Constitution to the level of a technicality, police show their disdain for the Bill of Rights and the blueprint of American due process. Defense lawyers, for the most part, point out and exaggerate the errors of the police and the prosecution; they seldom manufacture them.

Error-Free Investigations

There will be mistakes during the investigation and during the trial. There are no perfect trials or investigations. A perfect investigation is suspect. Yet if police officers cannot conduct a perfect, error-free investigation, why should they try?

Although error-free investigations are unattainable, attempting to achieve them is highly desirable. The never-ending efforts of the police to perform the perfect investigation will be recognized and will bear fruit both in and out of the courtroom. The investigator who leaves no stone unturned will be more successful in investigating a crime than will the investigator who rushes to judgment based on hastily gathered information and evidence. The investigator will be successful, that is, if we define success as investigations that lead to convictions or rigorous plea bargains.

Loose ends are errors that have been made by omission and can be just as costly as errors of commission. It is not very helpful to discover at the time of trial

that the defense has found a witness who places the defendant at a different location than that alleged in the indictment or who has the defendant departing the scene
hours before the crime was committed. Errors of omission are the easiest to avoid.
If investigators do the job they are paid to do and in the way they are paid to do it,
errors of omission will be kept to a minimum.

How do you explain to a prosecutor how you failed to discover the existence
of an alibi witness? How do you dispute testimony that you never knew existed?
How do you prepare for trial when there is relevant information missing? How do
you explain to the jury your efforts to convict a possibly innocent person? How do
you explain the failure to discover **exculpatory evidence** (evidence indicating innocence)? All these are questions that investigators, prosecutors, and judges would
rather avoid. They can be avoided by striving for perfection and following all leads
even after the puzzle has seemingly been solved.

Ethical Testimony

Prior to a suppression hearing or the trial, the prosecutors may discover problems
with the case being prepared. Hasty conferences with investigators may be called
and a joint exercise in damage control undertaken. Often damage control is accomplished by suggesting that the investigating officer's recollection of an event,
handling of evidence, or personal philosophy needs to be modified. The result is per-
jury no matter the motivation. It is easy to believe that the end justifies the means:
The defendant has done a bad thing and deserves to be punished, and lying to ensure
punishment is OK. Months, sometimes years, of hard investigative work might be at
stake. It is difficult to tell the truth when you know that the truth may set free a
defendant you believe to be guilty. It is at this point that one's personal philosophy
becomes an issue. The decision to lie, fabricate evidence, or deny **culpability** (criminal responsibility) is determined well before the opportunity to lie, fabricate evidence, or deny culpability arises. An individual's character and personal philosophy
are part of what he or she carries around in dealing with the world. The forming of a
personal philosophy begins in early childhood and continues in the home, church, and
school and on the street. An individual's personal philosophy never achieves finished
form, but is constantly evolving. If nurtured, it grows; if not, it slowly begins to die.

It is not the big issues, such as police corruption, but rather the day-to-day
decisions that reflect what a police officer's personal philosophy is. A personal philosophy does not come wired from the factory. A person does not awaken one morn-
ing and make the decision to be honest or dishonest. That decision is the result of
a long series of incremental steps. Many in criminal justice believe we need to teach
ethics by preaching about what is right and pointing fingers at those who do wrong.
Yet the basis of ethical conduct resides in the personal philosophy we bring to our
encounters. It is not unique to police work. The same philosophy accompanies us
no matter what it is we choose to do with our lives. The early lessons we learned
have stuck and grown, or they have died. If the latter, their death was not a quick
and painless one. Those values and lessons die a slow, lingering death; but they

---

1. Complete all documentation in a timely fashion (as information, evidence, and data are obtained).
2. Examine all evidence prior to trial.
3. Compare all evidence to references in documentation and relocate any identifying markings or characteristics.
4. Gather all field notes and sketches and place them in a separate folder (examine for extrinsic information).
5. Confer with the prosecutor prior to trial in anticipation of trial.
6. Contact all lab technicians and forensic scientists, and discuss laboratory findings.
7. Contact the medical examiner, and discuss the examination and documentation provided by that office.
8. Contact all witnesses to reconfirm information provided and the validity of statements made.
9. Select appropriate apparel, and ensure appropriate grooming.
10. Arrive at the courthouse early.
11. Remain at the courthouse until dismissed by the prosecutor.
12. Testify objectively and truthfully.
13. Treat the defense attorney with the same courtesy that is extended to the prosecution (especially if the defense attorney's conduct does not warrant it). The old adage "Don't get mad, get even" is self-defeating and should be replaced with the saying "Don't get mad, don't get even, win."
14. After testifying, do not leave the courthouse until excused by the judge.
15. Celebrate your victory with the team.

FIGURE 11-1 Checklist for testimony preparation.
(*Source:* R. F. Becker)

nonetheless die unless they are nourished. Nourishment is easy: You just use them. Every time an opportunity arises to do the right thing and you do it, the probability of doing the right thing in the future has increased. As you sit reading this book, you know whether you are an honest or a dishonest person. Nothing in an ethics curriculum, or anything that could be included in this book, could change your degree of honesty.

REVIEW QUESTIONS

1. Of what interest is chain of custody to trial lawyers?
2. What is an admissibility predicate? Provide a sample predicate for admitting a handgun.
3. What is a multiple predicate? Under what circumstances might one be necessary? Why?
4. How does the state authenticate a piece of evidence?

5. Why must the state authenticate a piece of evidence?
6. How can a lawyer ethically defend a defendant the lawyer believes is guilty? Include in your discussion comments on the ethical obligation a lawyer has to a client.
7. What must the state prove in each and every criminal case it tries?
8. How does police jurisdiction differ from judicial jurisdiction?
9. What is a motion for a directed verdict of acquittal?
10. Why is an in-court identification of the defendant required, and how is it made?
11. What role does case law play in understanding penal code offenses?
12. What is an affirmative defense, and what effect does it have on the burden of proof in a criminal trial?
13. What are the three basic tactics employed by a defendant in an effort to win a criminal trial?
14. What is the chain of custody, and what problems arise in attempting to maintain it?
15. How is a personal philosophy formed, and how does it evolve?
16. What are the advantages to a defendant of delaying a trial?
17. What is a motion to suppress evidence, and what role does it play in a criminal investigation?

REFERENCES

BECKER, R. F. 1985. *The underwater crime scene: Underwater crime investigation techniques.* Springfield, IL: Charles C. Thomas.

BECKER, R. F. 2002. *Criminal investigation.* Gaithersburg: Aspen Publishing.

MCCORMICK, I. 1982. Scientific evidence: Defining a new approach to admissibility. *67 Iowa L. Rev.* 879:911–912.

TABLE OF CASES

Daubert v. Merrell-Dow Pharmaceuticals, Inc., 113 S Ct. 1993.

Frye v. United States, 293 F. 1013 (D.C. Cir. 1923).

Chapter 12

A Look Back—A Look Forward

In the evolution of public safety diving, no single group has contributed more than our firefighters. Many of the teams that came together to provide recovery services for police operations were from fire departments from around the country. With recreational scuba gear, they accepted the responsibility for providing recovery operations because in most instances they were already providing rescue service. Before there was anything "glamorous" about public safety diving, even before it was called public safety diving, they were there. Many of these teams are still providing the same services with the same equipment.

We have come a long way in the interim. We have training organizations from around the country providing public safety diver training. It seems to be in vogue to criticize the equipment that early teams used and to establish a list of equipment basics that would put many teams out of business. That may not be an entirely bad thing, but the reality is that simply because a team does not have the "proper" equipment does not mean they are going to stop recovery operations. In the Southwest, many teams began and continue with the bare necessities. They have wish lists that will most likely not become a reality in their lifetimes. What responsibility do we have to train these teams? Some trainers have a bottom line: inappropriate equipment, no training. That kind of thing leaves these teams—and there are more than we might imagine—without training. In some instances it may be necessary to provide training for those teams, beginning with where that team is. When I began working with teams in Texas, recreational scuba gear was what they had, and recreational scuba gear was what they used. We started there and watched as some teams increased their equipment inventories (most often at their own expense) while others continued with what they had. Much of the public safety diving in Texas is done by small teams without the budgets to provide the kind of equipment we recommend they have. But they still dive. One day perhaps all public safety dive teams will have the "appropriate" equipment, but in Texas we still teach based on where they are.

In the writing of this book, part of the process included reviews from knowledgeable people in the industry. Their comments made this a better book. Evident throughout, however, were notably adamant views that there is only one way to do a certain thing. Much of what we know about underwater operations is a product of trial and error and numerous deaths from unsafe or uncalculated practices. Everyone's motivation is good in that the holy grail of underwater operation instruction is that all the divers go home.

The differences in practices considered sacred in one school of instruction but violated or substituted for other practices in other schools makes it clear that this industry, and more specifically underwater recovery operations, needs standardization not only in implementation, but also in instruction. The easiest thing to do is to examine the practices of the various schools of thought and bring together those that appear to work the best. But that is a chore that should not be left to the individual schools. Anyone teaching public safety diving has made contributions to its evolution, some perhaps more than others. However, those practices that are embraced by osmosis and adopted as working models are hard to label as belonging to any one school or person. Practices taught in one part of the country have been adopted by some teams but not by others. This text attempts to bring together the best of all information presently available, give credit where due and recognizable, and fashion some semblance of a protocol that can be taught and employed in processing an underwater crime scene.

The war over standards began the day it was determined that there was a difference between rescue and evidence recovery and that recovery was not a police function. As long as the operation was rescue and recovery, with no concern for the evidentiary nature of the item sought, any safe method of getting to the bottom and back was considered acceptable, and that is the standard in many places today. Many people associated with underwater operations, be they rescue or recovery personnel, have attempted to develop a safe approach. The safety of any particular method of public safety diving is still debated by different commercial training enterprises. The advent of considering submerged items as having evidentiary and forensic value gave rise to a new day in the underwater operations business. That new day is still in the predawn hours.

Some of the reviewers of this text were offended by the notion that fire departments and firefighters should not be in the evidence recovery business. There are volunteer teams, fire department teams, police teams, and hybrid teams all vying for the sobriquet "underwater investigator." We have examples of police organizations throughout the country that have adopted underwater investigation as a police function, yet there are still those enclaves wedded to the notion that fire departments and volunteer groups can do it. The basic question is not whether they can do it or not; to me, the fundamental question has always been "Should they be doing it?"

The key word in underwater recovery operations for the recovery of bodies and evidence is *investigation*. With all the myths that have been debunked in this text, one is led to the single conclusion that recovering bodies and evidence is, or should be, a law enforcement function. Most who understand the principles set forth in this text regarding the investigation of underwater secondary crime scenes do not disagree with that, but for their own mostly self-serving reasons, they believe that it does not require police personnel to provide that function. Semantics aside, underwater investigation, by definition, is a police function regardless of who is doing it. It has always been amazing to me that Canadians recognized this distinction early on and gave the responsibility to the Royal Canadian Mounted Police, who were pioneers in the evolution of the underwater investigator. No one associated with this industry can deny the contribution of Cpl. Robert Teather (RCMP). His kindness and generosity accompanied accompanied him wherever he went, and he left only goodwill and fellowship in his wake.

Because commercial training enterprises are a business, it is highly competitive, and the competition is for the same group of consumers. That competition often leads to unflattering comparisons and claims that one school surpasses another in quality, instruction, equipment, faculty, etc. Competition has been good for the evolution of ever-safer methods of deploying public safety divers, but it has been counterproductive with respect to moving us to a standard within the industry.

I know the arguments: If fire departments don't do it, in some jurisdictions, no one will. If the need exists and it is a recognized need, police departments should not be able to ignore their responsibility for the sake of convenience. It has been convenient for too long to let the fire department do it; after all, they have the equipment and the training. It's time to place the responsibility where it most properly belongs: with the criminal justice system.

Except for arson investigators, firefighters fight fires and cops enforce the law, which includes the search of crime scenes. It makes no more sense to have fire departments recover underwater evidence than it does to invite them to a homicide crime scene and ask them to process that.

Those who dispute this view are generally among the following:

• Fire departments that wish not to relinquish the responsibility
• Police departments that do not want the responsibility
• Volunteer teams that have established a niche
• Commercial enterprises that make their living training divers

Inertia is a peculiar proposition; change is not likely to take place unless someone actively promotes that change. There are so many reasons for leaving things the way they are that it is frustrating to those who recognize the winds of change and the need for the change those winds bring.

Step one in placing responsibility where it belongs is to relegate to fire departments the responsibility of rescue operations on the water (not to include spontaneous rescues provided by on-the-scene Samaritans and police who acquiesce to fire department jurisdiction upon their arrival), and to police departments crime scene investigation on, off, or under the water. There really is no rational argument for allowing civilians, firefighters, or any combination thereof to be working crime scenes. This seems so logical that it is hard to accept the arguments against it.

In the future the need for recognizing the police nature of the underwater investigative function will ultimately become apparent. Police will accept the responsibility of underwater investigation as they are subjected to vigorous insinuations and allegations of irresponsibility during closing statements by lawyers who pose to juries the same question we have been discussing: Why are firefighters processing crime scenes?

In the future there will be a national standard for water rescue operations that has little to do with evidence recovery operations. There will be a separate standard for underwater recovery divers (underwater investigators) that has nothing to do with rescue operations. There will also be a set of standards adopted by the reputable training facilities offering underwater investigation training, wherein an agreement will be reached among different schools as to the basic requirements of underwater investigator instruction, students, instructor training, and performance standards. It will take time, soul-searching, argument, and compromise, but it will happen.

In the future, once the world of underwater investigation has been accepted as a law enforcement function, there will come a day when commercial private training of underwater investigators will end. I envision a day when police academies offer specialized training for those among their own who will perform underwater investigations. I see a day when the commercial trainer for police divers is obsolete, and police organizations assume the responsibility not only for the performance of underwater investigations, but also for training the investigators just as they do for land-based investigations. There are few commercial enterprises that train police to investigate rapes, robberies, aggravated assaults, kidnappings, etc. There are few commercial enterprises that train police cadets, SWAT teams, hostage negotiation teams, etc. There are few commercial enterprises that teach police to shoot, drive, write reports, measure traffic accidents, etc. Most police agencies train their own. To that list one day will be added underwater investigation.

Index